Chinese Exclusion versus the Open Door Policy 1900-1906

Map of China Indicating Principal Boycott Centers

CHINESE EXCLUSION VERSUS THE OPEN DOOR POLICY 1900-1906

CLASHES OVER CHINA POLICY IN THE ROOSEVELT ERA

DELBER L. McKEE
Westminster College

Wayne State University Press Detroit 1977

Library of Congress Cataloging in Publication Data

McKee, Delber L   1923-
    Chinese exclusion versus the open door policy. 1900-1906.

    Bibliography: p.
    Includes index.
    1. United States — Foreign relations — China. 2. China — Foreign relations —
United States. 3. Chinese in the United States. 4. United States — Immigration and
emigration. 5. United States — Foreign relations — 1901-1909. 6. Roosevelt, Theodore,
Pres. U.S., 1858-1919. I. Title.
E183.8.C5M29   327.73'051   76-47024
ISBN 0-8143-1565-8

To My Wife
Margaret

Contents

Illustrations

Preface

America's former China policy is usually defined in terms of the open door, but there was a second policy. The exclusion policy, often overlooked, was important in its own right and played a significant role in American relations with China. Its influence was especially evident between 1900 and 1906 when misunderstandings were prevalent.

The time has surely come to take a closer look at this policy's abrasive and psychologically damaging effects — and examine the dynamics of the policy in the early 1900s. Four questions will receive special attention in this study: (1) What role did the policy play in American politics and society? (2) Why was it continued? (3) How upsetting was it in relations with China? (4) How much of a threat was it to the open door policy?

Within the United States this policy of national and racial discrimination in immigration proved seriously divisive and produced a continuing tug-of-war among business, labor, religious, and other groups over what American policy toward China should be. An examination of these internal dynamics will give one a better grasp of why relations with China were allowed to reach the serious point that they did after the turn of the century.

The crisis in the early 1900s was real enough when more and more Chinese resentment was stirred up by the exclusion policy. Chinese diplomats objected vehemently to the enactment of new exclusion laws and intervened extensively in American domestic politics to reverse the trend. China also abruptly terminated a treaty which acquiesced in these restrictions and sought one of a less discriminatory type. When other forms of protest failed, Chinese merchants resorted to a boycott of American goods; this in turn led to American military threats and plans to seize Canton. Certainly the period was a stormy one.

Yet while this was going on, the open door policy, announced in 1899 and 1900, was seeking to promote trade and friendly relations. Since it tended to challenge the exclusion policy, one would expect efforts to be made in the United States to introduce a more consistent arrangement. Such indeed was the case, but these endeavors ran into major obstacles. Trade opportunities were correspondingly adversely affected. It is surprising that more attention has not been given in recent times to the exclusion policy since it touches on the themes of racism, discrimination, the problems of ethnic groups, and American policy in Asia all at the same time. Too often the policy is assumed to have been a static one. It was not.

A reexamination of the issue is surely warranted when it is remembered that the standard work is still Mary B. Coolidge's *Chinese Immigration* (New York, 1909). New insights are now possible from the Bureau of Immigration records, diplomatic correspondence, and private collections which were not available to Coolidge. From these records and with the perspective now possible, a dynamic new stage in the movement beginning at the turn of the century may be discerned, which I have labeled the Powderly policy. Once the new stage in the exclusion drive is exposed to full view, the Chinese boycott of 1905-1906 as a reaction to it becomes more understandable. Many aspects of this complex movement have still not been carefully studied. The role played by Chinese-Americans in its beginnings, for example, has been largely overlooked. Nor has much attention been paid to the activities of the Chinese Empire Reform Association in America in this connection. Consideration needs to be given as well to the boycott's link with treaty negotiations and how and why the movement came to an end.

As for President Theodore Roosevelt's policy toward China during the boycott, this important subject has been examined before. But while Howard K. Beale's *Theodore Roosevelt and the Rise of America to World Power* (Baltimore, 1950) emphasizes the imperialistic attitudes of the times and portrays the president's resort to military threats in that context, another viewpoint — offered here — is that Roosevelt's military posture was primarily a defensive measure, designed to protect American citizens in China against a second Boxer-type uprising.

Throughout the period, the activities of the Bureau of Immigration represent a bizarre intrusion into the diplomatic decision-making process. The unconventional lobbying techniques of Chinese diplomats in the United States is another curious sidelight. The involvement of Chinese-Americans in influencing United States foreign policy is a story worth telling also. Indeed, for Chinese-Americans the boycott may be seen as a unique civil rights movement. Nor should the San Francisco earthquake of 1906 be overlooked as a novel and significant factor in affecting the direction of events.

Exclusion cannot, of course, be dismissed as a domestic policy, since it was based on treaties with China and remained so until 1904 when it was arbitrarily transformed into internal policy through new legislation. Even then it did not abruptly cease to be a major issue in relations between the United States and China; and, to be understood properly, it must be explored in both international and domestic political terms. Although enormously complicated, the subject is also unexpectedly fascinating.

Acknowledgments

Although my graduate student days are not of recent vintage, I should acknowledge, nevertheless, the influence of diplomatic historians such as Thomas A. Bailey, my former major professor, Fred H. Harrington, and Richard W. Van Alstyne. In East Asian History and International Relations, I owe much to Claude A. Buss, Theodore Chen, Franz H. Michael, Kazuo Kawai, and others.

Concerning the book at hand, I am especially grateful to Paul A. Varg for reading and criticizing an early draft and to Bailey for wise counsel on important points. For help on special aspects, I wish to thank Samuel C. Chu, John K. Fairbank, and Harold Z. Schiffrin. Charles C. Cook provided much valuable assistance regarding style. Colleagues past and present who have helped with inspiration and criticism include Arthur L. Jensen, Wallace N. Jamison, Martin Ridge, and Harry G. Swanhart.

Among libraries, I wish to recognize my indebtedness to Allegheny College Library, the Carnegie Library of Pittsburgh, Catholic University of America Library, Georgetown University Library, Grove City College Library, Houghton Library of Harvard University, Library of Congress, University of Pittsburgh Library, Stanford University Library, Westminster College Library, and Yale University Library. Many librarians and achivists have been most kind. I especially wish to thank W.H. Bond of the Houghton Library, Moreau B.C. Chambers of Catholic University of America, Mabel Kocher of Westminster College, Donald Mosholder of the National Archives, Buford Rowland of the Legislative Records Section, and Dorothy Smith of Allegheny College. W. W. Rockhill papers were used by permission of the Harvard College Library.

12

For help with translations, I wish to thank Joannie Chang Hung, Philip Liu, and Fifi Lee Servoss. Sally Atkinson was a most efficient typist, and Connie Sharkey gave valuable assistance in preparing the index.

I am grateful too for the help and forbearance of members of my family: my wife Margaret, son Richard, and daughters Anne and Mary.

Finally, I am most appreciative of the grants provided by the Faculty Research Committee and Administration of Westminster College.

The Two Policies: The Conflict

As a people we have talked much of the open door in China, and we expect, and quite rightly intend to insist upon, justice being shown us by the Chinese. But we cannot ask the Chinese to do to us what we are unwilling to do to them.

> Theodore Roosevelt, "Annual Message,"
> Dec. 5, 1905, U.S., Congress, *A Compilation of the Messages and Papers of the Presidents*, 20 vols. (New York, 1902-1908), 15: 7009.

"An Open Door for our merchants, our railway projectors, our mine operators, our missionaries," we cry, and at the same moment we slam the door in the face of the Chinese merchants, travelers, and students — the best classes who seek our shores.

> Luella Miner (missionary, teacher),
> "American Barbarism and Chinese Hospitality," *Outlook* 72 (Dec. 27, 1902): 988.

From every point of view this discrimination is a loss to the American people, diplomatically and from the point of view of the extension of American trade.

> Wilbur T. Gracey (consul) to Herbert H. D. Peirce,
> Nov. 29, 1904, National Archives, Record Group 59, Consular Dispatches, Nanking.

After contending so vigorously all these years for the open door in China, it would be the crassest of folly for us to shut the door against ourselves by our own act.

> *New York Daily Tribune*, Aug. 14, 1905, p. 6.

1
The Two China Policies
of the United States

Can a merchant insult a man and sell goods to him at the same time? In 1900 Americans seemed to think the answer was yes as their government announced the open door policy for China. The new policy — new at least on paper — contained in the open door notes of 1899 and 1900, signified the desire of the United States to preserve and expand the China market for American businessmen. But this was not the only policy held by the United States, even though President William McKinley and his secretary of state, John Hay, acted as if it were. In the background the exclusion policy, which had by treaty and legislation singled out and barred Chinese laborers as early as the 1880s, constituted a major policy too and one that reflected a distinctly different approach to China from that offered in the open door notes. For reasons peculiar to the situation, only a few perceptive Americans grasped that the United States had come to have two markedly different policies. Even fewer suspected that the earlier trend would seriously interfere with the later one. Yet the six years after 1900 saw much evidence that the first was indeed a formidable handicap. Offending a potential customer, as exclusion obviously did, was simply not good business.

Nevertheless, the two policies seemed unrelated on the surface; the contradiction between them tended to be obscured. The confusion was compounded because the open door policy applied to China but was not really a policy which had been made with that country. Since it was directed mainly at nations with spheres of interest in the Middle Kingdom, China was not even notified at the time the policy was instituted. Nor did these developments in the heady arena of international politics appear to have anything to do with the exclusion laws which followed soon after the 1880 treaty with China. It is possible, of course, that no conflict would have arisen if the original exclusion arrangement had not evolved subsequently into something different — a point for our consideration later.

As for the open door policy, its basic provisions are well known.[1] Within the spheres of interest of the various nations, the United States was requesting that harbor dues, railroad rates, and tariff duties remain the same for all foreign nationals. After the sending of the notes in 1899 to the great powers, the United States took a more forward position in 1900, when the Boxer Rebellion created a new set of circumstances, by insisting also that China's territorial and administrative integrity be preserved.

A survey of the interest groups behind the open door policy helps to explain its nature. By far the most prominent and powerful was surely the American Asiatic Association. Some scholars have gone so far as to give this organization most of the credit for persuading the nation to adopt the policy. Charles S. Campbell, Jr., for example, contends that the first set of notes was based on a memorandum that "reflected faithfully the propaganda of the American Asiatic Association." [2] Organized on January 6, 1898, with James McGee of Standard Oil Company presiding at the meeting, this group started out with 38 members who wished to promote trade and closer ties with China. By 1900 it had grown to 100 members and counted among them outstanding names in the business community.[3] Diplomats, scholars, and clergymen were also included in its membership. It inspired the formation of the American Association of China and maintained close ties with the American Asiatic Association of Japan and the China Association of London. At its annual meetings, it made a special effort to secure the attendance of the secretary of state, the ministers of China and Japan, and House and Senate members of the committees on foreign relations. Its secretary, John Foord, was able and forceful, and its monthly *Journal* was well edited and influential.

Confronting the enthusiasm and drive of this group, one is amazed at the small economic stake of the American businessman in China in 1900. Present in that country were 81 American firms and only 1,908 American residents of all types. The investment figure stood at a modest $17,500,000. Sales to China for 1900 were valued at only $23,745,000 ($60,598,000 for all of Asia) in contrast to sales to Europe of $1,111,456,000.[4]

It was evident that dreams about the future, not present reality, supplied the motivation for American businessmen. Former minister to China Charles Denby made that point clear in his remarks at the annual meeting of the Association in 1900. "The Eldorado of commerce," he proclaimed, "lies before us in the Far East."[5] Wu T'ing-fang, minister from China, at the same meeting, added his bit to the optimism of the hour. China was a great potential market, he agreed. "With your Pacific a fine highway and the Philippines at our door, you have great opportunities. If you don't come up, it is your fault."[6] Hopes were high among businessmen that the sale to China of cotton goods, kerosene, flour, machinery, and even railroads would grow in volume at a rapid rate.

Next in importance to the businessmen as an interest group were the missionaries whose connection with the open door policy was less obvious but significant nonetheless. By 1898, 23 American Protestant societies were represented in China by 276 ordained missionaries, 155 stations, and even more out-stations.[7] American missionary properties in 1900 were valued at $5,000,000.[8] Measured in both spiritual and material terms, the investment in China was substantial. With such a vested interest, Protestant churches and their missions could not be indifferent that their beachhead in Asia rested upon specific treaty terms. Preachers, missionaries, and church publications aroused a lively regard for China among church members. This special fascination with China, in turn, encouraged the government of the United States to take action on behalf of missions. Nothing in the open door notes pertained directly to religious bodies, but the churches and missions could read into the notes a restraining hand placed upon pro-Catholic European countries and a general endorsement of the status quo which worked to their own advantage.[9]

Another interest group is often overlooked. Educational institutions in China, founded by missionaries, were growing so rapidly that they were taking on a distinct identity by 1900. The figures for 1898 showed 1,032 schools and 74 higher educational institutions which altogether embraced approximately 20,000 Chinese students enrolled in American schools.[10] Therefore, American educators should also be counted as a force on the China scene. And they benefited too from the open door policy.

Other interest groups, some non-American, might be added to the list. The Chinese Imperial Maritime Customs Service, for example, had its own bureaucratic motives in lobbying for the open door policy.[11] The American navy, which would have preferred a base on the China coast, was definitely not in favor of the open door.[12] American policymakers, from McKinley and Hay to William W. Rockhill, State

Department authority on China, had to sense and respond to many domestic and international considerations in structuring a policy that would best serve the national interest. At that time, they had to be especially sensitive to the fulminations against imperialism of an articulate anti-expansionist minority.

Thus, the open door policy emerged as a compromise. It fitted admirably, however, the temper of the times with its incredible mixture of both idealistic crusading and self-seeking imperialism. The policy represented expansion without territorial acquisition or, as one scholar has described it, "a most interesting hybrid of anti-colonialism and economic imperialism."[13]

The Boxer Rebellion crisis, a brief but ugly encounter in the summer of 1900, was a severe test of the will of Americans to hold to their goals of commercial and cultural penetration, but they held firm. Despite the discouraging outlook, missionaries preserved an air of grim optimism. In June 1900, while the outcome of the uprising was still in doubt, the Reverend D.Z. Sheffield prepared to return to his station, even though, he wrote, "I know that my own work is wiped out."[14] Thirty-two members of the American missionary community had lost their lives. Yet it was certain, the *Missionary Review of the World* declared in September, "that the glorious Gospel will not suffer defeat or expulsion, but, instead, the day of its complete victory will be marvelously hastened."[15] The Progressive Era was dawning in the United States, and the reform spirit of the day saw a challenge in China. Education would be the key; by exposing Chinese to American schools that country could be induced to adopt the American model.[16] High hopes were held for the future relationship between the two countries.

Various aspects of the open door policy were manifestly important to China. Rockhill, writing in *Forum* in May 1900, contended that his first set of notes had "put a stop to the grab policy" and had "rendered a vast service to China."[17] Unrealistically, he envisioned future collaboration between the United States and China; together, they might even the odds in the balance of power in Asia.[18] In any case, he assumed that China would welcome the policy.

Public reactions of Chinese officials in the United States were indeed favorable. Ho Yow, consul general at San Francisco, writing in *Forum* in June 1900, hailed the new posture as "the most important diplomatic event" since the treaty of 1842 which had opened five ports to trade.[19] He held that the merchant class at the trade centers would especially favor the United States for its stand.

Minister Wu, in June, urged the United States to resist addition-al colonization in Asia. Since America now had the Philippines, he argued, it should not want other nations to encroach further upon the Asian mainland: "No man can tell how long the 'open door' can be maintained . . . unless further aggressions are prevented."[20] In early July Hay's second set of notes, which stressed the need to preserve the territorial integrity of China, seemed to be in accord with Wu's think-ing. In July Wu also elaborated on the theme of "mutual helpfulness." China could be the market; the United States could supply capital and build railroads; both sides would benefit. Moreover, China "was well disposed toward Americans."[21] However, contradictory currents pre-vailed. On the one hand, on July 13, 1900, only two weeks after the Hay circular came out, the Chinese officially extended the right to build the Canton-Hankow railroad to the American China Develop-ment Company. On the other hand, at this same time the Boxers were attempting to destroy all foreigners or drive them out of China.

To a western mind certain features of the open door policy should have seemed especially appealing to China, which, presuma-bly, was desperately eager to preserve its territorial integrity and should thus have been gratified to have the United States uphold the cause. As for the principle of an even-handed treatment of merchants, since China for years had pursued a deliberate course of treating all foreigners alike, it should have welcomed the stand of the United States on this point also. But China had its ancient tradition of en-couraging barbarians to fight barbarians, and the empire was not noted for allowing traditions to die quickly. For China to adopt a long-range policy of cooperating with one foreign power against others would have been a radical and improbable shift in strategy. Moreover, while the self-interest of the two countries in some areas may have occasionally coincided, in others it did not. As the Chinese officials in America viewed the situation, the United States should pay a price for China's trade; America might even go so far as to give up its une-qual treaties. Reciprocity, wrote Wu, "must be the key-note of every arrangement."[22] By inference, he challenged the foundations of the American position in China.

In more concrete terms, however, the price demanded by the Chinese was the abandonment of the exclusion policy. Both Ho and Wu seized every opportunity to point out the improbability of future American trade advances so long as exclusion remained in effect. Ho, insisting that the exclusion laws harmed trade and industrial growth, predicted in one article that these laws, unless repealed, would destroy "the very thing which the President and his advisers are trying so hard to establish: namely, commercial preeminence for the United States in the East."[23] Wu complained that, while China's door was open to Americans, the American door was "slammed in the face" of the Chinese.[24] The *New Orleans Times-Picayune* had reason to express reservations about the new open door policy in that it might undercut the exclusion policy.[25] China certainly wanted it to do just that. Wu in January 1900 had announced that exclusion would have to give way to the open door. "It will not do," he informed the American Asiatic Association, "for you to expect China to keep her door open all of the time if you shut the door on Chinese merchants who come to your gate."[26] Not only would trade not increase, he warned; it might even drop off altogether and there might be a large scale boycott of American goods. The Association should work for juster laws, and should "instruct the people here as to what we need and what is fair treatment."[27]

China's position as presented by Wu posed a major challenge to the open door policy. Trade would not grow — the open door policy would fail — unless the exclusion policy was eliminated. Wu insisted that a merchant could not sell goods to a man he was insulting. But in that imperialistic era, western nations took for granted that they could override opposition and impose their control and trade upon the peoples of other lands. For this as well as other reasons, many Americans were inclined to take lightly these angry Chinese warnings. By looking into the origins and characteristics of the policy, the full import of the exclusion issue can be grasped.

"It is the only question between us,"[28] wrote Minister Rockhill in 1905 to the Chinese Foreign Office, as he discussed a new immigration treaty in the final days before the Chinese instituted their threatened boycott, a remark which many American diplomats on relations with China from the 1870s on might have made. From its inception, the exclusion policy had been a constant irritant. "I don't ask any privileges for my people; I only ask equality," asserted Wu to a reporter in 1901.[29] His wish was a forlorn one. Special treatment, not equality, was the lot of the Chinese from the time of their first arrival in America. The treaties, the laws, the court decisions, and the reactions of localities were all evidence of this exceptional treatment.

It is officially recorded that the first Chinese to arrive in California were two men and a woman from Hong Kong who landed in San Francisco in February 1848.[30] As more arrived, some worked as laborers in San Francisco; others soon found their way into the gold mining areas. In 1852 alone 30,000 Chinese left Hong Kong for San Fran-cisco.[31] Opposition did not commence immediately, but discriminatory taxes were levied by 1852. Nevertheless, California in the 1850s needed cheap labor; Chinese were welcomed in certain occupations such as servants and laundrymen. Then in the 1860s, when the federal government sponsored the building of a transcontinental railroad, the promoters looked to China for large numbers of unskilled labor and found them.

With the depression of the 1870s, however, opposition to Chinese immigration arose in California and reached a high pitch. Scholars are not in agreement as to the reasons for this rising hostility. Some writers have stressed racial prejudice and have pointed to the large number of people in California from southern states. Others have emphasized cultural differences, noting that the Chinese clung to their traditional attire, language, and exotic "Chinatowns." Others have given special attention to economic factors: the willingness of Chinese to work for low wages; the fact that they were usually bound by contract to a Chinese broker in a manner reminiscent of slavery; the discovery that they could be employed as strikebreakers against unions and were so used in eastern states; and the tensions built up by a depression in California in the 1870s. One scholar has also empha-sized that Chinese, unlike other immigrants, were planning to live in the United States for a limited time only and would then return with their earnings to their families in China; therefore, their goals were markedly dissimilar from those of the people around them.[32] All of these factors were doubtless important, but there is no simple explan-ation for the rise of extreme anti-Chinese sentiments. Furthermore, this hostility, although most dramatically expressed in California, proved to be a national phenomenon.[33]

How this anti-Chinese feeling developed can be traced by re-viewing the immigration treaties from 1868 to the end of the century and examining the exclusion laws that evolved in the 1880s and 1890s. Article V of the Burlingame Treaty of 1868 was an open invitation to Chinese to come to America. Although condemning involuntary im-migration, it recognized "the inherent and inalienable right of man to change his home and allegiance, and also the mutual advantage" of the movement of people "from one country to the other, for purposes of curiosity, of trade, or as permanent residents."[34] In the same cordial tones, article VI supported the right to travel and reside in the two countries, as accorded to "the most favored nati⹁n," and article VII extended educational privileges.

But in spite of the benign spirit of the 1868 treaty, there was a peculiar quality about it in that immigration had become a subject for diplomacy. Article VI also stipulated that "nothing herein contained shall be held to confer naturalization upon citizens of the United States in China, nor upon the subjects of China in the United States."[35] Were nationals to be only temporary sojourners in the other's land? What about citizenship if they decided to be permanent residents? Whether the arriving Chinese intended to make the United States their permanent home or not, the increasing numbers coming to California seemed to point in that direction. In the 1850s over 40,000 arrived, and in the 1860s over 60,000 more had come.[36] In the 1870s, in the era of the Burlingame Treaty, the number of Chinese residents attained the peak figure of 123,201. Conditions in China during and after the Taiping Rebellion of 1850-1864 were bad enough to drive more Chinese away from their homeland; the news of the gold rush of 1849 in California added further incentive;[37] and then the need for workers on the Central Pacific railroad in the 1860s continued the trend. William H. Seward, secretary of state at the time of the negotiation of the Burlingame Treaty, was especially interested in the railroad labor factor.[38] Nine out of ten of the 10,000 laborers on the Pacific railroads in 1869 were Chinese.

With the completion of the Pacific railroads in 1869, the troubles of the Chinese in California mounted.[39] There was no other work for them to take up the slack quickly, so they drifted, over 9,000 strong, into San Francisco, desperate for jobs of any kind — and at any wage. To add to this already existing labor glut, workers from the east migrated to the west over the new Union Pacific railroad. New economic calamity struck the west coast with the nationwide panic of 1873. Since about one third of the white population of California was from the south, racial antipathies were already present. Added to the race factor were the explosive economic pressures of the 1870s.[40]

Dennis Kearney, an Irish Catholic, became the leader of the Workingman's Party, which was organized in 1877.[41] Although this party lasted only five years, it significantly advanced union organizing efforts in the state. The unions found that their most useful rallying device was opposition to the Chinese; ties with the national labor movement of the day, the Knights of Labor, "carried across the land their slogan *The Chinese Must Go*."[42]

As the Chinese issue rose to prominence in California, both Democrats and Republicans in the state embraced it and secured discriminatory legislation. Racially oriented court decisions also came out of California, and legislative action on the national level was earnestly sought. A California memorial to Congress stated that California if necessary would forego the benefits of trade with China in return for an end to Chinese immigration.[43] The alarm expressed by the memorial and implied by a referendum on the issue was undoubtedly heightened as the number of Chinese residents in California increased to 100,000 by 1875; moreover, by the late 1870s the "male adults almost equaled the voting population of the state."[44] By 1882 the Chinese population had risen to 132,000 and seemed to be accelerating at an alarming rate.[45]

Although Californians believed their civilization was being threatened, the rest of the country was not convinced. The tradition of open and free immigration was not easy to reverse, and the resort to violence in California against the Chinese was especially difficult to understand elsewhere. In Congress, however, the even balance between the two parties helped the California cause. Although President Rutherford Hayes vetoed a bill in 1879 that would have restricted the number of Chinese immigrants to 15 per vessel, he realized that it would be advisable to seek a new treaty with China to modify the immigration provisions of the Burlingame Treaty. Since China was reluctant to agree to a new treaty, the outcome was a compromise that only partially satisfied the Californians and other anti-Chinese elements. The treaty concluded on November 17, 1880, allowed the United States to legislate against Chinese laborers: the United States could "regulate, limit, or suspend such coming or residence, but may not absolutely prohibit."[46] Fair treatment of other Chinese was promised in the treaty, which contained no time limit and was presented as a supplement to the 1868 treaty.

More obstacles developed as exclusionists pressed for restrictive legislation under the new treaty. Through the use of petitions and memorials, the pro-Chinese fought hard against new laws. Centered in the northeast, especially New York and Massachusetts, business interests and missionary-minded Protestants stood for the status quo. The anti-Chinese, however, overcame the opposition, but with difficulty, and obtained a bill suspending Chinese immigration for 25 years. Among the anti-Chinese forces labor unions were especially active; throughout the country they joined with California to secure the new bill.[47] Which were more desirable: racial homogeneity and labor progress within the United States or trade with China and Christianizing activity in a foreign country? Although the issue was perhaps not quite that simple, Congress in approving exclusion appeared to be subordinating trade and missionary interests.

But the matter was not yet settled. Another hurdle loomed.

President Chester Arthur sided with the pro-Chinese groups in veto-
ing the new bill on the grounds that 25 years went beyond anything
authorized by the treaty. He did, nevertheless, accept the law of May
6, 1882, which suspended the immigration of Chinese laborers for ten
years and prohibited states from granting citizenship to Chinese.[48]
Other legislation followed in the 1880s that further broadened the incredibly elastic definition of *laborer* which appeared in the 1882 law.
Special certificates also had to be obtained by those who went to
China and then returned; they also had to be processed by consular
officers and treasury officials. Although the number of immigrants
dropped to 61,711 for the decade,[49] back where it had been in the 1860s,
violence broke out in Rock Springs, Wyoming, in 1885 and resulted in
the death of over 20 Chinese.[50]

The most controversial legislation of the 1880s was that of September 13, 1888, which was signed by Grover Cleveland. This act
made no pretense of excluding laborers only; it prohibited the entry of
all Chinese persons except "teachers, students, merchants, or travelers for pleasure or curiosity."[51] These special classes of Chinese, as
named in the law, had to be approved by the Chinese government in
certificate form, and by an American consul. Another provision
barred laborers returning unless they had a family in the United
States or property worth one thousand dollars.

In less than a month the Scott Act of October 1, 1888, voided certificates which had already been issued and denied entrance immediately to returning laborers. "By it," charged a Californian in the
North American Review in 1900, "twenty thousand certificates were
declared null and void, twenty thousand promises, on the honor of the
United States, that the holders should be allowed to return, were
ruthlessly broken."[52] This act, he maintained, "completely demoral-
ized the Chinese in this country, which was the intention."[53]

While the Scott Act was enacted without reservations, the act
just preceding it, on September 13, 1888, stipulated that the law was
to go into effect after a pending treaty with China had been ratified;
China, however, infuriated by the earlier actions of Congress, failed to
ratify the treaty.[54] The legality of the September 13 legislation could
then be challenged, but on July 7, 1899, the solicitor of the treasury
ruled that sections five to eleven, which dealt with this matter, were
not dependent upon treaty ratification.[55] In spite of the growing number of restrictions on Chinese immigration, the exclusionists were
never satisfied. In the early 1890s bills introduced in Congress called
for the exclusion of all Chinese except officials.[56] Although these bills

did not get far, they revealed the long-range goal of the exclusionists.

Since 1892 was an election year, it was not surprising that a new law, the Geary Act of May 5, 1892, should pass. This law, in contrast to the Scott Act, allowed Chinese laborers to travel to China and re-enter the United States, but its provisions were, in general, more restrictive than anything preceding it. The new law, although perhaps designed primarily to apprehend violators of the exclusion laws, had the effect of bearing heavily upon Chinese-Americans in general. For example, the Geary Act, in addition to continuing all Chinese immigration laws for another ten years, required Chinese to register, secure a certificate, and use this as proof of their right to be in the United States; in certain circumstances bail was not allowed. The law also "authorized arrest without warrant or oath ... and shifted the burden of proof to the defendant."[57] Imprisonment and deportation were the penalty for those who failed to have a certificate.

Another act further increasing the already tight restrictions quickly followed in 1893. Chinese-Americans, thoroughly aroused by this time, hired able lawyers and tried to get favorable decisions from the courts, especially on the registration requirement, but their efforts ended in failure. From then on, the burden of proof lay with any Chinese in the United States to demonstrate his right to reside in the country.

In the 1890s the Chinese government, for the third time in the nineteenth century, agreed to an immigration treaty. Although by this time all Chinese were excluded except "officials, teachers, students, merchants or travelers for curiosity or pleasure," the new treaty of March 17, 1894, still referred to the original purpose of "regulating, limiting, or suspending the coming of Chinese laborers."[58] It extended the prohibition of laborers for ten years, and authorized laborers in the United States to return to China and then come back to the United States; it also allowed Chinese the right of transit, and provided for the reciprocal registration of laborers. The designated classes, as indicated above, were still allowed entry.

A review of the laws and treaties pertaining to Chinese immigration cannot ignore the conflict between them. Many court cases dealt with the position of the Chinese in the United States and with the lack of consistency between treaty and law. In one instance, the Supreme Court frankly conceded that a conflict existed between a treaty and a recently passed law. Nevertheless, the Court took the view that the morals of another branch of the government were its own affair and that if Congress wanted to violate a treaty it had the power to do so.[59] An article on the Scott Act in *Arena* stated, "there was no question but that the act was a violation of treaty stipulations; no one denied it."[60]

The reaction of Chinese in America to the trend of events is easily surmised. One missionary to the Chinese in California spoke at a Senate hearing of the hostility toward Christianity among the Chinese. When he tried to bring the Christian message to the Chinese, stated the Reverend Nathan R. Johnson, they would reply with finality, "Kearney is a Christian."[61] In California, the plight of the Chinese saddened and alarmed a segment of the Protestant clergy, who were convinced that such treatment would "provoke retaliatory Chinese exclusion and persecution of the American missionaries in China."[62]

In China the reverberations began to spread also. In 1903 Lee Chew told of his experiences as a boy in a village in the Canton area. He said that he learned from his grandfather "about the American foreign devils, that they were false, having made a treaty by which it was agreed that they could freely come to China and the Chinese as freely go to their country. After this treaty was made China opened its doors to them and then they broke the treaty that they had asked for by shutting the Chinese out of their country."[63] Some parts of Lee Chew's story raise questions about the factual authenticity of his grandfather's teachings, but his statements about what was probably beginning to happen in the Canton area in the 1880s and 1890s have a plausible ring.

Minister Wu argued that trade relations between the two countries began to suffer when the United States turned against the Chinese immigrants. He presented statistics on trade between 1871 and 1901 to support his argument, and insisted that trade had dropped sharply after the passage of each new law.[64] The frustration of the Chinese government was acute because it could not block the trend or show its resentment convincingly.[65] After 1884, diplomatic relations grew steadily worse.[66] By the time of the Harrison administration of 1889-1893, according to Tyler Dennett, "a condition amounting practically to non-intercourse existed between the Chinese legation and the Department of State."[67] When the United States proposed Senator Henry W. Blair as a new minister to China in 1891, his nomination was rejected by China because of statements that he had made in the Senate on immigration.[68] Americans in China, however, were not singled out for retaliatory treatment.[69]

Although Chinese reactions, both officially and unofficially, had become more hostile by the 1890s, the exclusionists seemed unconcerned. Their momentum had acquired enough strength to override the protests of China-oriented business and religious groups who expressed growing alarm over retaliatory steps which China might take against them. In Congress, the exclusion policy was clearly receiving priority. In this arena at least, trade and missionary interests were fighting a losing battle.

Another policy toward China, however, had seized the center of the stage as the nineteenth century came to a close. An exciting war with Spain had just been fought. Expansion had caught the popular imagination. Hawaii and the Philippines represented new links with Asia. An Isthmian canal, which was a frequent subject of discussion, would open a shorter highway into the Pacific. And beyond the horizon lay the "Eldorado of commerce," in matchless splendor, the world of East Asia! In the open door policy, the McKinley administration staked out its claim to a voice in the politics of Asia and identified the national interest of the United States with the promotion of trade with China and the protection of missionary interests.

Here were two policies toward China, each backed by powerful vested interests. Congress gave priority to exclusion; the executive branch appeared more sensitive to trade and missions. Could the two policies be maintained simultaneously? In one sense, the new policy of the open door signaled a counter attack against the exclusion policy. Was it possible that the exclusion policy, after dominating the scene since the 1870s, might be uprooted?

2

The Powderly Exclusion Policy

At least one spokesman for the missionary community insisted that exclusion should make way for the open door. Mrs. S. L. Baldwin, in a letter to President Theodore Roosevelt in 1900, drew attention in forthright terms to the contradiction between the two policies. "What kind of a 'bargain' are we driving," she asked, "when we demand that *every* door in China shall be open to us — to exploit for our benefit — not even making any conditions as to who of our people . . . shall enter those forced open doors while we reenact laws to exclude all Chinese?"[1] The letter was referred to Roosevelt's commissioner general of immigration, Terence V. Powderly, the former leader of the Knights of Labor, who replied by disclaiming responsibility and directing her to Congress "as the question of re-enactment of the exclusion laws is a matter which will come before Congress during this session."[2]

Determined to have the last word, Mrs. Baldwin, president of the Women's Foreign Missionary Society — and wife of a former missionary — wrote again to Powderly to argue that labor should not support exclusion: "It becomes an insult to *labor* and ought to stir every *laborer* against this, for us to demand every door in China to be open to *all* of *our people* and refuse to open any door here to them. The injustice cries to heaven."[3]

Mrs. Baldwin's letters suggested that missionary groups were seeking a significant modification of exclusion and thought they had a lever in the popularity of the open door policy. Unlike Mrs. Baldwin, however, most Americans did not appear to be troubled by inconsistencies in policies toward China.[4] If they could, they wanted to keep both the open door policy and the exclusion policy, apparently assuming that China would remain passive or too weak to be considered.

Whatever the reason, the exclusion policy refused to fade away.

Contrary to a view that gained wide acceptance among scholars, the older policy not only held its own after 1900[5] but, in fact, took on dimensions by 1900 and thereafter which made it into a new policy. Although keeping the same term, its character became greatly changed.

The term *exclusion* causes difficulty because it is flexible and has changed meanings as frequently as the term *open door*. Probably the word was originally selected because its extremist implications would appeal to Californians; nevertheless, in its inception in the 1880s, it meant restricted immigration but by no means *total* exclusion. At first skilled and unskilled Chinese laborers were denied entrance. By the changing definitions and then by the controversial legislation of 1888, the term came to mean all Chinese except teachers, officials, students, merchants, or travelers — the so-called exempt classes — and the policy remained at approximately that point until almost the end of the century.

The new Powderly policy, as it unfolded after 1898, was one that worked consciously and actively for *total* exclusion. It followed the concept outlined in 1900 by J. M. Scanland in *Arena:* "The 'Exclusion' law does not exclude."[6] Pointing to loopholes, he concluded: "The only way to check this flow is to repeal the favored clause — excluding all except diplomats."[7] Although its main thrust was directed at preventing the entry of all Chinese, the plan had two other significant features: the deliberate harassment of Chinese within the United States with the intent of driving this minority group out of the country entirely — the Boston raid and mass arrest of October 11, 1903, being an extreme example of this constant molestation; the geographical extension of the policy beyond the limits of the United States proper, notably to Hawaii and the Philippines — both of which had sizeable Chinese minorities.

Since the new design did not come about through specific legislation or in a sudden, dramatic manner, it escaped the notice of most people of that day unless they were directly affected by it. It was further disguised because innovators like Powderly denied that they were doing anything new. In form, the policy was a subtle and silent administrative revolution carried out by the Bureau of Immigration. Congressmen became faintly aware of this revolution by 1902 as they gave their legislative blessing to an accomplished fact. Although no sudden departure from the past ever occurred, some features of the program were already discernible in 1898; by 1900 the most sweeping elements had been instituted.

At the turn of the century, the Bureau of Immigration served as an excellent vehicle for developing and carrying out a drastic exclusion program. The new agency, established by Congress in 1891 within the Treasury Department, was in the throes of developing professional standards. Starved for funds, it was inclined to use any means available to extract larger appropriations from a parsimonious Congress. Thus, the temptation was great for the bureau's spokesmen to exaggerate the extent of fraud and abuse which took place in carrying out the Chinese laws and regulations, which in turn called for more and more severe measures.[8] But the mastermind of the new approach, and the person setting the tone for the whole department, was Powderly. The former labor leader had earlier shifted into a career in law in Pennsylvania. He was active in politics and had worked hard for the Republican party in the election of 1896. McKinley, needing help badly against Bryan among the workers, was indebted to Powderly for his vigorous support. After the McKinley victory, Powderly asked for and was granted the post of commissioner general of immigration; he assumed office on August 3, 1897. With his arrival the spirit of Dennis Kearney took over the young bureau; Californians soon realized their fondest hopes.[9] With Powderly in command, labor's influence also became pronounced within the bureau. Although Lyman Gage was secretary of the treasury and nominally in charge of immigration affairs too, Gage seldom interfered with bureau affairs. Powderly had a free hand to make policy and to place men who saw matters as he did in strategic positions. James R. Dunn, who became Chinese inspector at San Francisco on May 15, 1899, was one of this type. Dunn, a union man in background, was a man with a mission, an energetic and resourceful leader in the crusade against the Chinese. Although Dunn appeared to need no encouragement, Powderly showed a marked favoritism toward those officers who took the most severe attitude toward the Chinese.[10]

Prominent among the rising social forces at work behind these personalities and the Bureau of Immigration was the growing power of organized labor. The American Federation of Labor, organized in 1886, had attained a size by 1896 that attracted the attention of men in public office. The president of the American Federation of Labor, Samuel Gompers, had campaigned against McKinley but found the new president willing to meet with the Federation's Executive Council.[11] In addition to this surprising innovation, Gompers found McKinley willing to meet with him personaily on labor matters.

Gompers, a remarkably energetic and effective labor leader, threw his heart and soul into the anti-Chinese cause. A cigar-maker' by occupation, he was especially sensitive to the upward movement of Chinese from the more menial jobs into more skilled ones like cigar-making, as well as into the shoe and textile industries. "More important," charged one biographer, "he loathed them as a race."[12] This was a time, of course, when racist ideas were prevalent. Gompers seemed sincerely to believe that the Chinese could not absorb American traditions and that their continued immigration would overturn western civilization.[13] Although no love was lost between Powderly and Gompers, the two men were in full agreement on the Chinese question. Already close ties between the Bureau of Immigration and the AFL became even closer in 1902 with Powderly's successor, Frank P. Sargent.

Although the initiative on anti-Chinese activities had fallen by 1900 into the hands of the bureau and the AFL, the Californians and others on the Pacific coast did not cease to be important. In Congress a regional bloc of votes could be counted on for tighter laws and higher appropriations. If the issue of race was emphasized, most southerners in Congress could be counted on to join in also.

Intellectual currents at the turn of the century also tended to favor the anti-Chinese side. Patriotic organizations had been growing in number and size since the 1880s.[14] These groups agitated against alien influence and demanded legislation against European immigration. Racial antipathies, propaganda in behalf of Anglo-Saxon superiority, and Social Darwinist "survival of the fittest" doctrines were part of the spirit of the times as well. Thus, receptive ears across the nation were ready to listen to proposals to tighten even more the restrictions on the Chinese. The reformist attitudes of the Progressive Movement also contributed their share by their sympathetic support for causes espoused by labor and by their reaction against the immoral aspects of the "Chinatowns."

By 1900 a creeping national consensus in favor of Chinese exclusion had emerged. Attorney General John W. Griggs, for example, had no labor ties and was from New Jersey, not California; nevertheless his opinion of July 15, 1898, opened the way for the bureau to move ahead. Rejecting the broad statements of the earlier treaties and laws, he asserted that "the true theory is not that all Chinese persons may enter this country who are not forbidden, but that only those are entitled to enter who are expressly allowed."[15] He specifically ruled on the word *merchant*. A *trader* — salesmen, buyers, clerks, and such — was different from a *merchant* and should not be admitted. This narrow definition of the merchant class dealt a heavy blow to one of the remaining groups still allowed to come in, but this measure was only the first of many steps to follow. On June 15, 1900, for example, the solicitor of the treasury placed the *student* in the same position as Griggs had placed the *merchant* by ruling that a student "is a person who intends to pursue some of the higher branches of study, or one who seeks to be fitted for some particular profession or occupation for which facilities of study are not afforded in his own country; one for whose support and maintenance in this country, as a student, provision has been made, and who, upon completion of his studies, expects to return to China."[16]

Only a few days before, on June 6, 1900, a law had given the commissioner general direct control of the exclusion laws and had specifically authorized him to make regulations.[17] The speed with which the new rulings followed revealed how impatiently Powderly had waited for the day when he could move ahead more openly. His cleverest and most effective move was the issuance in 1900 of a new set of regulations.[18] Superficially these were only rules and precedents selected from earlier laws, court decisions, legal opinions, and decisions made by former officials. From the many choices, however, which included both pro-Chinese and anti-Chinese rulings, his selections were invariably the harshest. By carefully choosing among the alternatives, he achieved a policy of exclusion that went far beyond anything that had previously been in effect. And yet, while revolutionary in scope, his new policy was ingeniously disguised as old regulations which had court endorsements.[19]

Still the relentless Powderly moved ahead. The transit question next received his attention. Convinced that many Chinese who were refused entry into the United States crossed over into Mexico and then returned illegally, he introduced new regulations on December 8, 1900, requiring Chinese to have a through ticket, furnish a bond of $500, present four photographs, and satisfy the collector of customs of a true intent to travel through the United States for the purpose stated.[20] To carry out the various parts of his program, Powderly preferred to have legal authorization, but he seemed not unwilling to proceed without it. When he requested Congress for a new law, he blandly admitted that in this instance he had been functioning outside the law:

> Your attention is called to the fact that the recent arrest of one Sam Wah Kee and six Chinamen, whom he was smuggling into this country, was made by an immigrant inspec-

tor, and resulted in the deportation of the six Chinamen and the prosecution of the smuggler, Sam Wah Kee. It is clear that if the said Chinese had knowledge of the lack of said immigrant inspector's authority to make said arrest they could have successfully resisted it.[21]

In the enforcement of the exclusion regulations, much responsibility for interpretation devolved upon officials at the various ports, especially at San Francisco, where most of the Chinese landed. One point of concern to an official was whether a returning merchant had to prove that he had performed no manual labor at all. Powderly replied that he would not lose his status as a merchant by washing his own clothes or those of his family. The commissioner general commented further, however, that if the official was in doubt about where to draw the line, "you may easily relieve yourself thereof by rejecting the applicant in any such case, leaving him to his own recourse by appeal to the Department."[22] Such a policy would mean expense and delay for the merchant; in addition, the tendency in Washington was to uphold the rulings of the port officials. Thus, Powderly had developed another device for barring or deporting Chinese.

Under James R. Dunn at San Francisco, Powderly's favorite among enforcement officials, the port acquired a reputation for draconian measures. The Reverend Ira Condit, who worked there with the Chinese, described the procedures in unflattering terms:

When they do arrive, merchants, laborers are all alike penned up, like a flock of sheep, in a wharf-shed, for many days, and often weeks, at their own expense, and are denied all communication with their own people, while the investigation of their cases moves its slow length along. The right of bail is denied. A man is imprisoned as a criminal who has committed no crime.[23]

Although the description is by a partisan observer, it demonstrates the role played by delay, expense, incarceration, and annoying investigations to discourage Chinese from seeking entry.

Soon after his arrival in San Francisco, Dunn became a center of controversy because Ho Mun, who had become ill in the detention shed, died in the county jail on November 21, 1899. The Chinese community was convinced that Dunn had denied Ho Mun medical attention; they obtained a lawyer who brought charges against Dunn in vitriolic language and denounced him especially for his arrogance. Rallying to his defense, however, his fellow officials insisted that the man who had died was trying to enter under false pretenses and that those bringing the charges were not really his relatives. The Building Trades Council of San Francisco, which claimed a membership of 8,500, also defended Dunn. Its resolutions, directed at the president, both houses of Congress, the secretary of state, and the secretary of the treasury, declared the council's "unqualified support to such officials as J. R. Dunn, Esq."[24] Calling him a victim of the mercantile and transportation interests, the council emphatically endorsed the procedures of the Chinese bureau. Thus, Dunn became and remained a hero of labor and other anti-Chinese elements in California in ensuing years, and the Treasury Department quickly cleared him of all charges.

Dunn, while enforcing rigorously the regulations that came down from above, urged Powderly for sterner measures, and these recommendations were frequently adopted. Because of his insistence, for example, the policy described earlier toward Chinese in transit had taken a sharper turn. In fact, the inspiration for Powderly's regulations of December 8, 1900, was supplied by Dunn, whose careful checking of baggage and individuals in the latter half of 1901 led to the rejection of 200 out of 1,000 such travelers.[25] By contrast, not one of the 37,000 Chinese in that category prior to 1901 was known to have been rejected. In Dunn's era, according to Mary R. Coolidge, "Treasury regulations culminated in a sort of reign of terror."[26] He was known to be hard of hearing, and his investigation of a Chinese immigrant through an interpreter — who was often unacquainted with certain Chinese dialects — must have been a fascinating spectacle to witness.

To Powderly, Dunn and his cohorts were ideal public servants. "Attention is specially called," wrote Powderly to the secretary of the treasury in his 1901 annual report, "to the report from San Francisco." The official in charge there (Dunn's superior) was "energetic, intelligent, and capable." Moreover, "nearly two-thirds of the applications were found to be fraudulent, and the applicants were denied admission."[27] In his first year of administering the exclusion acts, Powderly could point to other fruits of his tighter policies. Of 2,702 who had claimed membership in the exempt classes, the bureau had rejected 918. In addition, 328 had been deported who were illegally in the country.

But the commissioner general was still not fully satisfied. He had found many obstacles, he reported, to enforcing the laws. In his 1901 annual report, he expounded on how to evade them. Minor sons, he thought, were often not true sons. Returning laborers were not the same people who had acquired certificates earlier. Stricter rules were needed to prevent illegal entry across the land borders. And the term *merchant* needed a still narrower definition.

One point that he stressed in his report of June 1901 was the early expiration date of the exclusion laws, May 5, 1902.[28] In guarded language, the treasurer's report relayed the wishes of the Immigration Bureau. "If the laws should be renewed, or their provisions extended," wrote Secretary Gage, "the Department would be pleased to furnish a statement covering certain administrative betterments suggested by experience in their enforcement."[29]

Outside of the Bureau of Immigration, the exclusion policy was advancing on other fronts. By act of July 7, 1898, the policy was extended to the Hawaiian Islands; most of their 20,000 Chinese were thereby prohibited from emigrating to the mainland; only a few Chinese could continue to enter Hawaii from China. On November 25, 1898, an immigration official from the United States found procedures in the Islands different from those at home. He then changed the rules to conform. This meant the detention of Chinese travelers who had planned to sail to China on the steamer *Belgic*, he reported, but he had found a "cordial acquiescence of all parties interested."[30]

As to the Philippines, the State Department notified Minister Wu on August 1, 1899, of the step taken by Major General Elwell S. Otis to introduce the exclusion policy into that area.[31] This step, explained the same note, had been taken by the military administration for the Islands; the course was subject to review by Congress, which would ultimately determine the permanent policy. Wu's reply chided the State Department for not previously informing him of a policy that had been established almost a year earlier, on September 26, 1898. He was surprised, he said, to be apprised of an act that had already been enforced for a long time.[32] In other correspondence, China estimated that approximately 100,000 Chinese were in the Philippines and held that substantial trading had been carried on with the Chinese mainland.[33] Hence, an important Chinese interest was affected by the extension of the policy to the Philippines.

The exclusion policy was also expanded to include Puerto Rico, but the number of Chinese there was small. As for Cuba, although the policy was not applied during the United States military occupation, an extension occurred in a surprise move only a few days before the government was turned over to the Cubans. Since the Cubans were too afraid of the United States to dare to make alterations, this sudden action at the last minute developed into a permanent measure in Cuba.

All of these activities, representing a new exclusion policy, may be seen in their broadest sense as part of the social upheaval stirring the United States in the early 1900s — as part of the controversy over big business, expansion, the rise of organized labor, sweatshops, the nature of American citizenship, and the race question. In a narrower sense, the new policy was inaugurated by Powderly and the Bureau of Immigration with the enthusiastic acclaim of California and the AFL, and with a confused and indifferent general public riding along. Exclusion had become a national policy based upon a national consensus.[34]

But if the trade and friendship of China were desired, it was a dangerous policy. It not only struck at the inarticulate coolie class of China, which had been shut out sometime earlier, but, like the Stamp Act of American revolutionary days, it also aimed at the most articulate and powerful elements — the wealthy merchant, the student, the journalist, and the members of the educated upper class. Reluctantly, the Chinese government had adjusted to the older arrangement, but the new procedures affected the pride and dignity of the influential classes. Chinese diplomats were compelled to be deeply concerned with this problem.

3
Chinese Protests

Two news items appeared in the *New York Daily Tribune* on June 15, 1901. The first told of the arrival in New York City of *Taot'ai* Loo Chiu On, a young Chinese official, twenty-seven years old. A progressive, he spoke with enthusiasm of the reforms starting in China and especially of the new schools springing up. In his view, the Boxer Rebellion had turned out to be "a blessing in disguise."[1]

Speaking through an interpreter, he expressed friendship toward America. "You are the only people in the world which stood up for us," he declared, "and had you not, no one can tell what would have become of China."[2] Trade between the two countries, he predicted, would grow rapidly. But if his remarks could be viewed as an intriguing sample of pro-American sentiment building up in China in response to the American policy of preserving China's territorial integrity after the Boxer Rebellion, something quite different was happening in America.

The *Tribune* on the same day, also on the front page, reported that the Chinese in the United States were preparing a memorial urging repeal of the exclusion act, "on the grounds," wrote a reporter, "of fair play and as a sort of reciprocity for the opening of Chinese ports."[3] The plan was to get the 15,000 Chinese in New York to sign the memorial and then to reach other Chinese east of the Mississippi River. The account further noted that the most powerful and wealthy Chinese merchants in New York were leaders in the movement, that it was counting on help from the counsul general at New York, Chow Tsz-chi (Chou Tzu-ch'i), and that Wu T'ing-fang had recommended the project.

The two articles pointed up the dilemma that Wu had constantly faced after becoming minister to the United States in 1897. He did not find it easy to adjust to Americans who were, according to one scholar, "simultaneously fearful and contemptuous of the Chinese yet confident of a favored role as China's friend and benefactor."[4] Regardless of whether America's open-door policy was making friends in China, never before had the Chinese-American minority of approximately 90,000 complained so bitterly about being mistreated.

Personally as well as officially, the astute diplomat was caught in the middle. Since he had worked energetically and successfully in 1898 to get the Canton-Hankow railroad contract for the American syndicate,[5] he had a stake in the success of this venture and in good Chinese-United States relations. In addition, he also saw the United States as a nation that might help China resist Russian pressure in Manchuria,[6] he got along well with Americans, and "became the spoiled child of the American press."[7] Nevertheless, since he was from the Canton area of South China, he was keenly aware of the disaffection felt in that section; neither could he ignore the distress signals that were coming from the Chinese in San Francisco. For a solution to his problem, Wu preferred the one of obtaining a reversal of the exclusion policy — no easy matter. As Powderly and Dunn pressed their attacks on upper-class Chinese, Wu found his task more and more difficult.

Wu began a diplomatic offensive against Powderly's policies in 1898. An example of this was his lengthy note of November 7, 1898, challenging the Griggs ruling which maintained that the latest treaty, that of 1894, warranted excluding all Chinese except those groups specifically named. The treaty, Wu insisted, was intended to bar only laborers; he therefore urged the secretary of state to advise the president "to place a check upon those limitations which are being added to solemn treaties by opinions and new Treasury orders."[8] But nothing came of his appeal. Wu continued to object to other recent interpretations that added new restrictions. He also warned that if the new rules were extended to Hawaii it would be another "serious aggravation."[9] He was particularly perturbed over the prospect that, while Chinese might be barred, Japanese would not. Nevertheless, despite his protests, the exclusion policy followed the flag to Hawaii.

In 1899 Wu devoted a large share of his attention to the threat that, once the United States annexed the Philippines, Chinese immigration would be stopped there too. Although Spain's policy had for many years been capricious and discriminatory, especially in the field of taxation and jobs, Wu seemed much more alarmed over American intentions. When he asked the State Department for information, it

first professed to be uninformed about the plans of the military authorities. From the Chinese consul general in Manila, however, Wu
learned that the exclusion policy had been put into effect. Indeed, the
policy took an even more extreme form than that in the United States,
since for a time all Chinese were being barred. "I have to ask," Wu
finally wrote the State Department, "that instructions be sent to Major General Otis to cease the violations of the treaty of 1894 by the
exclusion of merchants and other exempt classes mentioned in Article
III of said treaty."[10] On December 5, 1899, Hay informed him that instructions had gone out to military officials to observe the treaty and
admit members of the privileged classes.[11] From then on the exclusion
policy was applied in the Philippines as it was in the United States.

Wu was also vexed about the growing use of minor technicalities
to exclude members of the privileged classes from the United States.
One celebrated case in 1899 involved Yee Ah Lum and 30 other merchants who were denied entrance on the grounds that their certificates in English lacked some of the information required. The fact
that, as merchants, they had a right to enter and that they had filled
out the forms correctly in Chinese was of no avail. Wu's note of October 2 charged that the "spirit and intent of the treaties and laws" had
been "entirely lost sight of."[12] The new restrictions were not intended
to affect Chinese officials; nevertheless, in some instances they did.
One case involved an acting consul general and a naval attaché who
were on their way across the continent from London to Vancouver.
When their train stopped at Malone, New York, they were forced to
get off by an American official and spend the night there while he
checked their credentials. Although a small incident in itself, the in-
sensitive tone of American policy was demonstrated when no official
apology and no offer to pay for the night's detention in a hotel were
forthcoming.[13] These omissions were duly lamented by Wu.

In the next year, 1900, Wu was again questioning the barring of
Chinese from the Philippines. On May 7, 1900, he proposed that the
policy for the Philippines be kept separate from that of the mainland
and asked that Congress be notified of China's views.[14] But Congress,
informed of his statements, proved unresponsive.

Then came the Boxer Rebellion in June 1900 and with it more
trouble for Wu. With the news of atrocities and the murder of foreigners in China, United States officials turned in anger against local
Chinese. In addition, treasury officials ruled that at San Francisco no
Chinese at all would be admitted; the reason — according to the explanation given to the Chinese consul general — was the occurrence of

Wu T'ing-fang, Chinese Minister to the United States, 1897-1902, 1908-1909. (Library of Congress.)

Cartoon Attack on Minister Wu T'ing-fang. *(New York Daily Tribune,* November 30, 1901. Library of Congress.)

further "outrages on Americans in China."[15] But this time the immigration people had gone too far, and the local official had to rescind this particular order very soon. The spirit of revenge did not vanish so quickly from that city, however. Even under these adverse circumstances Wu had continued his struggle, though more guardedly. His ability to do so was a tribute to his previous success in establishing good rapport with the American people. Indeed, his personal popularity was so great that the assistant secretary of war seriously proposed that the old dynasty be "thrown off a cliff" and Wu be made the new emperor.[16]

A new problem for Wu in 1900 was the narrow definition of *student*, given on June 15 by the solicitor of the treasury. By this time, Powderly's recent general regulations had also gone into effect, and the right of Chinese to appeal rulings had become more circumscribed. In addition, immigration officials were now assuming the right to investigate the accuracy of information contained on the Section VI Certificate (so-called from a provision in an 1884 law), which the exempt classes procured from the Chinese government and then had visaed by an American consul. On the student issue, the Chinese Legation chose to make a test case out of Yip Wah, a young man who had proper credentials according to the earlier interpretations. In his note of November 30, 1900, Wu pointed out that the student had every right to enter, based on treaty stipulations, and yet he had been refused admittance; his appeal had also been denied. Wu denounced the new requirement that a student must know the English language — to learn it was a reason for coming to the United States. Although America presumably wanted China to become westernized, the broader implication of the decision was that the United States was blocking that process. This case, he maintained, was important enough for the president to "exercise . . . his supreme authority to bring about a proper observance of these international stipulations."[17]

Officials at San Francisco maintained, however, that their action was in accord with the solicitor's definition. Yip Wah was too young to enter a university, did not know English, and seemed uncertain if he would practice medicine, the career he was supposed to be preparing for in the United States, when he returned to China.[18] These arguments satisfied the secretary of the treasury, and he refused to reverse the decision.[19] And the president, Hay informed Wu, believed that the final judgment lay with the secretary of the treasury.[20] Thus, Wu lost another important round. Yip Wah was deported, and others were also forced to return to China, much to the chagrin of Wu and American missionaries and exporters.

The student question had many sensitive aspects. One showed up in a letter from a missionary at Swatow to Hay in March 1900. Missionaries were getting the impression, he wrote, that students as well as laborers were being barred. If students came to the United States, the practice "would not only give us an educational ascendancy here, but it will also increase our prestige and stimulate commercial as well as intellectual intercourse."[21]

A related principle involved was whether there would be wider intellectual and cultural contact between China and America. The decision by the United States to discourage such exchanges came less than a year before an imperial decree calling on officials to send students abroad from their respective areas to study "industrial science" at government expense. Hay saw that the secretary of the treasury received three copies of the decision.[22] But to the immigration authorities another aspect was more important. The treasury official at San Francisco seemed to envisage a mass migration of Chinese if the rules, which had not been in effect before 1900, were not maintained. Without them, he wrote, "all Chinese youths will be enabled to avoid the protection afforded to this country by the Exclusion laws."[23] The statement was a revelation of the spirit and purpose behind the new regulations.

Wu ran into another snag in 1900. In addition to officials, merchants, students, and travelers, the treaties with China specified that teachers should be permitted to enter the country freely. Along with other privileged groups, however, they were now being kept out. In a note of April 11, 1901, Wu discussed the lot of the teacher, Tan Shi Tak, who had arrived on December 22, 1900. His papers were in order, but the Chinese inspector asked detailed questions about school and pupils. Then the inspector, reported Wu, interviewed the parents. All of the information was correct with one exception: the person named was not at the address given. The one discrepancy was used as a reason for not admitting the teacher.[24]

Wu complained not only about the new restrictions but also about the insulting treatment of the immigration inspectors.[25] One long protest elicited an angry rejoinder from Dunn in San Francisco, who declared that even "a Chinese Inspector, like the worm, may turn, and protect his name, his good repute and his official dignity."[26] He denied the charges, and nothing came of them.

While the minister was interceding on behalf of Chinese arrivals at ports, he was also objecting to a stepped-up policy of official harassment of Chinese-Americans within the country. On January 8, 1899, for example, he denounced the mass arrests of Chinese by an immigration official in Portland, Oregon, and on July 10 he objected to the deportation of two merchants from Buffalo. Why, he asked in another instance, were two merchants kept in jail in Los Angeles? "This," he declared, was "persecution and not prosecution."[27] He made charges in 1900 about arbitrary searches and arrests — in Philadelphia, for example — and pointed to the bureau's disregard for due process of law. Article IV of the 1894 treaty, Wu reminded Hay, promised Chinese all of the rights of citizens "of the most favored nation."[28] He also stressed the American government's promise "to exert all its power to secure protection to the persons and property of all Chinese subjects in the United States."[29]

During the Boxer period, Wu learned, a miniature reign of terror was sweeping through Illinois. Hong Sling, a Chicago merchant, described how he had received rough treatment from a deputy United States marshal and also maintained that several Chinese in that area had been arrested recently and deported. "When the men are arrested," he wrote, "they are usually taken before the United States Commissioner at once, and before the Chinaman has an opportunity to confer with friends he is tried and ordered deported."[30]

In responding to Wu's outcries on these matters, Hay was coldly polite but not encouraging. He ordinarily referred cases involving immigration treaty interpretations to the secretary of the treasury or the attorney general; he then relayed their answers, which relied heavily upon Supreme Court cases and legal precedents, back to the Legation. Upon receiving charges of mistreatment of Chinese within the United States, he sent the accusations to the governor of the state involved. Hay was not altogether indifferent to Chinese grievances, but he seldom let anyone know his real feelings. His last diary entry on June 19, 1905, only a few days before his death, was directed to the decision of the president to terminate "the barbarous methods of the Immigration Bureau."[31]

From 1898 to 1901 Wu's official notes provide a running account of China's discontent with the trend developing under Powderly. Wu did not question the exclusion of laborers. His objections were principally concerned with three developments: the extension of exclusion to Hawaii and the Philippines, the rejection or humiliation of visitors from the privileged classes, and the harassment of Chinese-Americans. Wu had emerged in this brief time as the major spokesman challenging the drift toward the total exclusion of Chinese, but he seemed unable to reverse the trend.

Wu found that he could accomplish nothing through the conventional diplomatic channels and, therefore, tried some that were unconventional. The remolding of American public opinion and the persuading of Congress to accept a more liberal immigration policy were formidable undertakings; nevertheless, Wu set to work. Fortunately for him, potential allies were not lacking. For a starter, he could count on the wholehearted support of Chinese communities in San Francisco, New York, and elsewhere. The church and educational elements that might be induced to come to his aid were more important politically. He also had a good chance of gaining the support of large steamship and railroad interests; exporters in the kerosene, textile, and flour lines; and agricultural groups seeking cheap labor. If he could harness these interests, he would have a powerful political instrument.

Early in 1900 the versatile diplomat had already begun his campaign. Indeed, his concluding remarks to the American Asiatic Association on January 26, 1900, had been a clear call to arms: "This society is composed of educated people, who should instruct the people here as to what we need and what is fair treatment."[32] His speech, the *New York Times* reported, had "made a marked impression."[33]

Other talks by Wu followed. Almost without exception they incorporated arguments against exclusion. To the 300 people at Delmonico's who were attending the banquet of the Silk Association of America, he announced, "We do not legislate against your coming. Our doors are open to you; we treat you as we treat all other people — not as you treat us."[34] At the dedication ceremonies for a new law school at the University of Pennsylvania, he suggested that in the Philippines local customs should not be changed any more than was necessary: no "race or class legislation should be tolerated."[35] One of his greater speaking triumphs was an address in 1900 to some thousand people at a banquet in Boston of the National Association of Manufacturers. As usual, his Oriental attire stood out, and he was cheered frequently as he spoke. He emphasized the opportunities to trade, and carefully pointed out that if Chinese merchants could come into the country to make purchases they might also "carry home with them a great many things which they had no intention of buying at the outset."[36]

Not limiting themselves to speeches only, the minister and others closely identified with him were responsible for articles in journals. In the *Independent*, Wu drew attention in 1900 to the growing Chinese trade and the impressive Chinese railway concession which had gone to an American group. He then asked the embarrassing question: "Why should the Chinese be singled out and excluded when others are allowed to come and compete?"[37] The drastic changes in interpretation since 1898, he declared, were "the last straw on the camel's back."[38] He urged that a commission travel to China to look into the entire matter. The consul general at San Francisco, Ho Yow (Wu's brother-in-law), followed with an article in the June 1900 *Forum.* Wider trade opportunities were beckoning; yet, there were "some dark spots on the disk of trade. . . . The spots to which I refer are the laws of this nation against Chinese immigrants."[39] Indeed, the exclusion laws, he contended, would destroy any chance the United States had of "commercial preeminence" in China.

Wu continued his offensive with an article in the *North American Review.* This time he proposed that "reciprocity" be the "key-note of every arrangement entered into" between the two countries.[40] He also reiterated the open door argument: "Her [China's] door is wide open to the people of the United States, but their door is slammed in the face of her people."[41] He suggested for an alternative restriction a literacy test based on ability to read and understand the Constitution. "That," he observed, "would give the Chinese a chance along with the rest of the world, and yet effectually restrict their immigration."[42] The "friendship of a nation of 400,000,000 people ought to be worth cultivating."[43] The minister even took the daring step of appearing before the Senate Committee on Appropriations to give testimony on a restrictive amendment then under consideration. Although some newspapers criticized him for this, the *New York Times* maintained that there were precedents for his action.[44]

No one followed Wu's endeavors more carefully than Gompers, who paid tribute in a negative way to the tireless diplomat. He wrote to the head of the International Typographical Union and other union leaders:

I should like to call your attention to the activity of the Chinese minister, Mr. Wu T'ing Fang in this country. There is never a social function in Washington at which he is not an honored guest. He mingles with the politicians at all political parties, making himself agreeable to everyone; he goes to a meeting of the southern manufacturers in the city of Philadelphia, and he points to the markets of northern China; he tells the cotton manufacturers of the south that there is the great market for their cheap cotton fabrics; he attends a meeting of the American bankers in Philadelphia, and he tells them that there should be an American bank in China . . . he goes to Atlantic City and addresses the Hebrew Chautauqua; he goes to Philadelphia on the Fourth of July and delivers a patriotic oration. All this activity of the . . . minister is plainly for the purpose of making friends in every direction against the time when there shall be a renewal of the efforts to keep Chinamen out of this country.[45]

Wu's spirited presentations made a marked impression on many of his listeners. "Almost everyone who heard him speak" reminisced Senator Benjamin Tillman on the Senate floor in 1906, "can recall . . . the way his mustache fairly got four or five additional kinks or curls in it when he alluded to the indignities and outrages put upon his countrymen."[46] But after pouring months of hard effort into his crusade, Wu saw events take a turn in 1900 that he could neither anticipate nor control. The ill will engendered by the Boxer Rebellion undercut much of the goodwill that he had been laboriously creating. "At the present moment," editorialized the *New York Times*, "any statement of the desires or intentions of the Chinese government can have little value."[47] In July 1900 news had been received of the murder in China of Baron von Ketteler and of bloodshed involving American naval forces. Because of the warlike atmosphere, Wu could do nothing but cancel his plans to deliver a Fourth of July oration at Independence Hall in Philadelphia.[48]

The Chinese officials, however, quickly adapted themselves to the Boxer trouble, and used it for an object lesson as to how neither Chinese nor Americans should behave. In speaking to the San Francisco Chamber of Commerce, for example, Ho Yow declared that his government would suppress anti-Caucasian bias, but "so must you here resist, discountenance, and denounce all anti-Mongolian prejudice and feeling in order that amity and comity may prevail."[49] Wu pointed out that Americans also committed outrages on Chinese and broke treaties.[50]

Although temporarily sidetracked by the 1900 disturbance, Wu soon returned to the lecture podium. On December 10, 1900, he was warmly received by a New York audience when he spoke on Confucianism and Christianity.[51] In February 1901 he refused to sit at the same table with General Otis, the man officially responsible for extending exclusion to the Philippines during the military occupation.

"Of course," scolded the *New York Times*, "the matter will be over-looked. . . . He shouldn't do it again, however."[52] Wu, undeterred, moved ahead and in June was encouraging the Chinese in New York to petition Congress not to extend the Geary Exclusion Act.[53] Wu tried another novel approach. On the rainy, dismal night of July 13 he sought out Powderly at his home in Washington and proposed to strike a bargain. If the commissioner general would gain labor's support for a law that would either place all nationalities on the same footing or allow upper-class Chinese to enter the United States, Wu would cooperate fully in suppressing the illegal entry of lower-class Chinese. But the wary Powderly, who had two close associates stationed secretly in the next room as witnesses, politely but firmly refused.[54] More articles by the minister and Ho Yow followed this unsuccessful venture.[55]

As Wu devoted his energies to influencing public opinion, his ally, Foord, and the American Asiatic Association, took the lead in Washington in early 1902. Foord, arriving in January, claimed that he found there no organization of consequence; rather, he "found the field virtually in possession of a knot of professional labor agitators who had the ear of the committee of Congress."[56] A consideration of Wu's earlier activities, however, makes Foord's statement hard to believe. For some time an impressive number of letters and petitions against exclusion had been finding their way to the president and to the appropriate committees of Congress. Some, though by no means all, must have been inspired by the minister. One significant interest group was the agricultural element and related industries of California. Walter Egbert, for example, identifying himself as a grain grower and stock raiser in Rio Vista, California, informed Roosevelt that Chinese were needed in "fruit raising, hop growing, beet sugar growing, canning and cooking."[57] "The East and middle West," wrote the president of the California Canneries Company, "has the European emigrant . . . and the South the negro! Why should the Pacific Coast alone be held to practice the virtue of exclusion?"[58]

Hawaiian and Philippine interest groups wrote or came to Washington. A delegation of Hawaiian planters paid a call on the president and on Secretary Gage.[59] The American Chamber of Commerce of Manila sent an appeal to Congress to admit Chinese laborers to the Islands subject to restrictions set by the Philippine Commission.[60] Chinese residents in the Philippines sent their own petition requesting the exemption of the Islands from the exclusion acts.[61]

Religious groups all over the country became involved in the is-

sue and played an important part in the controversy. Some churchmen were concerned with missionary activity among Chinese in the
United States. Others were thinking about their overseas efforts.
Nathan R. Johnson, representative of the former type, was a missionary to the Chinese in the San Francisco area. He wrote President
McKinley on May 24, 1901, of his work on behalf of an anti-exclusion
memorial. The current law, he charged, violated the treaty and the
Golden Rule. He hoped to secure 100,000 signatures to amend the law
so as to avoid discrimination.[62] General O. O. Howard, the well-known
former head of the Freedmen's Bureau, was a prominent layman appealed to by the Christian missions of San Francisco and Portland to
speak in churches for better treatment of the Chinese and a less restrictive immigration policy.[63] He accepted this call to duty and traveled and lectured throughout the country.

More attuned to the foreign mission side of the question was
Mrs. S. L. Baldwin, another active campaigner. "Is it not a screaming
farce on decency," she wrote in the *New York Daily Tribune*, "to say
nothing of justice and Christianity, for us to continue our anti-
Chinese laws in view of our demands upon China?"[64] She challenged
Hay's public statements that the United States was being guided by
"the Monroe Doctrine and the Golden Rule."[65] How, she wondered, did
the exclusion laws fit in? "To favor an 'open door' commercially and a
closed door in every other sense," wrote a Methodist minister to Powderly, "is not very consistent."[66] Retaliation against Christian missions in China might occur, he cautioned. Other letters from members
of church groups expressed similar views; among them were Congre-
gationalists, Methodists, Presbyterians (USA), Reformed Presbyterians, and United Presbyterians. Pittsburgh and Chicago were two
urban centers from which a large number of church petitions came.

If other denominations had organized their protests as systematically as the Reformed Presbyterian Church, the effect would have
been more significant. Mobilized by the determined Reverend Mr.
Johnson, this small denomination, with fewer than 8,000 members at
that time, but with active missions in both China and San Francisco,
responded with petitions to Congress from congregations in western
Pennsylvania, Ohio, Kansas, and elsewhere.[67] His efforts, however,
impressive as they were for one man, fell far short of his goal of
100,000 signatures. Johnson was also present at a public meeting in
Boston on December 22, 1901, which adopted resolutions against the
reenactment of the Geary Law. Held in the Methodist Episcopal
Church, the assembly was presided over by William Lloyd Garrison,

son of the famous abolitionist. Wu's influence was suggested by the presence of Colonel Stephen W. Nickerson, an attorney who later became a consul for China in Boston.[68]

The religious memorialists, in contrast to the agricultural interests, showed almost no desire to admit laborers. Instead, since they were more concerned with the privileged classes, especially students, they opposed restrictions on economic or racial grounds, but they endorsed moral restrictions, such as those against prostitutes and criminals.

The business groups which had ties with the China trade, although slower to respond, were more specifically against or for particular legislation. On January 10, 1902, Charles Hamlin of the Canadian Pacific Railroad Company secured the unanimous adoption by the Boston Chamber of Commerce of a resolution to extend and limit the existing exclusion law to the expiration date of the treaty, which would occur in 1904.[69] The leadership in the business community, however, was mainly assumed by Foord and the American Asiatic Association. On January 28, 1902, the Executive Committee of the American Asiatic Association passed a resolution to set up a special fund for newspaper articles and other publicity to sway public opinion and obtain a more liberal treaty with China and terms that would promote trade.[70] In the same month Foord set up headquarters in Washington. In February, soon after Foord arrived, resolutions and petitions urging moderation on exclusion began to pour in from business groups. In that month the president and Congress heard from the Portland Chamber of Commerce, the Merchants' Exchange in San Francisco, the San Francisco Chamber of Commerce, the Philadelphia Board of Trade, and the New York Chamber of Commerce.[71] These resolutions stressed the need to let Chinese merchants enter the country and proposed that the Geary Act be allowed to continue only until 1904 to coincide with the end of the treaty of 1894.

Coincidental with the growing opposition to exclusion, Secretary Gage was said to be for the repeal or lapse of the exclusion law. "He is thoroughly permeated with the Eastern commercial idea," moaned the *San Francisco Chronicle*.[72] At approximately the same time, November 1901, Wu had shifted ground briefly to urge treasury officials to let the law expire and wait for a few months to see whether a new one was really needed.[73] This idea fell by the wayside.

Another step taken by Wu was to seek the support of the president. Hay arranged the appointment.[74] The audience with Roosevelt was a great disappointment, however. From the minister's remarks to reporters afterward it was evident that Roosevelt was reacting to demands of press and public opinion for maintaining rigid exclusion and that he would propose more restrictive legislation. "Why can't you be fair?" Wu angrily asked the reporters, in complaining about disparaging anti-Chinese references appearing frequently in the press. "Would you talk like that if mine was not a weak nation? Would you say it if the Chinese had votes?"[75]

For approximately two years before Congress was ready to take up the exclusion issue, Wu had been pressing his case in ways not normally used by diplomats. He had sent note after note through diplomatic channels, and had become a frequent visitor at the Treasury Department; he had also helped organize protests among the Chinese communities. In his speeches and writings he had tried to develop a pro-Chinese public opinion. And, most important, he had built up a powerful political coalition from various moral and economic forces in American society. As Congress convened in November 1901, Wu and his allies, with the open door forces prominent among them, prepared for a final struggle to get legislation upholding the right of non-laboring Chinese to come to America.

4

The Exclusion Law of 1902

"There is warrant for the belief," announced the *New York Times* in October 1901, "that at the next session of Congress there will be an interesting contest over the reenactment of the Chinese Exclusion Act."[1] According to the editorial, the East was still uncommitted while the South was shifting over in favor of cheap labor; the West Coast might no longer be adamantly anti-Chinese. "If . . . Minister Wu has been as successful as is reported," the *Times* speculated, "in securing a Southern and Eastern interest in an important modification of the present exclusion law, the question will have a great deal more interest than it has had for the past ten years at least."[2]

On the other side of the continent, the *San Francisco Chronicle* denied any softening of the West Coast's position. Secretary Gage, it asserted, was "wide of the mark when he assumed that public sentiment on the Pacific Coast has undergone any change on the subject of exclusion."[3] Furthermore, labor was determined to preserve exclusion, and the "interests of American labor are far superior to us as a nation than the petty profit which all the commerce we can hope to get from China will give us."[4]

Most of the country seemed to be unaware that two powerful and determined political groups were descending on the president and Congress. Other questions, such as breaking up trusts, regulating railroads, untangling labor-management problems, terminating the occupation of Cuba, and shaping tariff policies for the Philippines were also commanding the attention of Congress and the general public; but between November 1901 and May 1902 Chinese exclusion became a major subject of debate. Much more was at issue than the renewal of a law. Scholars have overlooked the fact that three impor-

52

tant questions were under consideration: first, should rulings of dubious legality by the bureau, having the practical effect of barring most upper-class Chinese, receive the full weight of statutory law; second, should the policy for the mainland also apply to Hawaii and the Philippines; and third, should the bureau be given a firm legal base to exercise the broad powers which it was in fact wielding.

That the anti-Chinese spirit had as much vitality as ever after 1900 was very evident in the 1902 hearings of the Senate Committee on Immigration and the debates in Congress. These same sessions disclosed that aggressive pressure groups were busily at work on both sides. By April congressmen were loudly denouncing the intrigues and sinister influences being exerted by "great transportation interests," or by the "pro-China lobby," or by "sentimentalists," or by "labor bosses."

Had an uninformed observer surveyed the effort to change the exclusion legislation, he might have been misled into thinking that California had become less anti-Chinese. When the *Chronicle* declared in 1901 that the assumption "that the exclusion law is ineffective is absolutely wrong," it might appear that it stood for moderation.[5] If the added severities imposed upon the Chinese after 1898 are taken into account, however, the statement would not seem so moderate. Furthermore, before Congress adjourned in 1902, the *Chronicle* had adopted a more extreme position. Of course, one newspaper's views are suggestive in a limited way only of the state of mind of Californians. Another, more significant indication was the position assumed by California congressmen. They were diligently occupied in 1901 and 1902 both in seeking tighter restrictions and in securing the support of legislators in their region and elsewhere. Their efforts led to the foundation of a powerful exclusionist bloc in both the House and Senate.

Too much emphasis on geographical factors can lead to neglect of the social aspects of the anti-Chinese effort. Within California and on the national level as well, organized labor was the group clamoring loudest for sterner measures. Its efforts, however, cannot easily be separated from those of other elements on the west coast, of the Immigration Bureau, or of certain patriotic societies. Its presence was pervasive. It was the cement which held together the various groups and interests working for stricter exclusion laws.

Especially visible within the ranks of labor was the American Federation of Labor which by 1902 had attained a size and degree of organization large enough to exert considerable political pressure. At its annual convention in 1900 at Louisville, Kentucky, it had revived

the exclusion question in a resolution which demanded the reenactment and strengthening of the exclusion laws.[6] The local unions affiliated with the AFL on the west coast were taking the lead by the
summer of 1901.[7] By September the AFL Executive Council had authorized Gompers to hire a lobbyist to work for the continuance of the
existing law.[8] Gompers' choice, Herman Gutstadt, was a cigarmaker
from the east. He had moved to San Francisco and had been active in
editing labor papers and in anti-Chinese work. Gutstadt planned a
vigorous campaign to highlight the dangers in any loosening of restrictions. These dangers included possible unrest on the west coast,
enhanced labor competition, serious moral problems, and a threat to
democracy in the Chinese ignorance of American traditions.[9] "The
strenuous effort made by the Chinese minister . . . to defeat re-enactment of the exclusion act," warned Gutstadt, gave reason to fear "that
should Congress fail in its duty of re-enacting this law, no time would
be lost by the myriads of Chinese in flooding this country as never
before."[10]

Gompers, like the Chinese minister, went to see the president in
November 1901.[11] That his interview was more satisfactory than Wu's
was made obvious at the AFL Convention in December, when a resolution from the Portland, Oregon, Federation Trades Council commended Roosevelt for his support of exclusion in his message to Congress on December 3; the resolution further proposed that the AFL
thank the President and offer encouragement.[12] The same Trades
Council, after denouncing Wu for meeting with Roosevelt, charged
also that he had overstepped diplomatic proprieties in his comments
to the press afterward.[13] An AFL committee insisted that exclusion
had moral and social aspects as well as economic, and authorized
Gompers and the Executive Council, in the interest of maintaining
exclusion, to "concentrate all the resources of the organization upon a
supreme effort."[14] Preparing and distributing literature and cooperating with other groups were among the recommended measures.

The AFL had also been active on other fronts. Moves to establish
closer ties with the Bureau of Immigration were started by February
1901, when the AFL Executive Council decided to invite the commissioner general of immigration to meet with it. At the ensuing meeting
on February 19, Powderly and the assistant commissioner of the Port
of New York, Edward F. McSweeny, were very cooperative.[15] The bureau had much to contribute. Articles in magazines and press, based
on information contributed by the bureau, molded public opinion and
created a negative image of the Chinese. Violations of the law were

common enough to give the bureau a cause to dramatize; these bureau releases supplied an abundance of quotable material to the AFL and other anti-Chinese elements. On January 14, 1901, after the president's endorsement of exclusion, Powderly presented forceful arguments for exclusion in an article in *Collier's Weekly* entitled "Exclude Anarchist and Chinaman!"[16] He also advised Congress that race, religion, and economic factors necessitated the continuation of exclusion legislation.

Meanwhile, the California wing of the AFL had become very active. The *Chronicle*, in November 1901, wrote of the approaching meeting of the state AFL convention and the need to give "convincing proof" to Congress "of our absolute sincerity."[17] The San Francisco Labor Council, claiming a membership of 30,000, had already, on May 17, 1901, given such proof by sending a resolution to President McKinley expressing the fear that Asians coming from the new territories would break down the exclusion barriers; the memorial asked for protection for American labor "against all classes of Asiatics."[18] By June, Dunn had become much concerned over the labor agitation and urged Powderly to come to California, explaining, "The labor element of the entire coast has been organized within the past year or two as never before and has grown very powerful."[19]

To demonstrate that other classes of Americans would join with labor against the Chinese, the California labor movement supplied the inspiration for a mass meeting in the Metropolitan Temple in San Francisco on November 21.[20] Delegates from business, civic, and labor groups were encouraged to gather from all over the state and the west coast. Senators George C. Perkins and Thomas R. Bard indicated that they would attend. The California press supported the effort by daily expressing concern over attempts by Chinese officials to overturn exclusion. A ten-page memorial to Congress that called for the renewal of the Geary law of 1892 was adopted at the California Convention, attended by some 3,000 delegates.[21] The Convention also selected a five man commission to work for exclusion legislation in Washington. This commission, with the official endorsement of the governor, included a former governor, Edward J. Livernash, a reporter for the *San Francisco Examiner*, and Andrew Furuseth — a member of a sailors' union affiliated with the AFL. Since the commission was comprised of three Democrats and two Republicans, its activities always had political ramifications. After the commission arrived in Washington, it became a powerful voice in the exclusion controversy, and its demands went far beyond the original memorial.

The anti-Chinese forces in other states were also forwarding petitions and resolutions to Congress and other arms of the government. An Oregon resolution, read in Congress on February 11, 1901, urged that exclusion be made permanent and be extended to Japanese and other Orientals.[22] The Montana and Idaho state legislatures also produced resolutions, but were satisfied with a ten-year extension of existing legislation.[23] That there was a great deal of labor influence behind these resolutions from mining states, may be presumed.

Supporting the state memorials and resolutions from the West were petitions from local labor unions throughout the country. Indeed, these petitions were very effective weapons for labor. An impressive flurry of them came from the San Francisco unions in November 1901, addressed to the president, the secretary of the treasury, and the commissioner general; they combined requests to raise Inspector Dunn's salary, keep him in San Francisco, and reenact the Geary Act.[24] Around the country Gutstadt was constantly prodding the local unions. "When Dennis Kearney, the Sand Lot orator of the Pacific Slope, fired his rhetorical guns at the Chinese," declared Gutstadt to the New York City Central Federated Union in November, "he builded better than he knew."[25] When the issue was again presented at the AFL convention in December, the Central Federated Union voted to favor reenactment. President John Mitchell of the United Mine Workers Union was also urging local unions to send similar resolutions to Congress.[26]

Hundreds of labor petitions, with thousands of signatures, poured into Congress. They came from locals, from city centrals, and from the headquarters or conventions of the international unions. The files of the Committee on Foreign Affairs of the House were jammed with them. Duplicates found their way to the Senate Committee on Immigration in late 1901 and early 1902. In the *Congressional Record* three pages of fine type were needed merely to list the names of those organizations.[27]

The American Federation of Labor, although the ringleader, was not the only labor voice to be heard. The Western Labor Union, for example, also called for exclusion; so too did the Knights of Labor and the Railroad Brotherhoods (the Industrial Workers of the World was not organized until 1905). Among the Brotherhoods, the Order of Railway Conductors was at first noticeably remiss in not sending a petition. On February 19, however, its leader, E. E. Clark, gave his endorsement: "Our legislators must not be permitted to misunderstand our attitude on this matter and to thus mistake our silence . . .

RESOLUTIONS TO EXCLUDE CHINESE LABORERS
From the United States and Their Insular Possessions.

WHEREAS, The act excluding Chinese laborers from the United States will expire May 5th, 1902, and it is held, by those who favor the unlimited immigration of Chinese laborers, that the passage of an Exclusion law would be detrimental to the commercial interests of the United States, when as a matter of fact, the limited benefits of trade to be obtained by the so-called open-door policy for China can not, in even the smallest degree, recompense our people for the immensely greater loss caused by the displacement of so many of our own countrymen who are consumers as well as producers, while the contrasted consuming power of the Chinese laborer is limited almost exclusively to products of China, and the surplus of his earnings is sent out of this country, where it is earned, checking its prosperity; while the money paid as wages to our own people remains and correspondingly enriches us, stimulating our own industry and trade, thereby tending to continue national prosperity—the very opposite effect as obtained by the employment of Chinese; and,

WHEREAS, The exclusion of Chinese is no more a question of cheap labor than it is a question of American citizenship, the quality of which is largely determined by the general economic condition of the individual citizen; and,

WHEREAS, The presence in our country of a people entirely out of harmony and training with American comprehension of liberty and citizenship, who are alien to our customs and habits; as different from us in political and moral ideals as it is possible for two peoples to be; who are so thoroughly grounded in race characteristics that even the generations born and reared amongst us still retain them, can not but exercise a most demoralizing effect upon the body politic, the social life and the civilization of the people of our Nation, now and for all time; and,

WHEREAS, The fifty years of residence of Chinese in the United States, notably in California, has demonstrated their utter disregard for all of our laws, civil or criminal, while enforcing their own illegal edicts of blackmail and murder, emanating from representatives of their Tongs or Companies; and,

WHEREAS, Official investigations have exposed a condition of affairs in the State of California, the people of which had and still have to bear the brunt of this Asiatic contamination, almost incredible to our people, in which gambling hells, opium joints, dens of iniquity and vice, are but superficial evidences of a moral standard as degrading in its exhibition as it is demoralizing by its contact; and,

WHEREAS, By reason of their low wages the Chinese have successfully invaded a number of trades and callings, displacing many thousands of our own people, and lowered the standard of wages, living, and morals of all others, affecting thereby the most important factors essential to our industrial and social development; and,

WHEREAS, Failure to enact an effective Chinese Exclusion Law, both for the mainland of the United States and for our insular possessions, would open the gates of the United States and afford the opportunity for millions of this, the most dangerous and undesirable element, to further invade and utterly ruin trades and callings now providing a living to American mechanics and laborers to whom such immigration would be nothing short of a calamity; therefore, be it

Resolved, That we *Amalgamated Sheet Metal Workers I. A.* Union, No. *17,* of the city of *Galesburg* State of *Illinois* the *3th* day of *March* 1902 in meeting assembled, most respectfully but urgently request the Congress of the United States to speedily and before the termination of the present law enact Senate Bill 2960 or House Bill 9330, excluding Chinese persons from entering any part of the United States or its domain; and, be it furthermore

RESOLVED, That we view with alarm all proposals to indicate to China or to the Department of State of the United States any desire on the part of the United States to recede, in any degree, from our present National policy of excluding Chinese laborers; and we strongly protest against the adoption of any Exclusion Law limiting the continuance of that exclusion policy to December 7, 1904, and we urgently favor that feature of the bill hereinbefore mentioned as Senate Bill No. 2960, and House Bill No. 9330, which fixes no time for expiration.

Resolved, That a copy of these Resolutions be transmitted to our Representative in Congress and to the two United States Senators from this State, with the urgent solicitation for their co-operation in the passage of the bills enumerated.

Therefore, the above preamble and resolutions are respectfully submitted to you, with the request that the same be presented to the United States Senate or to the House of Representatives as a petition from the above organization. Respectfully yours,

W. A. James President.

Attest: *Ed. C. Nelson* Secretary.
Address *185 Laurel Ave / 178 Phillips,*
Galesburg Ills.

Typical Anti-Chinese Labor Petition. (Petitions, Senate Committee on Immigration, 57th Cong., 1st sess., 1901-1902. National Archives.)

for indifference."[28] While the most active unions were the cigarmakers, typographical workers, and miners, the petitions represented throughout the ranks of labor an unusual display of unity and intense feeling.

Other allies in the anti-Chinese cause were the patriotic orders, many of which engaged also in organized petitioning. The Junior Order of United American Mechanics, which showed its greatest strength in eastern Pennsylvania and New Jersey, was particularly active. Also at work in the Pennsylvania-New Jersey-Connecticut-Maryland area was the Daughters of Liberty, which combined a call for the continuation of Chinese exclusion with requests for general restrictions on immigration, a more severe law against those who attempted to assassinate government leaders, and a law to keep out or deport anarchists.[29]

Variations in the exclusionist theme showed up in the petitions. While many of the signers seemed content with the exclusion of Chinese laborers alone, others wanted to reject Chinese of all classes. Still others sought the extension of exclusion to the new territories. The most extreme approach called for the exclusion of all Orientals. These petitions clearly affected the temper of Congress. While pro-Chinese sentiments continued in a steady stream, the petitions against the Chinese became a deluge. The legislative chambers rang with eloquent speeches on behalf of the "home and hearth of the workingman." On every hand conversions were avowed. Representative Robert R. Hitt, for example, Republican chairman of the Committee on Foreign Affairs, announced early in January 1902 that he was for exclusion. "I was the only bad member," he told the press, "and I am perfectly amiable now. Nobody wants this legislation more than I. . . . There is nothing to argue about and nobody to take the negative."[30] Indeed, by January 1902 triumph seemed near at hand for the powerful anti-Chinese forces. All that remained was for Congress to process a new exclusion bill that would carry out the wishes of the alliance between labor and the California Bureau of Immigration. A long statement to the Senate from Wu protesting exclusion went unheeded.[31]

For the Republican Congress the administration's position was understandably of great consequence. Republican presidents before Roosevelt had opposed and vetoed exclusion legislation as secondary in importance to the fulfilling of treaty obligations and the encouragement of trade with China. Neither Hayes nor Arthur, however, had been faced with a labor movement as powerful as the AFL; nor in their day was the pressure for restrictions nationwide. Since their time the western, largely pro-exclusion states of Montana, Washington, Idaho, Wyoming, and Utah had also entered the Union. Another significant factor was that Roosevelt had been president only since the tragic death of McKinley in September; the timing was such that the insecure new president had only until December to prepare his first annual message to Congress. Roosevelt was further entrapped because the Democratic party platform of 1900 had supported "the continuance and strict enforcement of the Chinese exclusion law, and its application to the same classes of all Asiatic races."[32] Although the Republican platform had said nothing, political realities nonetheless dictated that Roosevelt endorse exclusion.

On November 20, 1901, Representative James C. Needham of California was delighted when he called on President Roosevelt and learned that he would recommend continuing and strengthening the law.[33] Since the announcement came on the eve of the convention on exclusion in California, the political timing was good for both the president and the Republican party. In his annual message on December 3, the president kept his word by once again recommending "as necessary" the passage of "the law excluding Chinese laborers" and the strengthening of it "wherever necessary in order to make its enforcement entirely effective."[34] This stand was deplored by the *Jewish Exponent* of Philadelphia which contended that the United States was saying to the Chinese "You must take our goods, the missionaries, and anything else we choose to send you . . . but you must not show your faces within our borders, for you are too far beneath us to be fit company for us."[35] The AFL, of course, was overjoyed with the president's statements.

Roosevelt's position, however, was not entirely determined by political expediency. In 1894, he had concluded that to admit Chinese "would be ruinous to the white race."[36] Howard K. Beale has stated that Roosevelt looked down on China and believed the Chinese to be a backward race. By excluding Chinese an important question was raised: How far did Roosevelt wish to go? The State Department, in a memorandum prepared by Rockhill, favored a bill that would simply extend the existing Geary Act until December 8, 1904, to coincide with the end of the ten-year period of the 1894 treaty.[37] But Roosevelt chose the more restrictive approach of the Lodge bill of December 4, 1901, which proposed to extend the Geary Act indefinitely.[38] Then two days later Powderly sent the president a draft of a lengthy, complicated, and much harsher bill. It was, he informed the president's secretary, "prepared here in the Bureau under my directions."[39] On the same day, December 6, Representative Julius Kahn of California presented Powderly's draft to the House as his own bill.

Aggressive promoters of the Kahn bill were Gompers and the AFL. "The simple re-enactment of the present law," Gompers informed his Executive Council, "would leave us in the most precarious condition."[40] He was fearful of the possibility that Chinese might immigrate by way of the Philippines. Eventually, the California Commission lined up behind the Kahn bill. Indeed, as Gompers informed Senator Boies Penrose, chairman of the Senate Committee on Immigration, the bill had the support of the west coast congressmen and was "a measure framed by representatives of the American Federation of Labor, and by members of the California Exclusion Commission, and as to the administrative features, acceptable to the Bureau of Immigration."[41] Before the entire question was settled, Roosevelt, under heavy pressure from Gompers and the California Commission, had also shifted his support to the Kahn bill.[42]

The Kahn bill — or Mitchell-Kahn bill as it was later named in recognition of the sponsorship — was the most extreme version of 17 anti-Chinese bills. It contained a listing of the new rulings and regulations that had become anathema to Wu and his supporters. Definitions of terms like *student* and *merchant* were so circumscribed as to bar these classes in all but name. Other provisions struck down more permissive parts of the 1894 treaty with China, such as the stipulation that Chinese in transit could pass through the United States. Another part of the bill excluded Chinese from the Philippines and Hawaii, and also prevented their migration from those islands to the mainland.

In the early months of 1902 both the House and Senate held hearings on the subject, but the spotlight focused primarily on the Senate hearings which John Foord claimed to have procured.[43] Foord, taking advantage of his opportunity, organized a formidable group of businessmen, including exporters and textile manufacturers from both north and south, to attend the sessions and to attack the Mitchell-Kahn bill. Of special import was the presence of Clarence Cary, leader in the American China Development Company, which had as stockholders such financial giants as J. P. Morgan, Carnegie, Harriman, Rockefeller, Vanderbilt, and Schiff.[44] Foord's group alone was a potent combination, but closely allied with it was the Pacific Mail Steamship Company, a subsidiary of the Harriman group. This company had for its attorney Maxwell Evarts, who was well known

and the son of a former Republican secretary of state. Also present
was Democrat Charles S. Hamlin, an acting secretary of the treasury
in the 1890s. Hamlin officially spoke for the Boston Chamber of
Commerce and the New England cotton-mill owners, but was understood unofficially to be representing the Canadian Pacific Railroad of
the Hill-Morgan interests.

It is difficult to believe that Foord's group and the other prominent business and financial people would have taken such a keen interest in the exclusion issue if Chinese officials had not been in the
background prodding them. The most obvious spokesman for China's
interests at the hearings, however, was John W. Foster, former secretary of state and occasional legal adviser to China. Ostensibly appearing as a private individual representing the public interest, he was
charged by the *San Francisco Chronicle,* nevertheless, with being "a
Hessian in law and diplomacy . . . willing to give his services to the
highest bidder."[45] And on the floor of the Senate, Penrose, fellow Republican, unkindly labeled him "the representative of the Chinese
Empire and not a disinterested witness or writer."[46] Another person
who probably had close ties with Wu was Stephen W. Nickerson, who
appeared against exclusion at a public meeting in Boston on December 19, 1901, and also as "legal adviser to three of the foreign consulates" in that city.[47]

At the hearings former Secretary of State Foster explained in
great detail the treaty violations inherent in the Mitchell-Kahn bill.
He also condemned the current abuses and insults meted out to
Chinese visitors and predicted that they would worsen if the bill were
passed. Furthermore, he pointed to the bill's threat to future trade
with China. The open door policy had been developed to promote the
commerce of the United States in China, he asserted, but "what will
that avail us, if, by our own rash legislation and injustice, we ourselves close this door to our manufacturers, farmers, and merchants?"[48] Evarts charged that the bill was inconsistent, unconstitutional, in violation of treaties, burdensome to shipping interests, and
likely to provoke innumerable court cases. Foord stressed the disad-
vantages in barring students: "We would like to take the youths, and
educate them to American ideas and lead them up to American trade
probably."[49]

The hearings were lengthy and acrimonious. Both sides were
resourceful and determined. Edward J. Livernash, reporter on the
California Commission, was an especially aggressive collaborator
with Gompers in supporting the Mitchell-Kahn bill and in preserving

it intact. Thus, it was reported favorably to the Senate by the Penrose Committee, even though resolutions against the bill continued to be sent to Congress by merchants in California and by other business groups such as the New York Chamber of Commerce.[50]

The Senate hearings lasted from January 21 to February 15, 1902. On March 12 the Senate committee reported its bill to the Senate. On March 25 the House committee presented a milder bill (HR13031) than the Senate version. It eliminated, for example, a definition of *Chinese* that was intended to cover mestizos in the Philippines and prevent their entering the United States. But once again the power of the anti-Chinese side was vividly demonstrated. Champ Clark, Democrat from Missouri, submitted an anti-Chinese minority report that closely approximated the original Kahn bill. Then he proposed amendments to the majority report which the House accepted one by one. At last, he could announce in triumph, the House had acceded to his original requests.[51] Now the Democrats could also take credit for a tight exclusion policy. With Clark's amendments, the House bill was not fundamentally different from that reported in the Senate.

Although the outlook for China was discouraging by March 1902, Wu kept on fighting. On March 22 he wrote the secretary of state of his opposition to the Mitchell-Kahn bill. He recounted past instances of mistreatment of Chinese, then dissected the bill, and concluded that it afforded no remedies for past problems and promised to create new ones in relations between the two nations. If the bill passed, he warned, Chinese merchants would go elsewhere to buy, and students would go elsewhere to study. The overall effect of the bill, he stressed, was to nullify the 1894 treaty.[52] In Peking the Chinese Foreign Office had also presented a memorial to Minister Edwin H. Conger against the reenactment of an exclusion law. The memorial emphasized in particular the importance to the Chinese of the Hawaiian and Philippine Islands.[53] Vice Consul Lock Wing denounced the existing exclusion act as "barbarous" in a speech before members of a Presbyterian Church in New Jersey. Before missionaries could be effective in China, he declared, Christians in America had "to live up to the principles of the Great Master."[54] The Chinese effort was an intense one, directed at American public opinion as well as at officials in Washington.

As the Senate began to debate the Mitchell bill, Wu's side rallied once again. On April 4 Wu himself was present to hear Senator John H. Mitchell's presentation of the bill. He was surprised, he remarked afterwards, that only ten Senators were present to hear the address.[55] In succeeding days well-known names in the Senate joined in an attack on the bill — Orville H. Platt of Connecticut, Joseph B. Foraker of Ohio, Shelby M. Cullom of Illinois, Marcus A. Hanna of Ohio, Matthew S. Quay of Pennsylvania, and others. Senator Jacob H. Gallinger of New Hampshire seemed best informed about the views of China and most willing to enter them into the record. Senator William P. Dillingham of Vermont kept in touch with the pro-Chinese Pacific Mail Steamship Company, whose vice-president remained nearby much of the time.[56] Occasional allusions were made to the possible undermining of the open door policy. "All of the resources of American diplomacy," cried Senator Gallinger, "have been directed to securing an open door in China for American products. . . . Are we now to neutralize the advantages thus gained with so much difficulty by hostile legislation?"[57] Retaliation by China, he admonished, would surely follow the passage of such a bill.

After six days of heated Senate debate, a new climax was reached on April 10 with the sudden appearance of the Platt amendment, a major challenge to the anti-Chinese side. Disguised as an amendment to the Mitchell bill, it really proposed to cut out the Mitchell bill entirely and continue the existing exclusion laws until December 7, 1904, or for the duration of the treaty if it were allowed to extend for an additional ten years.[58] In essence this proposal was the same as the earlier state department position, which had received some support at the Senate hearings in the form of the Proctor bill. On April 16, in spite of violent opposition by the anti-Chinese side, the Platt substitute passed by a vote of 48 to 33. The *New York Tribune* proclaimed the defeat of the Mitchell bill in large headlines on its front page.[59]

This surprising victory for Wu's side was only temporary, however. As the House was still committed to the extreme version, a conference committee was necessary to find a compromise. Representatives Hitt, Perkins, and Clark joined Senators Platt, Dillingham, and Clay to seek a middle ground, but finding one was not easy. "I desire to say," reported Platt at the end, "that the conference has been in some respects a strenuous one."[60]

The bill finally passed by both Houses, in contrast to the Mitchell bill, was brief. In a few paragraphs it extended the existing exclusion laws, including certain sections of the 1888 act, for the duration of the treaty and "so far as the same are not inconsistent with treaty obligations."[61] In addition, the laws were to apply to the island territories; Chinese were not allowed to migrate from one group of islands to another, or to the mainland. The secretary of the treasury was authorized to make rules to implement the act.

As the bill went to the president for his signature, Wu made a final effort to destroy it. On April 29, 1902, he wrote Hay to convey to the president China's appeal for a veto. His principal objection was to the part dealing with Hawaii and the Philippines. "I respectfully submit," he reasoned, "that it is not in conformity with international law and the comity of nations to include in the operations of a treaty numbers of people and a great extent of territory which were in no respect the subject of the treaty."[62] On that same day, however, the president signed the bill. Hay could only inform Wu that his message had arrived too late to be considered.[63]

The importance of the enactment of the 1902 law has largely gone unrecognized. Many scholars have seen it as merely a continuation of the earlier policy with a few minor modifications. A serious reappraisal of the law, however, leads to the conclusion that it represented a significant step forward for the exclusion forces. First, by upholding past restrictive legislation, Congress was, in effect, bestowing its blessing on the increasingly harsh administrative regulations of the Bureau of Immigration and was by statute barring nearly all upper-class Chinese. To be sure, Powderly's own particular brand of exclusionism had received full legislative endorsement, even though Roosevelt had replaced Powderly by the time the law was passed. Second, Congress was spreading the exclusion principle to the new territories in a permanent sense, even though this meant the destruction of significant trade and travel exchanges between China and the Philippines. Third, Congress allowed the new commissioner general (by means of the secretary of the treasury) almost a free hand, by the terms of the law, to impose additional restrictions to his heart's content.

The new law clearly represented a more restrictive policy than anything that had previously been in effect. It retained everything from the past and added several new controls. Indeed, the result contained more of the Mitchell bill than either side cared to admit and offered no concession of substance to China in the interest of trade or of the promotion of American missionary or educational enterprises in that country. On the contrary, the new law seemed destined to have an adverse effect upon such endeavors. Thus, exclusion was given primacy by Congress over the open door policy.

The outcome was no victory for moderation even though some

pro-Chinese and a few scholars later declared that it was. Some observers were misled because of the earlier defeat in the Senate of the Mitchell bill.[64] Senator George F. Hoar, consistent enemy of exclusion legislation for a long time, genuinely believed, according to his memoirs in 1903, that a "more moderate Statute was enacted in 1902."[65] Former Secretary of State Foster, who undoubtedly knew better, gave the impression in a diplomatic history, published in 1903, that moderation had won out.[66] Foord also indicated a victory for the pro-Chinese cause. China should be grateful, he wrote, for the conciliatory course being pursued by the United States.[67] Such rhetoric, however, was not likely to comfort or convince Wu, who was soon to return to China and receive, after a brief interim appointment, a position in the Foreign Office.

A matter of future importance was that the anti-Chinese, despite their impressive achievement, refused to be satisfied. Gompers denounced the new law as a "Bunco Bill" and saw it as "one of the most conspicuous pieces of bungling or vicious legislation, or both, ever enacted by Congress."[68] Following his lead, the *San Francisco Examiner* also took a scornful attitude toward the new legislation.[69] Perhaps only in politics and war do the defeated cry victory and the winners shout defeat. In any case, these declarations of dissatisfaction by the exclusionists signaled the probability that additional anti-Chinese legislation would be sought in the future. Wu and the open door forces, trounced this time, had no grounds for feeling confident about the outcome of the next round.

5
Clashes over Exclusion: A Treaty Termination

The passage of the 1902 exclusion law left the Chinese more disillusioned and unhappy than ever. Wu notified the State Department of China's disatisfaction. Applying the principle of reciprocity, he informed Hay, China "would be expected to prohibit the coming . . . of all civil and mining engineers, of all railroad contractors . . . and of all merchants who did not have an established place of business."[1] He demanded modification of the administrative regulations and then consideration of a new treaty.

Apparently shaken by Wu's vehemence, Roosevelt indicated to the Treasury Department his desire for less restrictive rules, but the department brushed aside the president's wishes in an answer that was relayed by the State Department to the Chinese minister. The regulations were required, insisted the secretary of the treasury, "to counteract . . . ingenious devices" to get around them.[2] In July 1902 the secretary similarly rejected objections to the new and tighter regulations contained in a new circular (Circular 52).[3] He denied the charges of treaty violations.

While official remonstrances were proving futile, Lee Chew, a laundryman, expressed the unhappy reaction of a Chinese-American. "The treatment of the Chinese in this country," he wrote in 1903, "is all wrong and mean."[4] It continued thus, he believed, because China was not strong militarily. His disenchantment with Roosevelt was great: "we thought him a brave and good man, but yet he has continued the exclusion of our countrymen. It would not have been so if McKinley had lived."[5]

The growing displeasure of Chinese-Americans with the president in 1902 and 1903 was justified. Roosevelt, attuned primarily to his own political fortunes in California, carefully scrutinized a political analysis of the state by his talented friend John Barrett. Writing the president in 1902 from Honolulu on his way to the Orient, Barrett maintained that, despite the divided nature of the Republican party in California, the different factions supported the Roosevelt administration. His "clear position on Chinese Exclusion" had been of great help in this. In the same memorandum Barrett called the political power of labor in California, especially in San Francisco, "the key to the situation."[6] He recommended the naming of a Californian to the Cabinet, and mentioned Victor H. Metcalf among others. Roosevelt was planning a trip to the west in 1903 and delayed acting on Barrett's recommendation until 1904, when the appointment of a Californian to a Cabinet post would have its greatest political impact. The president's eagerness to strengthen his political base in California was to have fateful consequences for Chinese-Americans.

Chinese-Americans grew more fearful of the Roosevelt administration as a number of changes in personnel and administrative structure dealing with immigration became increasingly weighted against them. In 1903 the Bureau of Immigration was detached from the Treasury Department and became part of the new Department of Commerce and Labor. Its first head, George B. Cortelyou, followed the existing tradition of allowing the commissioner general of immigration to go his own way.[7] The administrative shuffle left the bureau with greater autonomy and more freedom to adopt anti-Chinese tactics.

Frank P. Sargent, the new commissioner general, was directly in charge of policy toward the Chinese from May 1902 until his death in 1908. He was a hard working and tenacious man.[8] "His diplomacy," said the *Tribune*, "is the art of gaining by seeming to yield."[9] He was also a friend of Gompers and, having been a labor leader, was disposed toward labor. At the Senate hearings of 1902, one of the pro-Chinese speakers had accused Powderly of forgetting that he was "a paid employee of the Government and not the president of the American Federation of Labor."[10] The same complaint could have easily been leveled against Sargent.[11] But Roosevelt thought him, after the first year, a decided improvement over Powderly.[12]

Sargent was for restrictive immigration laws in general; he also worked zealously at enforcing the Chinese exclusion laws. Although Powderly had already carried through an imaginative policy in this regard, Sargent demonstrated talent along the same lines beginning with his first full-year annual report for the fiscal year ending June 30, 1903. Appropriations for the year, he reported, had been raised from $215,000 in the preceding year to $250,000.[13] He was looking forward to instituting the Bertillon system of identification with some of the funds authorized by Congress. Deportations of Chinese in the preceding fiscal year, he announced, numbered 704 as compared with 519 in the 1902 fiscal year. Members of the exempt classes admitted, mainly resident merchants, numbered 1523 out of 1759 who claimed that status.[14]

Among the recommendations by Sargent for new legislation were: allowing the right of appeal for the government in appeal questions; requiring Chinese merchants to keep an up-to-date list of their members; appointing immigration inspectors to go to China and carry out examinations at the consulates; and not permitting releases on bail for Chinese who were arrested.[15] These recommendations, appended to the information in his first report of larger appropriations and greater numbers deported, added up to a vigorous forward movement in the exclusion effort in 1903. Two goals could be detected in Sargent's subsequent annual reports: to bar new entries and to purge America of its Chinese-American minority of less than 100,000. Nor did all of this activity take place on the west coast.

The Boston mass arrests of October 11, 1903, were a sample of the harassing devices used to induce Chinese-Americans to leave the country. The incident itself grew out of claims by immigration authorities that large numbers of Chinese had illegally entered the country. According to Chinese Inspector Izard, 35 percent of the 12,000 Chinese laundrymen in New York City in November 1902 were there illegally. A wholesale raid at that time, he suggested, would net hundreds of Chinese who ought to be deported.[16] Sargent in his annual report of June 1903 charged that 10,000 Chinese had been smuggled into the United States.[17] The numbers stated were unbelievably high, but they offered an excuse for the bureau to take action.

As Sargent later explained the immediate background of the raid, the Boston Police Department had asked the United States district attorney of Boston for help in dealing with the Hop Sing Tong, believed to be blackmailing Chinese who were subject to arrest and deportation. Then the district attorney had turned to the Bureau of Immigration for assistance, and the bureau, "with considerable reluctance," had agreed to help.[18] On the night of October 11 arrests were made of 234 who did not have certificates on their persons; the deportation of five immediately followed, and later 45 more were deported.

The pro-Chinese version was very different. In an article in the

Atlantic Monthly Foster described the sudden raid on the Chinese quarters of Boston on a Sunday evening. The officials, he wrote, had entered restaurants and private homes without warrants and had arrested at least 250 persons; had transported them to the Federal Building in such a rough way that one man had his ribs broken; had then demanded that they produce certificates of residence; and had kept them crowded through the night in two small rooms, where they were so closely packed that they had to stand from eight at night until late afternoon the next day.[19] On the next day, Monday, wrote Nickerson, in a pro-Chinese article, a United States district judge had declared the proceedings legal. "Would the judge in question," he asked, "have decided that such proceedings were legal, if three hundred British or German subjects or French citizens had been raided and arrested without warrants?"[20] In their articles Foster and Nickerson charged that the action was both unconstitutional and a violation of the treaty rights of the Chinese.

The whole affair, contended Sargent in 1906, was "an incident which stands . . . isolated in the general enforcement of the Chinese exclusion laws."[21] However Sargent justified it later, the episode appeared at the time to represent a bolder and more aggressive anti-Chinese thrust on the national level than any other previously instituted by an agency of the Federal Government.

Since Sargent tried to outdo Powderly in anti-Chinese zeal, he was bound to clash with the open door interests. The most highly publicized instance of this was the case of Miss Luella Miner and the two Chinese students who planned to study in the United States. Miss Miner, a survivor of the Boxer crisis, was a Presbyterian missionary and teacher of English in a college in China. Her two young charges, one of whom was a descendant of Confucius, had risked their lives to save foreign missionaries. They had been admitted to Oberlin College in Ohio.

Miss Miner and the young men instead encountered one hurdle after another. At San Francisco, upon the arrival of the party on September 12, 1901, immigration officials decided that the students should be rejected, primarily on the ground that Viceroy Li Hungchang had issued the certificates in place of the properly certified person under him, the superintendent of imperial customs at Canton.[22] Additional errors were that the certificates were in Chinese rather than English and that all of the required information was not contained on the Chinese form. Consul James W. Ragsdale had approved the forms, however.

Appeals to the Treasury Department, although supported by Wu, were at first denied.[23] Then Powderly had a change of heart and allowed the students to remain, "as a special act of executive clemency."[24] This action led to the confinement of the young men, one of whom, H. H. Kung, would become China's finance minister, in the detention shed until the records could be sent back to China and returned in proper order. Meanwhile, Miss Miner stood by and came to know intimately about the horrors of the "Shed." "Suicide is common," she wrote in the *Independent;* "death is not infrequent."[25] Disease and crime were rampant there too.

Miss Miner had influential friends and secured another privilege for her students. After they had spent a week in the detention shed, she persuaded John Endicott Gardner, a much respected interpreter in the immigration service, to transfer the young men to a hospital. There they remained for about a year until she could again cut through the red tape. On August 8, 1902, she wrote Dr. Gardner asking if she could take the students to Oberlin in time for the next term of college. "Receiving no response to that letter," she later wrote the infuriated Inspector Dunn, "I assumed that silence gave consent and started on the journey east."[26]

Miss Miner's foray might have succeeded if she had not decided to travel east by the northern route, which took her party across the Canadian border and back into the United States at Portal, North Dakota, where her students were intercepted by the watchful inspectors at that station. Unlike "the famous 'Open Door,' of China," she wrote, "this portal was closed."[27] After remaining at Portal for six weeks, she and the two Chinese went to Toronto to await a decision on the case. In the meantime, Viceroy Li had died.

Sargent was inclined to take a hard view of the episode. The students would have been better off, he wrote Treasury Secretary Leslie M. Shaw, to have been returned to China by the next ship.[28] Considering "all of the circumstances of the case," he wrote to the Ministers Union of Oberlin, "the Bureau is at a loss to suggest any means by which the two students . . . could be afforded relief."[29] Nevertheless, it was not easy to ignore letters on behalf of the two men from the president of the American Board of Foreign Missions; from the renowned missionary, Judson Smith; from the Ministers Union of Oberlin, which included the president of Oberlin College representing the Oberlin faculty; from Representative Theodore Otjen of Wisconsin;

from the widow of a missionary who had been murdered by the Boxers; and from O. F. Bird, a businessman in Milwaukee.[30] Some wrote to the president, some to the secretary of state, and some to the secretary of the treasury. The Chinese Legation joined in the effort.

In January 1903, over a year later, the certificates at last arrived, and the odyssey finally came to an end in Oberlin. "Now I know," remarked one of the students, "that it is easier for a camel to go through the eye of a needle than for a Chinaman to enter the United States."[31]

Few writers stirred up as much public sentiment against the bureau's policies as Miss Miner. As a heroine of a sort, who could write well and with authority on Chinese matters, she reached a wide and sympathetic audience through articles in *Advance, Independent, Outlook,* and elsewhere. Her appeals were to the ideals of the Declaration of Independence and the Christian religion, but they pointed also to the self-interest of merchants and missionaries. "We are very proud of our 'Open Door in China' policy," she wrote, but this did not jibe with "our 'Shut Door in America,'" A time might come when "our commerce and missionary operations may stand waiting at unopened Portals."[32] Miss Miner stressed the special folly of antagonizing students of whom her proteges, Mr. Fei and Mr. Kung, were examples. They had already written of their experiences to a young official who "was in almost daily contact with a club consisting of about three hundred of the most progressive men in Peking, literati and officials representing most of the eighteen provinces."[33] At a time when students were being encouraged by imperial edict to study abroad, they were being alienated by the exclusion policy and were turning to Germany, Russia, England, and elsewhere. Trade opportunities, she warned, would undoubtedly be lost in the process.

The Miner incident was not the only one of its kind, but others seldom ended on such a happy note. In July 1903 Teng Hu Lee, a Yale graduate, arrived from the Dutch East Indies to take graduate work in political economy at Columbia University. He had been assured by the American consul in Batavia that his diploma would establish his status as a student and that he would be allowed to begin his studies. In short order, however, the authorities had him deported.[34]

Such occurrences demonstrated that resolutions like those adopted on June 20, 1902, by the International Missionary Union were in vain. Noting that the exclusion laws were being continued, the resolutions asked the secretary of the treasury to "modify the regulations" as to remove "unnecessary obstacles . . . placed in the way of students . . . and of preachers of the gospel."[35]

While missionaries and educators were encountering conflicts between their purposes and the exclusion policy, businessmen with interests in China were also having their problems. A noteworthy instance of this was in connection with preparations for the Louisiana Purchase Exposition, scheduled to be held in St. Louis in 1904. Congress, giving its blessing to this event, had exempted Chinese from the exclusion laws for purposes of participating in the exhibition. In 1902, Barrett had gone to China to publicize the affair, which intended to highlight the new territories and the influence of the United States in the Pacific.[36] Although China expressed some misgivings over the exclusion policy, it was persuaded to contribute an exhibit.[37] Indeed, it authorized the expenditure of $300,000 for the occasion; and Barrett, good salesman that he was, induced the empress dowager to send P'u Lun, prince of the royal blood, to head the imperial commision to the Fair.[38] Several merchants also planned to come, announced Wong Kaikah, imperial vice commissioner to the Exposition.[39]

The usual clash of interests soon appeared on the American scene, however. In a departmental circular of January 7, 1903, the bureau stipulated that Chinese arrivals had to supply evidence to the collector of customs that they were entitled to attend the Exposition. They also had to provide a photograph and undergo a physical examination and then must go directly to the Exposition, do their designated work there, return to a port by the most direct route, and leave by the first vessel. In addition, they were expected to furnish a $500 bond to ensure the following of regulations.[40]

Chinese objections soon followed. In May 1903 Chentung Liang Ch'eng, the new minister in Washington, complained to David R. Francis, president of the Exposition, that the regulations were not in keeping with the original invitation.[41] He urged that Chinese have the same privileges as other exhibitors. From Conger in Peking came word of "painful surprise" at the regulations and of sharp criticism of them in the press.[42] Indeed, for a time China was on the verge of withdrawing. Anxiously Roosevelt intervened with the secretary of commerce and labor to direct that the "utmost liberality be shown."[43] Some bending occurred; the rules would not apply to the prince and his staff, decided Secretary Cortelyou, and new guidelines would be prepared for merchants. But the existing rules would still apply to employees and laborers.[44]

In the course of the 1903 exchanges, the bureau came in for severe criticism by the American press and business community. The *New York Times* saw the merchants of China as being "treated practically as intending criminals."[45] The American Asiatic Association *Journal* spoke of the "barbarous restrictions" in use against the Chinese.[46] But none of these complaints seriously deterred Sargent and his staff. Rumors reached Sargent that a plot was underway to smuggle in coolies as laborers on an exhibit. Lee Toy of Philadelphia, who had applied for a concession, had a past record as a smuggler and was thought to be organizing a stock company for the same purpose again.[47] Francis, Senator Penrose, and others wrote to urge further modification of the rules. No, replied Cortelyou on January 4, 1904, in a letter of refusal prepared by Sargent, the "general welfare" had to be given first consideration.[48]

Wong Kai-kah contributed an article in 1904 to the *North American Review* entitled, "A Menace to America's Oriental Trade," which aroused the businessmen in an important way.[49] So much ill will had been stirred up in China, he declared, that it would have been better not to invite the Chinese to participate at all. Wong also raised the specter of a boycott or some other form of commercial retaliation. Goaded into action by the threat, the Indianapolis Commercial Club printed his article in pamphlet form and passed resolutions deploring the ill treatment of merchants, scholars, students, and travelers. Club members, many of whom knew Wong personally when he had lived in their community, called on commercial groups to unite in getting the laws better administered.[50] These resolutions, which found their way into the files of the Bureau of Immigration, were approved by the New York Chamber of Commerce, the Board of Trade and Transportation, "and similar organizations."[51]

In 1904, as in the preceding year, the American Asiatic Association kept up a steady drumbeat of disapprobation. It lashed out more sharply than usual against the commissioner of immigration at San Francisco in April. "He undertakes," charged Foord, "to exclude a Canton merchant because his 'appearance and conduct were those of a common laborer,' and a visiting Chinese student because he had 'little or no knowledge of the English language.' "[52] "In the one case five weeks elapsed between the date of arrival and the reversal of the commissioner's decision; in the other case, there was an interval of seven weeks."[53] Francis A. Carl, an American employed by the Chinese government as vice commissioner to the Exposition, gave personal testimony to the oppressiveness of the regulations. When he arrived early in 1904 with a working force, he found H. H. North, the commissioner at San Francisco, rude and suspicious. It "makes me very much disgusted with my own countrymen," wrote Carl to the

Chinese minister, "to see the injustice with which they treat respectable Chinese."[54] Although Carl's party had tried carefully to clear with consuls in China before leaving, one report complained that it still "took many weeks before they were allowed to land and proceed with the commissioner to St. Louis."[55]

A temporary improvement in relations came with the opening of the Exposition on April 30, 1904. The Chinese contribution was described as "a most exquisite exhibit,"[56] and Prince P'u Lun "made warm friends" and "won the hearts" of those attending the much publicized event. He was, said Hay, "a handsome and delicate young gentleman of 29 who looks much younger."[57] At the White House, the president received him cordially, and the American Asiatic Association made great efforts to charm him.

Despite the brief upturn, reports persisted of the tactless handling of Chinese visitors. The Bertillon system, which had been adopted by the bureau not long before, was the object of special condemnation by the pro-Chinese side. An *Outlook* editorial explained the system to its readers as "a scientific method of identifying criminals by the accurate measurement and inspection of the naked body";[58] photography was also part of the procedure. The *Outlook* pointed out that incoming Chinese merchants, students, and travelers receiving such treatment sometimes included graduates of prestigious colleges in the United States. Technically the bureau restricted the use of the Bertillon system to laborers; but, in practice, any Chinese person suspected of being a laborer — and most Chinese were — had to undergo the examination.

For several months in the spring and summer of 1904 rumblings against the bureau's methods were still heard. Chester Holcombe, formerly acting minister in Peking, condemned the "petty, childish, and harassing regulations."[59] Even more outspoken was Charles Stewart Smith, a much respected New York merchant and banker, who described them as "star chamber proceedings" and "a travesty upon justice and fair play."[60]

In his June 1904 annual report, Sargent felt the need to acknowledge and defend himself against the "violent and continuous assaults."[61] "The authors," he reported, "resorted to the press, appealed to the trade associations and other commercial bodies of our great cities, holding up to the affrighted gaze of businessmen alluring views of the vast value of Chinese commerce to other countries."[62] And complaints had continued in spite of the bureau's efforts to placate. Yet the restrictions were necessary, he argued, quoting from a letter by

Treasury Secretary Cortelyou to Representative Eugene F. Loud, because of past experience with fraud. Moreover, they were justified by former court rulings and by interpretive statements which had been made by the United States commissioners who had negotiated the first exclusion treaty.[63]

No evidence appears, despite the mounting clamor against the bureau's rules, that any abatement of the general drive for total exclusion was made. An inspector from San Francisco told Dr. E. R. Donehoo, Presbyterian minister in Pittsburgh: "You are trying to get these people back into the United States, while we are determined to keep them out."[64] A former immigration official recalled later that he had been ordered personally, by a clerk in the bureau, "that if any Chinese merchants arrive at New Orleans and I have no time to examine them they shall be deported without examination."[65] Other officials around the country, he maintained, had been told the same thing.

The effort to reduce the Chinese-American population continued, and the hapless minority wondered where to turn next. Denied voting privileges unless born in the United States, Chinese immigrants wielded almost no political leverage. On June 29, 1903, the president of the Chinese Merchants Exchange of San Francisco appealed without success to the secretary of commerce and labor to use his "kind offices" to improve matters.[66] The home country was also too weak to help. What other solutions were there? China would have to become a strong military power; then there would be more respect for them — so concluded some influential Chinese-Americans.

Ng Poon Chew (Wu P'an-chao) is an interesting example of changing attitudes. The passage of the law of 1902 marked a turning point for him. Until that time Ng , as a Presbyterian minister, had taken exception to the views of younger Chinese who wanted to build up the armed might of China. They were wrong, he said; "it is Christianity which China needs."[67] In a lecture in New York in early 1902, he still showed enthusiasm for the United States: "The Chinese feel that America is a friend to China, notwithstanding the exclusion laws."[68] Ng, as editor of a Chinese newspaper, hoped to find a middle ground on exclusion. In the later stages of the debate on the Mitchell bill, for example, he suggested a literacy test in English and a "certificate of character" as an acceptable compromise.[69] But trade retaliation might follow, he predicted, if the Chinese became too greatly incensed.

Three years later, however, in 1905, his mood was no longer conciliatory or optimistic. Nor did he see Christianity any longer as the answer. The exclusion act, he asserted, was both a violation of treaties and "contrary to the American spirit of justice."[70] In ten years China would have 800,000 men in its army; in a commercial way, "not in a military way," it would then be avenged. Thus, a man who had opposed military power for China only a few years before became alienated against the United States.

The Chinese-Americans, looking for a government that would be stronger and more capable of acting as their champion, were bound to be attracted to leaders and groups that stood for reform in China or possibly even revolution. United States policy unwittingly encouraged this trend by permitting political refugees and reformers from China to enter and make their appeals to the Chinese communities. A notable example of the arrival of a young reformer was Su Shih Chin, who entered at San Francisco in 1901, even though the empress dowager was reputed to be offering a reward of $50,000 for him.[71]

A more famous reformer admitted was Liang Ch'i-ch'ao (then often called Liang Kai Cheu or Liang Ki-chao). This man, follower of K'ang Yu-wei, a leader in the Chinese Empire Reform Association, as the Protect the Emperor Society was called in America, was described in 1903 by the *New York Times* as thirty years old, dressed in western clothes, and looked "like an Americanized Chinaman, although he does not speak English."[72] At this time Liang was advocating the restoration of the emperor who had been removed in 1898. He also favored a constitution for China, representative government, and educational reform.[73] On his arrival in San Francisco, the population of Chinatown turned out enthusiastically to welcome him. In a procession headed by a brass band "were fifty hacks filled with Chinese merchants and men of prominence in the colony."[74] The Reform Association was reported to have 10,000 members in San Francisco out of a total Chinese population estimated officially at that time as less than 15,000. In December 1902 the *Times* believed the Association's membership in the United States totaled 20,000, the increase occurring during Liang's visit.[75]

Other reformers finding their way to America included Tong Chew, who came from Yokohama to New York City to start a weekly newspaper intended to be an official organ of the Reform Association.[76] The Association, according to Tong, had 5,000,000 members in the world. K'ang Yu-wei's daughter arrived to prepare for studies at Wesleyan College. Her father soon followed. Sun Yat-sen, in his travels about the country, appeared at New Orleans in August 1904.[77] The appearance of such figures revealed that a great deal of intellectual ferment was taking place in the Chinese communities in the United States. The exclusion policy did not keep these leaders out, nor did it silence them.

With reformers and revolutionaries increasing in numbers and gaining influence among Chinese overseas, the Chinese government had to be more alert. But it had other priorities to consider, too. Should it try some drastic action to reverse exclusion, or was American support in preserving China's territorial integrity important enough to warrant keeping on friendly terms and continuing normal commercial relations?

Barrett, the confidant of Roosevelt, wrote with assurance that China would accept the exclusion policy more readily than the seizure of its territory. Chinese would say, he informed his readers in 1902, that exclusion was a "mere bagatelle or incident compared to the forcible acquisition of China's territory by foreign nations."[78] If Barrett was correct in his analysis remained to be seen; there was no doubt, however, that China in 1902 was on the verge of losing territory. Two years after the Boxer Rebellion, Russia had still not withdrawn its troops from Manchuria in spite of China's alarm and of the protestations by Japan and the United States. Manchuria, seeming to be so vulnerable, was a tempting prize for the Russians to retain. The worried Chinese leaders had good reasons to look for help from all possible quarters.[79]

If China did nothing else about exclusion, it could at least send diplomatic notes of protest. And this it did. A more drastic recourse would be to seek a new and better treaty when the existing one came up for renewal in 1904. In the Chinese view the termination of the 1892 treaty would automatically restore the Burlingame Treaty of 1868 with its assurance of unrestricted immigration. As 1902 came to a close, however, Chinese-Americans appeared to be losing a powerful advocate in the legation when Wu was called home; they must have grieved to see him on November 18 turn his office over to the *chargé d'affaires*.[80] One of his final acts was to make Nickerson, the Boston lawyer who had been a vigorous critic of exclusion, an "Honorary Vice Consul of the Chinese Empire" at Boston.[81] The step intimated that the exclusion battle would continue.

Up to the time of his departure, Wu remained popular with the

American public. At one time it was rumored that he had been offered the Chair of Chinese literature at Columbia University.[82] Another rumor was that, if assigned to another country, he would resign and stay in the United States. One newspaper naively suggested that he might lose his head when he got back to China for being so popular in the United States.[83] For a person not raised or educated in the United States, he was amazingly successful in mastering the American idiom; yet he remained distinctively Chinese. The American Asiatic Association whose members viewed him as a "highly interesting personality," with a "sense of humor" rarely found among educated Orientals, expressed "genuine regret" at his departure. In addition, Foord thought, he had "earned the right to tell the American people some wholesome truths about the absurdity of their legislation in regard to Chinese immigration."[84]

Wu's career in China proved important to the United States also. He did not know what his next post would be when he left America; first, he became first vice president of the Board of Commerce; but then, early in 1904, he was promoted to the Foreign Office as second secretary. Conger seemed pleased to see a person with experience abroad join the Foreign Office.[85] No American appeared apprehensive that a proud Chinese from the Canton area, whose career in America from 1897 to 1902 had emphasized a continuing if futile struggle against the exclusion policy, had acquired a prominent place in shaping the foreign policy of China.

Sir Chentung Liang Ch'eng replaced Wu as minister in Washington. He was thirty-nine years old in 1902, and had earlier been sent by his government to the United States for his education. He was an imposing figure, standing six feet high and with a powerful build; he had distinguished himself at Phillips Andover in 1887 as a good baseball player. At the British Diamond Jubilee, he had been "knighted by the Queen in recognition of his tact and diplomacy."[86] When he learned of his new appointment, he remarked that he was glad to have this post instead of the one in Paris, since in Washington he would be among "good friends, and old college chums."[87] Secretary of State Elihu Root later referred to him as "a very intelligent and perspicacious man."[88] Such qualities would be greatly needed for his somewhat turbulent sojourn in the United States, which would cover the cancellation of the American China Development Company concession and the Chinese Boycott of 1905-1906.

When Liang returned to Washington in April 1903 he was accompanied by ten students, which implied that students felt obligated

Sir Chentung Liang Ch'eng, Chinese Minister to the United States, 1903-1907. (*Harper's Weekly* 49 [December 23, 1905]. University of Pittsburgh Library.)

to go to great pains to avoid rough handling at American ports. Liang took up the exclusion question immediately, but judiciously. When interviewed upon arrival he said, "I should be pleased if a greater part of the present Chinese immigration restrictions were taken off by the United States, but my nation cannot hope for much more than is now received."[89]

Liang's reticence on exclusion rapidly disappeared when the bureau instituted the Bertillon system in 1903, further curtailed the transit privileges of Chinese, and established the controversial regulations for Chinese attending the St. Louis Exposition of 1904. The whole issue came close to him personally when his brother and entourage arrived from the Philippines and experienced the difficulties. The brother, Liang Hsun, consul general at Manila, arrived at San Francisco on September 30, 1903, with his wife, daughter, maid, and a young woman who was a friend of Liang's daughter. The visit was at the invitation of the Chinese minister, and Washington had been officially notified in advance. Yet the immigration officials refused to admit any of the party, except Liang Hsun himself, without a certificate from Washington. Minister Liang was "indignant" over the matter and talked of registering a strong protest with the State Department. Orders to admit the group soon arrived from Washington.[90]

Two other incidents in 1903 involving indignities toward officials evoked protests by the Chinese minister. One of these concerned Chow Tsz-chi, the first secretary of the legation, making a trip from Washington to San Francisco in September. His story was that at Flagstaff, Arizona, an inspector had asked him for identification. He had replied with his name and official status. The inspector had insisted upon more than his card; and then, reported Chow, "he grasped me by the arm."[91] When informed that he was being placed under arrest, Chow protested, but the official went on, "Even if you were the Chinese Emperor I would arrest you."[92] This statement infuriated Chow even more. When a conductor confirmed Chow's identity, the inspector allowed him to continue on his way. But, first, the angry Chinese notified the State Department of his experience and asked for "proper authority at San Francisco."[93]

The Chow affair brought forth a formal complaint by the Chinese Legation. In a written defense of the bureau, the secretary of commerce and labor informed the president that the laws were merely being carried out; the Chinese secretary had erred in failing to provide proper identification quickly enough. The inspector was only doing his duty in checking and was not lacking in politeness.[94] The

Chow issue, examined more closely, reveals how deeply problems of communciation and differences in culture compounded an already abrasive situation. The inspector may have been sincere in believing his conduct to have been polite and inoffensive. Nearly every word and act, however, were tactless and insulting from the viewpoint of an educated Chinese. The inspector had first used pidgin English, an indication to the class-conscious Chinese that it was presumed he was a laborer. Then the act of questioning an official, the doubting of his word, the patronizing tone of the questions, the laying hands upon his person, and the semi-facetious remark about the emperor were all extremely offensive, whether intentional or not.

Another official, Tom Kim Yung, an attaché, encountered even rougher treatment in 1903; he was physically abused and then thrown into prison by the police in San Francisco. Humiliated by the experience, he committed suicide. Since no Federal agency was connected with this incident, the State Department turned the matter over to the governor of California to settle.[95]

Liang, while forcefully denouncing the perpetrators of these anti-Chinese deeds, reserved his most scathing remarks to condemn the Boston mass arrests of October 11, 1903. Never before, he informed Hay, had "there been a case attended with such signal disregard of the assurances and pledges of just and humane treatment given by the United States, such flagrant violation of treaty obligations, and such utter defiance of the Constitution and laws of the Federal Government."[96]

When the ill will generated by these incidents is considered, the willingness of the Chinese government to negotiate a commercial treaty favorable to the United States on October 8, 1903, is amazing. In being willing to do so, it gave away a major bargaining point for extracting concessions on exclusion. China had its long tradition, however, of treating all foreigners alike, and the British had already obtained a new treaty. Furthermore, Peking had hopes — never to be realized, however — of securing American help in resisting the continued Russian occupation of Manchuria.[97] In 1903 at least, the Manchu dynasty obviously regarded Manchuria as more important than the abuse of its subjects in a distant land.

The commercial treaty, broader in scope than the title implies, extended certain rights to American citizens in China and, in addition, contained an article ensuring comprehensive protection for missionaries and converts. It covered tariff questions, the *likin* (a tax on commerce) which was to be abolished, mining regulations, protection of patents, copyrights, and trademarks. It called for a uniform national coinage, for the reform of the judicial system, and for the banning of further importation of morphine. A provision especially pleasing to the American Asiatic Association was the opening of Mukden and Antung in Manchuria as treaty ports.[98] Even the Senate could find nothing objectionable in the treaty and approved it by unanimous vote. "The treaty," declared the *New York Times*, "is doubtless the most important convention made by the United States with any Oriental country."[99]

Since China was so cooperative about that treaty, American officials may have reasoned that China would be the same about the exclusion treaty which, unless denounced by one side or the other, would simply continue unchanged for another ten years. Toward the end of 1903 Peking had to make a decision on this point. As early as 1902 treaty revision was being advocated by the pro-Chinese side. Foord had seen his efforts to block tighter legislation as "preparatory to a more general movement, in which the Association would have to take the lead, in favor of renewing the treaty of 1894 with China on a more liberal basis."[100] Miss Miner, in a church publication of December 1902, wrote that the time had come "for friends of justice to bestir themselves, for the leaven to be working."[101] Liang, however, had not pursued the matter, although Wu had mentioned it before he left. The surprise and consternation of the State Department were great, therefore, when a telegram from Conger arrived, dated January 25, 1904, with the terse announcement that China had given notice of termination, according to the terms of the treaty.[102]

The State Department at first refused to believe that China was serious. The Chinese decision was made at a time of growing tension between Japan and Russia over Manchuria. On December 26, 1903, Conger had written that war was possible and that China might become involved; on January 2, 1904, he warned Washington that war appeared inevitable; on January 13 he predicted it was imminent. China could surely read the signs as well as Conger. If Russia forced China to join on the Russian side, China would find itself in a desperate position. To remain neutral, as it frantically desired, would require help from friends in all quarters. Nevertheless, a growing resentment against discrimination was becoming very strong in China and among Chinese outside the empire, so that the government could no longer ignore it. With a great deal of creaking in the joints, the Chinese Empire was shifting its priorities. Thus, it had chosen to take a stand against exclusion at a time when the movement was still gaining momentum within the United States — and to react against the uglier manifestations of the anti-Chinese efforts.

6

The Exclusion Law of 1904

The Chinese note of January 1904, which gave formal notice of the ending of the treaty, was brief. It explained, however, that China was acting nearly a year in advance, instead of the six months required by the treaty, so that a new and better treaty could be negotiated.[1]

On February 2 Wu, now in the *Wai-wu Pu*, or Foreign Office, proposed to Conger in Peking that the treaty be extended for a year so that the new treaty would be negotiated after the election. Conger replied that he should have received this proposal earlier. Wu explained that the Foreign Office had not thought of this aspect earlier. In haste, Conger telegraphed the information to Washington.[2]

Hay's answer to Conger was that the treaty did not provide for a one-year extension, only a ten-year extension. His telegram of February 11 instructed Conger to urge China to withdraw its official notification. "Impossible," warned Hay, "to secure ratification here of another even as favorable. Present moment seems most unfortunate to renew agitation of question."[3] His follow-up statement on February 19 explained that the Senate was not likely to approve a new treaty and that Congress would probably enact even more severe legislation once treaty restraints were out of the way.[4]

When Conger in February pressed Peking to keep the existing treaty, he included the inducement that new plans were being formulated with respect to the island territories. He also hinted that the president had China's interests at heart in other matters, presumably in the Russo-Japanese War, which had begun on February 8, 1904. Therefore, he urged, China should continue the treaty for another ten years when a better settlement might result.[5]

Prince Ch'ing's reply to Conger was not flatly negative, but it was not encouraging. He felt that because of the current and persistent complaints from Chinese coming to the United States, and from those living in Hawaii and the Philippines, ten years was a long time. He did not object to the exclusion of laborers "but to the construction given by the Attorney General to the 3rd Article, and to the severe regulations prescribed by the Treasury for carrying it out."[6] In confidence, Conger expressed his belief to Hay that Ch'ing's arguments had come from Wu, adding that he would continue to urge the Foreign Office to alter its position, but he was not optimistic.[7]

As Conger moved ahead with his delicate task, he found himself on the defensive with China over the rigid rules covering the St. Louis Exposition; Conger asked Hay if they could not be "more liberally construed."[8] The Chinese, he wrote again on March 15, could not understand why they had first been urged to participate and had then encountered so many obstacles when entering the country.[9] On the American side, some steps in the direction of leniency were taken, but Conger still made little headway with Prince Ch'ing. In April he went over the treaty issue again with Ch'ing but once more failed to get agreement on a ten-year extension.[10]

The Canton-Hankow railroad was another delicate problem between the United States and China in 1904. It was not being built very rapidly by the American China Development Company, and China had learned that the company had fallen under the control of Belgian interests, contrary to promises made to China. Conger was critical of the company in his dispatch of January 21, 1904.[11] Both nations were careful to keep this issue separate from the exclusion question; however, negative attitudes inspired by one set of circumstances could easily have induced negative attitudes in others.

On April 20 Conger sent Hay his correspondence with Peking, pointing out that the Chinese were determined not to retract their denunciation of the treaty. Conger was sure that Wu was "wholly responsible for the present position and action of the Chinese government."[12] Yet his exchanges indicated that a great deal of public pressure had been placed on Peking officials, especially by the Chinese in the United States, to obtain an improvement in conditions.

The Chinese note of April 1 "(Ching to Conger, by hand of H.E. Wu Ting-fang)" was significant in making clear exactly what the Chinese wanted changed. The note did not challenge the exclusion of laborers. It, first, objected to the narrow interpretation of the exempt classes and to the humiliating treatment meted out to them, and, second, it condemned the harassment of Chinese within the United States; in sum, the note took issue with the Powderly policy. China saw in a continuance of the treaty for another ten years an acquiescence by it in the expulsion from America of all Chinese.[13]

Conger ended his part of the exchanges on April 11 by warning the Chinese that, while his government was not unwilling to extend the treaty for less than ten years, the difficulty was that such changes would require Senate action and might produce unfortunate consequences; in the United States "signs of violent agitation" were already appearing.[14] Prince Ch'ing replied that he could not see how conditions could get any worse than they were; that he was receiving complaints also, particularly from Chinese in America; and "thus, since each of our Governments had its difficulties, we had better wait perhaps until the terms of the present Treaty shall expire and then discuss the matter again."[15]

While Prince Ch'ing was writing that conditions could not get worse for the Chinese-Americans, the dire predictions of Hay and Conger were partly fulfilled. Hay was first silent about the news of China's action, but on March 22 the secretary of commerce and labor was notified.[16] Two days later the news appeared in the press. The *New York Times* commented, "There is nothing in the treaty that could make its continuance desirable . . . and it is not surprising that it has been denounced."[17] China showed an inclination to work out a new treaty promptly; before April 2 Liang had received instructions from Peking to open negotiations with Hay.[18] But the signs in the United States were all pointing toward rough weather ahead.

Waiting in the House to pounce was Livernash, the veteran of the 1902 exclusion wars, who had been rewarded for his earlier efforts by winning the nomination in California of the Union Labor party and the endorsement of the Democratic party. Livernash, after winning the election, had taken his seat in the House only a few months earlier and had immediately become a center of controversy.[19] On March 31, 1904, he introduced a bill (HR 14619) to strike out the part of the act of 1902 that required the law to be consistent with treaty obligations, thereby ensuring that the law remain intact whether a new treaty were negotiated or not.[20]

In the Senate Thomas Patterson, an exclusionist-minded Republican Senator from Colorado, quickly followed suit on April 1 with a similar bill (S5343). He also secured the approval of the Senate to have a legal opinion printed which held that, when the treaty ended, all exclusion laws would automatically be nullified. Patterson's tie with the AFL was also disclosed when it became known that Gompers had originally obtained the legal opinion. In view of this opinion, Patterson maintained, his bill was essential to preserve exclusion. Platt, however, questioned the interpretation of Patterson and the law firm which had given the legal opinion.[21] Nonplussed by this turn of events, Cullom and Platt sought out Hay to ask what the State Department planned. Hay was not especially helpful: he would try to have a new treaty by December; if not, the matter would be up to Congress. "Whatever they do," Hay wrote caustically in his diary, "will be wrong and shameless."[22]

The president, who had found exclusion such a slippery and explosive subject in 1902, was also very much agitated. He had received letters on the Miner affair and on the St. Louis Exposition regulations. Sensitive to these complaints, he had made an effort in January to ameliorate the administration of the laws. The occasion grew out of an incident involving a partner of Quan Yick Nam, a New York Chinese, who was known and respected by Roosevelt. When the partner was not allowed to reenter the United States, Roosevelt interceded on his behalf, suggesting at the same time that the case be allowed to serve as a precedent for better treatment of merchants and students. He wrote the secretary of commerce and labor, "I have been for a long time uneasy about the way in which Chinese merchants and Chinese students have all kinds of obstacles thrown in their way when they come to this country."[23] Bureau officials would agree with this type of communication, but then proceed to ignore it; the Roosevelt gesture was futile.

Nineteen hundred and four was an election year, and Roosevelt was determined to win the large bloc of votes represented by labor and the Pacific slope. On April 5 he discussed the exclusion issue with his Cabinet and accepted the suggestion of sending a message to Congress recommending that the law be extended without regard for treaty obligations. He then asked Hay to write the statement, a task that Hay found peculiarly distasteful.[24] Obediently, the secretary prepared and sent his memorandum to the president the next day, but Platt urged Roosevelt to hold off, at least for a while.[25]

Roosevelt played the part of Hamlet for a few more days. On April 8 the Cabinet again discussed the matter. Hay and Attorney General Philander Knox advised the president that the existing laws were adequate and not to get involved. But, Hay entered in his diary, "the President and Moody fear that votes will be lost on the Slope, if something is not done to convince the people out there that the Executive will enforce the exclusion law, treaty or no treaty."[26] The same thinking was gaining support among Republicans in Congress. Patterson demanded that the stipulation regarding treaty consistency be removed to "banish fears," as Patterson expressed it, "fears that will increase day by day and hour by hour until the day of the election, and thereafter."[27] Since the current session of Congress was nearing adjournment, the question of the best way to get the bill up for an early vote was raised. Henry Cabot Lodge had formerly suggested attaching the bill as an amendment to a sundry civil bill, [28] an idea Congress eventually adopted. One alternative to legislation appealing to the administration was to obtain a ruling by the attorney general that the 1902 law would remain in effect after the lapse of the treaty; on April 10 the attorney general was reported to be preparing such an opinion.[29] But the opinion for some reason failed to appear. Instead, on April 18 the Hitt bill was introduced.[30]

The AFL's actions between 1902 and 1904 help to explain the background of the Hitt bill and the mood in Congress in April. The Cigarmakers' Union at the AFL's annual convention in 1902 had secured approval of its resolution for additional legislation or tighter administrative rulings to protect its members against "this dangerous and degrading competition of cheap Chinese labor."[31] Edward Rosenberg of the San Francisco Labor Council also urged the AFL to send a representative to Hawaii and the Philippines to report on labor conditions and to recommend steps to protect the interests of American workers. Rosenberg was subsequently appointed; he later supplied articles to the *American Federationist*, the AFL organ, urging tighter rules to prevent all types of Oriental labor from getting to the mainland.[32] The AFL, which agreed with this recommendation, and was also determined to bar any further immigration of Orientals into the new territories, carefully scrutinized the Taft Commission's policies as they unfolded in the Philippines.

The AFL Executive Council at the end of 1903 reported that it had failed to get more legislation on the exclusion question, "in view of the shortness of the session."[33] When Gompers learned, however, early in 1904, that China had denounced its treaty, he alerted Livernash and Patterson and secured the amendment to the "general deficiency bill remedying the defect."[34]

On April 18 the Hitt bill, in the form of an amendment to a general deficiency appropriation bill, got to the floor of the House late one night. Although it had been circulated widely, according to the chairman of the Commitee on Foreign Affairs, it did not have the formal approval of the committee. Representative Oscar W. Underwood, southern Democrat, thought it was important enough to be debated, but James A. Hemenway of Indiana remarked, "Of course I expect to pass the bill tonight."[35] Democratic representatives kept raising points of order until Representative William J. Wynn of California, Union Labor member and Democrat, asked them to stop. He informed the chamber that although his colleague, Livernash, was absent, Livernash had "studied the amendment," had found it "quite sound and should be passed without change," and had also "found it satisfactory to the labor leaders with whom he had consulted."[36]

Since the bill did more than continue the existing law regardless of treaty, congressmen wondered about certain parts. The legislation, Hitt maintained, was merely designed to separate the law from the treaty and to clarify some points.[37] James B. Perkins of New York, a Republican member of the Committee on Foreign Affairs, was franker. The bill, he said, was passing in substance what had been in the bill in 1902 and had then been cut out by the Senate. At this point in the debate, Livernash arrived and revealed more of the bill's origins. Extolling the virtues of Sargent and his legal adviser, Richard K. Campbell, he confided that "the amendment comes directly from these friends of that policy."[38] He also intimated that Roosevelt approved the provisions. Before the night of April 18 was over, the bill passed the House as part of a general deficiency bill and, as the *Chronicle* reported, "without a single vote being cast against it and without a word being said against it by anybody."[39]

In the Senate, even though time for adjournment was drawing near, more attention was given the measure than it had been accorded in the House. The House bill, as passed, was substantially different from the original Livernash and Patterson proposals, which would have continued existing legislation regardless of treaty stipulations. The Hitt bill was not long, but when it reached the Senate, it had eleven sections. The major points were as follows: it continued and extended previous legislation and included the island territories; it barred any movement of Chinese from one set of islands to another, or from islands to the mainland; it allowed Chinese who were citizens of the United States by birth to enter the United States; and most controversial, it defined *Chinese person* as "any person descended from an ancestor of the Mongolian race which ancestor is now, or was at any time subsequent to the year 1800, a subject of the Emperor of China";[40] it defined *laborer* as any Chinese except those specifically entitled by law to enter; it authorized the immigration officials to rule on claims to citizenship by Chinese; it brought Chinese under the stipulations of a general immigration act of March 3, 1903; it gave the

United States government the right of appeal against an adverse ruling by a lower court; and it allowed some latitude to the commissioner general to exempt Chinese who had been in the United States before 1894 or who had rendered special service to the government.

Belatedly, the pro-Chinese forces woke up and began to descend on Washington. The *Chronicle* reported on April 21, "R. P. Schwerin, Maxwell Evarts and John Baldwin, counsel for the Union Pacific, are already here, and the attorneys for the Northern Pacific and other roads are on the way."[41] One representative of a transcontinental railroad denounced the bill as a "monstrous law." It would, he exclaimed, "raise the dickins with us. The Chinese will boycott our railway and steamship line sure."[42] The rumor was that John W. Foster was once again being asked to fight against an exclusion bill. In addition to working on Senators, the "pro-China lobby," asserted the *Chronicle*, was trying to get the secretary of state to write a letter to the Senate, pointing out the conflict between the "Perkins-Hitt amendment"and treaty obligations.[43] The American Asiatic Association also alerted its members to write to their Senators against the pending bill.[44] On the other side, labor rallied its forces to push the bill through. On April 21 the AFL Executive Council met in Denver and adopted a resolution urging the passage of the Hitt bill.[45] Senator Henry M. Teller reported that a labor representative had solicited his support for the bill.[46]

In the Senate Platt led the attack on the bill. He was willing to exclude laborers, he said, but he challenged the extreme character of the proposed legislation; he noted that even Wu could not enter the United States as a private citizen, because the bill would classify him as a "laborer." Treaty negotiations were in progress, and it was important not to tie the hands of the American negotiators too tightly. The 1902 law, he asserted, would not lapse with the end of the current treaty; no new bill was really needed at all. Already non-laborers were excluded in many cases, and the new bill would extend the practice even further. One of the provisions would not allow Chinese laborers to be used in the construction of the Panama Canal. Furthermore, many Japanese, all Koreans, and many Filipinos would also be debarred. Another part, he charged, was unconstitutional. To him the extension of the 1902 law had become "a pretext for entering into this legislation, which is so difficult, so delicate, and so doubtful in its propriety."[47]

A motion by Cullom succeeded in eliminating parts unrelated to the extension of existing laws. This was in line with requests in telegrams which had come from the Boston Chamber of Commerce,

Charles S. Hamlin (the Hill-Morgan transportation system), and Judson Smith, secretary, American Board of Foreign Missions. "It seems to us," telegraphed the Reverend Mr. Smith, "that all the sections . . . passed by House except first section constitute new legislation completely changing present laws. We hope you can prevent any further legislation . . . except what is absolutely necessary to secure continuance of existing laws."[48]

Gallinger of New Hampshire, who had presented the telegram, spoke briefly but movingly of the long-range importance of the question. "China today is weak and helpless," he declared, "but China some day will be strong and aggressive; and I hope that the relations of this country with that Empire may be such that when that day comes we shall have the good will and the sympathy and not the hatred of that great people."[49] Finally the Senate passed the Cullom version of the bill.

When the House refused to concur, a conference committee followed with the end result favoring the Senate bill. The final outcome was a paragraph that extended the exclusion laws without a time limit and applied them to the insular possessions. In addition, the Chinese populations of Hawaii and the Philippines, unless they were United States citizens, were barred from the United States.[50]

Buried in a general deficiency appropriations bill, and hurried through at the last moment with little debate, this new law of April 29, 1904, failed to receive much attention either at that time or later. Superficially, all that it seemed to do anyway was reenact existing legislation; but, as in 1902, appearances were deceiving. In an article in the *Independent* on the Patterson bill, Gompers pointed out the deeper meaning of the passage of this legislation. His members, he said, saw the issue in broader terms than competition and lower wages; it concerned "a menace to our civilization."[51] Furthermore, exclusion was "no longer a question. It . . . may be considered, in the United States at least, as a closed issue."[52]

To be sure, Congress appeared to be in agreement with Gompers as it separated the exclusion policy from treaty ties. An American consensus had been attained. Labor and California had convinced the American public that the issue was one of "civilization." Even those opposing the Hitt provisions beyond section five — but accepting the first section — indicated their approval of the status quo, which meant nearly total exclusion. Thus, the question had become, as Gompers maintained, "a closed issue." The priorities of 1902 and before were reaffirmed. For once the AFL was satisfied with the action taken by Congress. "Just before the adjournment of Congress," reported Gompers in the *American Federationist*, "the view of organized labor as presented by Senator Thomas N. Patterson . . . was sustained."[53] And in the other camp, the American Asiatic Association claimed victory also in having staved off the attempts "to enlarge the discretion of the Immigration Officials and to give legislative sanction to some of their most arbitrary rulings."[54] The past policy might continue temporarily, it thought, until a new treaty could be concluded.

Although Platt had referred to delicate treaty negotiations in his statements in April, nothing had appeared on paper in the spring or summer to indicate that diplomats were actively working on a new treaty. Until June the State Department vainly continued to hope that the Chinese would reverse their action. In addition, the Russo-Japanese War, which had begun on February 8, 1904, was overshadowing other Asian issues in both Peking and Washington. China gratefully embraced Hay's suggestion that it declare its neutrality, and it looked to the United States for support. One difficulty for China was the appearance of belligerent vessels in neutral waters; another was whether Chinese officials were to continue collecting customs in the treaty ports in Manchuria. Throughout 1904 the Chinese government remained in a precarious diplomatic position;[55] thus, it found itself under heavy pressure to abandon the struggle over exclusion. That China did not do so was evidence of powerful counterforces at work.

To be sure, nothing on the American scene encouraged the Chinese to expect a better treaty. Shortly after the news of China's decision to end its treaty, the *Chronicle* was already emphasizing the need to watch out for "the artful efforts of the Chinese Minister to broaden the privileges of the privileged classes when entering the country."[56] And Senator Thomas R. Bard of California had warned the president that a more liberal treaty for China was out of the question.[57] The commissioner general urged that the new treaty authorize officials of the bureau to examine Chinese in Chinese ports and insisted that it conform so closely to the current laws, "as will leave no room for doubt or question as to whether there is agreement."[58] Even the ordinarily optimistic American Asiatic Association *Journal* conceded that there was "no hope" that a new treaty would be "more liberal" than the one that was soon to expire.[59]

If Minister Liang believed in omens, he would have been disturbed by an inauspicious one in June 1904. Roosevelt had at last made up his mind to appoint a Californian to his Cabinet and was inquiring secretly about Victor H. Metcalf, a graduate of Yale Law School, who had moved from the east to California and had been elected to Congress from there.[60] By June 16 Roosevelt had obtained the acceptance of Metcalf for the position of secretary of commerce and labor. If elected again, Roosevelt wrote, he really planned Metcalf for the navy or army, but that was for the future.[61] For the present, in any case, the Labor-California combination reigned supreme over matters affecting Chinese exclusion. With Metcalf as secretary of commerce and labor and Sargent as commissioner general, the Chinese minority within the United States, and those seeking to enter or reenter, could expect little mercy. Roosevelt's reasons for appointing Metcalf apparently had nothing to do with the Chinese question, but the end effect was the same.

Another discouraging sign for the Chinese was the platform of the Republican party in 1904. Pointing in two directions, it hailed the growth of trade with the Orient and commended the policies of McKinley and Roosevelt in promoting trade, but it also "cordially" approved "the attitude of President Roosevelt and Congress in regard to the exclusion of Chinese labor."[62] It promised to continue that policy. In the Democratic platform the exclusion issue was treated only by inference, but Roosevelt's reelection in November made the Republican stand more significant.

If anything, less sensitivity was shown toward the Chinese after the denunciation of the treaty and the 1904 legislation than had been the case before. New regulations were constantly tightening the screws. Incidents involving visitors to the St. Louis Exposition went on throughout the summer and early fall. One episode that did not help relations between the two countries was the detention of Yu Kit Men, a commissioner from China to the Exposition and head of a shipping firm in Shanghai. In traveling from New York City to St. Louis he was awakened in his stateroom and asked for his pass. Not having one that satisfied the inspector, he was placed in a "detention pen" near Buffalo until the inspector had checked to make sure that he was not a laborer.[63]

Although students did not entirely stop coming to the United States, reports indicated that more and more were bypassing it. An article in the *China Mail*, a Hong Kong daily, said that students from Nanyang College were going to Belgium to study engineering. They might have come to the United States if they had not feared mistreatment by immigration officials. In the first half of 1904, only one out of several young Chinese going abroad to study had "had the courage to select the United States as his destination."[64]

Among incidents involving students, one of some consequence concerned Alice (Ailing) Soong (spelled "Soon" in the records), a young woman sent to the United States to attend Wesleyan College in Macon, Georgia. Later she became the wife of Finance Minister H. H. Kung; one of her sisters married Sun Yat-sen and the other married Chiang K'ai-shek. She arrived with a missionary family and was detained on the vessel by an official who did not consider her papers in order. Her anxious father in Shanghai, a wealthy merchant and former Methodist minister, went to Murray Warner, a mechanical engineer and businessman, for help. By then he had received a telegram: "Am held and not allowed to land."[65] Infuriated, he asked Warner to telegraph her to return to China, but by that time she had been admitted.

The wheels moved more quickly for Miss Soong because many influential people interceded for her. One was Seth Ward, representative of the Board of Missions of the Methodist Episcopal Church, who got in touch through an intermediary with Senator George C. Perkins of California. Another was the president of Wesleyan College. The State Department also was doing its best to cut through the red tape. The problem here was whether a Portuguese consul general in China had the right to issue a student certificate to Miss Soong as a Portuguese citizen. An authorization was sought by the State Department from the Portuguese minister in Washington who was out of the city at the time. In a few days he was found and eventually supplied the proper face-saving clearance. The delay was from July 2 to July 19, 1904.[66] If the regulations were so rigid that even Miss Soong was detained for more than two weeks, the chances for a young Chinese without connections in high places to enter the country and attend a university were exceedingly slight.

The unpleasant incidents in the summer of 1904 were partly caused by a new regulation of July 22, 1903, that required officials at the ports to collect and hold the certificates of Chinese who were not laborers. The practice meant that privileged Chinese, while traveling within the country, lacked certificates with which to identify themselves to the satisfaction of inquiring inspectors. An example of this difficulty occurred in the case of a band of 15 students from the Canton area who were brought to the United States by a prominent Chinese official. The group included the nephew of the mayor of Pe-

king and sons of high officials and rich merchants. The students also
had connections with the Chinese Empire Reform Association. In
Portland, Oregon, they were questioned by an inspector and held up
so long that they missed their train. The Chinese official in charge of
the group told the press that, from the time they had arrived in the
country, the small band had been insulted and harassed; if this continued, he would urge the Viceroy to send students to Great Britain in
the future.[67]

In July Frederick W. Sutterle, of the American Chinese Company of Shanghai, sent clippings from the foreign press in China to illus-
trate the alienation of influential Chinese. A "strong antagonistic sentiment," he wrote, was "slowly but surely gaining ground in China
against the U. S. amongst the intelligent official and mercantile classes."[68] Unless the United States changed its policies in the near future,
he admonished, the favorable position of Americans in China would
be undermined and the Chinese might, in retaliation, discriminate
against American trade. A steady stream of letters from China repeated the points made by Sutterle. Mrs. Emma E. Fong, wife of the
president of Li Shing Scientific and Industrial College in Hong Kong,
in a letter to Roosevelt wondered if it was necessary to treat students
and businessmen "worse than dogs."[69] John Goodnow, former consul
general in China, wrote in a memorandum for the State Department
that, although Acting Viceroy Tuan Fang was pro-America and had
placed his own son in a Georgetown high school, he was not sending
students from the Nanking area to America "to be possibly herded
with coolies."[70]

To reconcile the rising tide of resentment in China against the
exclusion policy with the steadily growing consensus in the United
States favoring the total exclusion of Chinese was not an easy job for
diplomats. Not until August did a treaty draft emerge from either
side. On August 8, 1904, Liang submitted a Chinese draft and, on
August 12, sent a lengthy statement of 47 pages to explain its provisions. The minister's review of China's grievances contained little that
he had not complained about many times before. The statement added
up, however, to serious charges of treaty violations by the United
States and even a flaunting of its own laws. He spoke of hardships for
Chinese in being denied entrance, of mistreatment of those who were
admitted, and of harassment of Chinese who resided within the United States.[71] In the new treaty he was seeking to protect the rights of
laborers who wished to go back to China and then return to the United
States, to eliminate the detention shed ordeal, to end affronts to

Chinese within the United States, to stop other abuses in connection with technical errors and questioning procedures, and to clear the way for non-laborers to come to America.

The Chinese draft was not a long document. Article 1 contained a definition of *laborer* and agreed to the exclusion of all who fell within the definition. Article 2 affirmed the right of registered laborers in the United States to remain there. Article 3 stipulated the right of transit for Chinese. Article 4 proposed a certificate for non-laborers to identify and protect them from indignities. Article 5 was a "bill of rights" for Chinese-Americans and provided for bail in place of detention, right of appeal, and protection against arrest without warrant or detention of any kind without "due process of law." Article 6 provided for all the rights of the "most favored nation" except the right of naturalization. Article 7 extended the reciprocal right to both countries to register laborers. Article 8 proposed that differences arising out of the treaty should be submitted to an arbitrator. Article 9 recommended ten years as the time limit and longer if neither government objected. The draft also proposed admitting some laborers into Hawaii and the Philippines.[72]

Hay referred the treaty draft to his trusted adviser on Asian affairs, Rockhill, who after four days reported favorably on it. He called the section on laborers a "decided improvement on the Treaty of 1894."[73] And on the question of admitting non-laborers, he was unusually straightforward: "I am of the opinion that we should do everything possible to encourage and facilitate their coming to the United States."[74] His reasons were already well known to Hay, and his opinion was the same as "that of all Americans conversant with conditions in China or interested in promoting closer relations both political and commercial between our respective countries."[75]

Rockhill suggested some changes which, however, did not alter the basic features of the treaty draft. He was uncomfortable about the proposed principle of reciprocity, and inserted the reservation that nothing should impair the rights of the United States citizens in China as approved in the Commercial Treaty of 1903. He also changed some other words and phrases and inserted a provision to make revisions of the treaty possible after ten years without a cancellation of the entire treaty.[76]

In a handwritten note to Rockhill on October 6, Hay sounded favorably disposed toward the Chinese draft, but in the same note took steps to ensure its doom. He thought that Liang had made a "very strong case," and he expressed a liking for Rockhill's suggestions, including that of drafting an American treaty version. "But," he added, "have you any assurance that Liang and the Department of Commerce are substantially at one in regard to the draft treaty? It would be useless to sign a treaty without knowing how the Department of Commerce stands in regard to it."[77] On the same day Hay got in touch with Metcalf, who seemed, according to Hay, "very reasonable and fair."[78] Setting out on this optimistic note, Rockhill wrote to Sargent on October 7 to arrange for a time of meeting.[79] Since Sargent was out of town, Richard K. Campbell, his legal representative, would work with Rockhill.[80]

Sweet reasonableness then vanished. Campbell's formal analysis of the Chinese draft exposed a wide gulf dividing the State Department and the Department of Commerce and Labor. One point of agreement was that Hawaii and the Phillipines should be kept separate from the current negotiations. But from that point on Campbell wished to stress the preservation of past restrictions. Liang's proposals, which would be weakened by the approach taken since 1880, would be reversed. He defended past procedures and urged in addition the stationing of immigration officials in China to carry out more extensive investigations of Chinese applicants.[81] The basic difference between the two Departments appeared to be that, while the State Department was willing to settle for a treaty excluding laborers, the Department of Commerce and Labor was determined to bar all but a miniscule number of Chinese. The bureau within the latter felt compelled to destroy the Chinese draft, challenging as it did the bureau's intricate administrative structure developed since 1898 to accomplish total exclusion.

Between October 13 and 26 Campbell prepared a bureau counterdraft. Forwarded to Sargent on October 26, Campbell's draft did not define *laborer*, and it excluded all Chinese except those groups specifically designated. It proposed that bureau officials conduct the examinations in China. Transit privileges would remain the same, and detention would be continued, but no "longer than necessary." Certificates of residence would be required of non-laborers in the United States. The treaty would run for 15 years and another 15 might be added. For the most part the treaty preserved and confirmed the status quo; however, it also added new restrictive features. As Campbell forwarded the treaty drafts to Sargent, he stressed the "additional article . . . providing, in accordance with your views, for the registration of all Chinese persons lawfully in the United States either now or hereafter."[82] In effect, the bureau was using the treaty as a method of carrying exclusion a few steps further. Sargent's reply on November 1 was that he found Campbell's draft "very satisfactory."[83]

Metcalf seemed to have some awareness that the situation was not as simple as it appeared. After looking over the bureau's counterdraft, he ordered Campbell in November to see Rockhill and ascertain the reason for China's discontent.[84]

Evidently alarmed over the shortness of time before the treaty ran out, Rockhill sent his reply directly to Campbell instead of forwarding it through the usual channels. He gave a digest of Liang's long statement of August 12: China wanted 1) fewer restrictions on travel by Chinese laborers legally in the United States; 2) the end to detention sheds; 3) the end to harassment of laborers within the United States; and 4) clarification on which classes were exempt, verification of their status before they left China, and protection for them against indignities in the United States.[85] Two weeks later nothing had changed. Hay realized that the Department of Commerce and Labor would not budge. "Metcalf thinks," he wrote in his diary, "that there must be nothing not in harmony with existing legislation, forgetting that existing leg'n is founded on old treaty which will cease to exist Dec. 7."[86] On November 22 Roosevelt discussed the treaty issue briefly with his Cabinet. Afterwards, Hay asked Rockhill to confer once again with Metcalf and Sargent.[87]

Another sensitive matter in November was the continuing dissatisfaction of China with the behavior of the American China Development Company. Indeed, China was taking steps to cancel the Canton-Hankow railroad concession. Since the Roosevelt administration wished to preserve the concession if possible, China was in a stronger than usual bargaining position. But it would still need the help of the United States with the peace terms following the Russo-Japanese War to uphold its sovereignty over Manchuria, and no one could predict in November 1904 the outcome of that conflict. Nevertheless, on November 25 Liang urged Hay to press ahead on the railroad question.[88]

On November 28 the treaty draft of the Department of Commerce and Labor had won over the administration. The time factor was bothering Hay, however. On November 28 he wrote in his diary: "The Dept. of Commerce and Labor have [has] made a counterdraft of Chinese Treaty — which is not so bad in itself, but it departs so far from the Chinese draft that it cannot possibly be negotiated before Dec. 7th when the old treaty expires."[89] On November 29 Metcalf told

Hay that his counterdraft was the best that could be offered by his Department. "I asked Liang to see him," wrote Hay, "at M's request."[90] Hay was now worried about what would happen when the treaty expired. He foresaw trouble on December 7, "unless we can sign a *modus vivendi.*"[91] Hay sent the American draft to the Chinese Legation on November 29,[92] by which time it was clear that no treaty agreement was possible in the short time remaining.

The immediate question became what to do when the treaty expired. Campbell had prepared a memorandum taking the position that the laws would remain in effect regardless of the termination of the treaty.[93] China's official view was, however, that when the 1894 treaty expired all immigration restrictions were automatically at an end; this had also been Hay's opinion on November 18. At a Cabinet meeting on December 2, the Roosevelt administration decided to continue the laws in effect until a new treaty was ready.[94] When the Chinese minister saw Hay on December 5, Hay found him "in some dejection about the treaty."[95] The Department of Commerce and Labor, said Liang, would not agree to define the word *laborer* or to clarify the status of the exempt classes. Hay, trying to compensate in other directions, suggested that some adjustment of Boxer indemnity payments might be made by the United States in the future. Liang, preoccupied with the treaty issue, sought out Hay again on December 19. The conversation dealt with both the indemnity and the treaty. Hay discovered that Liang thought that he was "making some progress with Metcalf."[96] A few days later, on December 23, the Chinese minister informed him that the railroad concession was being cancelled because the Belgians had acquired control of the Company.[97]

In Peking Conger had been told very little of what had been transpiring on the exclusion question. On December 5, however, Hay's instructions contained a review of the background of the draft and counterdraft. The tone of the statement reflected the thinking of the Department of Commerce and Labor and signified that chances for reaching an agreement were dimming as time went on. Hay stressed the advantage of having officials in China who would check carefully on applicants for travel certificates and the importance of having the cooperation of the Chinese government in implementing the treaty provisions;[98] inferentially, he was hitting at the charge that certificates could be purchased from officials in the Chinese government.

Minister Liang was very busy those days considering the War, the concession cancellation, the indemnity question, and the immigration treaty. The fact that he had a reply and a new treaty draft ready by January 7, 1905, notwithstanding, suggested that the Chinese were giving high priority to the exclusion question. In his note the Chinese minister totally rejected the Department of Commerce and Labor treaty. The effect of the new American draft, he wrote, would be to exclude all Chinese except five classes. If China used a reciprocal yardstick, it could keep out American "bankers, brokers, commission agents or commercial travelers, expert accountants and clerks . . . physicians, lawyers, clergymen, and missionaries."[99] He also emphasized the importance of working out special arrangements for Hawaii and the Philippines. The type of exclusion envisioned in the American draft, he admonished, would undoubtedly ruin trade relations.

Rockhill saw no point in trying to respond to Liang; the Department of Commerce and Labor had taken over. "I would suggest," he wrote Hay on January 9, "that a copy of the Minister's note, together with the draft of treaty submitted by him, be sent to the Secretary of Commerce and Labor, and request be made him that he kindly communicate to the Department such suggestions as he may have concerning it."[100] Rockhill also proposed to Hay that a new form letter be prepared for those inquiring about treaty negotiations. "I don't see that we are in a better position now than we have been heretofore to give the writers of such letters any encouragement."[101]

The second Chinese draft, accompanying Liang's statement, was notable for being more assertive than the first one. It kept to its earlier position that *laborer* should be defined and that non-laborers should be allowed to enter the United States freely. One new feature was its demand of the right to bar American laborers from China on a reciprocal basis. Another was its request that Chinese laborers be admitted to the island territories on the same basis as other Asians. It also stipulated the right of the Chinese government to institute regulations against American citizens in China similar to those adopted toward Chinese in the United States. Families of the privileged classes, it added, should be allowed to enter America too.[102] Behind the new draft, three separate groups were distinguishable: 1) the privileged classes whose pride and self-interest were being challenged; 2) the Chinese-Americans who felt they were being driven out of the country; and 3) the commercial and sentimental interests pertaining to Hawaii and the Philippines, which had suffered a shattering blow through annexation by losing trade and travel privileges with China. The emphasis on reciprocity and the demand for equal treatment with other Asians showed a new assertive nationalistic spirit.

That the second Chinese draft, when it arrived at the Department of Commerce and Labor, would be flatly rejected was easily predictable. The draft of the United States, observed Metcalf in his statement of January 12, 1905, "represented the limit in the way of concessions . . . to which I as Secretary of this Department felt that I could with propriety go."[103] China had a right, he granted, as a sovereign state to insist on reciprocity, but this would not encourage him to change his mind; he proceeded to defend in great detail the departmental draft.

The department continued to resist all efforts to make it change its position. The commissioner general, in his June 30, 1905, annual report, sounded the confident note of a man who had won a great battle when he stated, in comparing the exclusion work of the bureau with other areas, that "in no branch" of its work had the bureau "so thoroughly succeeded in carrying into effective operation the purpose of the laws committed to its charge."[104] He acknowledged the opposition of missionary interests and commercial interests; the treaty negotiators had sought to exclude laborers only, but this, he declared, would have made the laws inoperative. He dismissed protests against the bureau's activities by denying that Chinese had ever been insulted or humiliated.[105] A few months before Sargent's annual report the bureau had demonstrated to the Chinese that it was getting ready to strike another blow. Sargent's new plan was to begin a census of Chinese. Under the new interpretations and regulations of the bureau, this might lead to the deportation of many Chinese who had entered the country in a less restrictive era; it would also catch up with some who had got into the country illegally. The Chinese minister, protesting this project, on March 31 argued that the step should not be undertaken during the treaty negotiations. Metcalf replied that the measure was needed for better administration of the laws and that there was no rule against doing so; this answer was relayed to Liang in a note of rejection from the State Department on April 13.[106] Court cases, particularly the decision of May 8, 1905, were also assisting the anti-Chinese side.[107]

In the spring of 1905, therefore, the restrictions were becoming even tighter, and the treaty negotiations appeared to be stalled. The Roosevelt administration had accepted the position of the Department of Commerce and Labor that any treaty should at least confirm the status quo, which meant the exclusion of most Chinese, including many merchants and students. Moreover, the American treaty draft contained a feature — the registration of non-laborers — that was even more restrictive than existing legislation. Far removed from this view was the Chinese position that only laborers should be barred, that Chinese in the United States should be better protected, and that the exclusion policy should not apply to Hawaii and the Philippines.

The anti-Chinese appeared victorious, whether there was a new treaty or not, since domestic legislation had been separated from treaty terms in 1904. Furthermore, the Department of Commerce and Labor seemed strong enough to dictate the terms of any new treaty. China could only accept defeat gracefully.

7
Boycott: The Open Door Closed

As treaty negotiations began to reflect the wishes of the anti-Chinese forces, the mood of the American Asiatic Association changed from one of cautious optimism to gloomy carping. Foord absolved the president, secretary of state, and James R. Garfield, head of the Bureau of Corporations, of blame, but castigated the "Trades Union Fanaticism" which dominated the Bureau of Immigration and the "gentleman from California" who was at its head.[1] He felt that "the only hope" for better treatment of students, merchants, and travelers from China was for "the commercial interests" to use their influence systematically on Washington. But other more drastic plans were getting underway among the disillusioned Chinese.

It was becoming apparent to those most closely connected with Chinese affairs that the alienation of China was reaching a dangerous stage and might result in events that would seriously damage American interests. Jeremiah W. Jenks, professor at Cornell University and member of the International Commission for the Gold Standard, after a trip to China, reported that even Chinese who had received their education in the United States were tempted to sympathize with "Boxer movements" after learning of insults to their relatives.[2] H. N. Cook Belting Company in San Francisco had been doing business with a Chinese firm for 25 years, but officers of the Chinese firm abruptly canceled a planned visit to San Francisco because they had heard "that their countrymen will meet with but scant courtesy from the hands of your officials."[3] The Pacific Commercial Museum, voice of the exporters of San Francisco, agonized because Chinese, who were planning to visit the United States and buy $200,000 worth of machinery and supplies, had decided to go to Europe instead.[4]

Students as well as merchants were declining to come to the

103

United States. John Goodnow, consul general at Shanghai, wrote on November 17, 1904, that students were going to Europe instead. He forwarded petitions complaining of this trend.[5] Wilbur T. Gracey, vice consul-in-charge at Nanking, wrote of an action taken by Viceroy Tuan Fang to select and underwrite the costs of 84 students to study abroad, which Gracey considered most unusual and notable. Yet none of the students would be sent to the United States because of earlier instances of mistreatment by officials. Gracey lamented that the exclusion laws were "one of the greatest points against which we have to contend in endeavoring to promote American trade and good feeling."[6] A petition from the Shanghai area with approximately 234 names on it, principally missionaries and educators, complained about the drift of "desirable classes of Chinese" to other countries.[7]

Americans in China detected a loss of patience with the United States by merchants, students, and local officials. In a dispatch on November 29, 1904, Vice Consul Gracey wrote that "higher authorities cannot appreciate our stand."[8] When he tried to explain, his words were "drowned by the quotation of . . . indignities placed upon them."[9] Danger signals were being noted and transmitted to Washington from all parts of the United States such as a statement from a meeting of church superintendents, missionaries, and teachers in New England[10] and a letter from John Fryer, authority on China at the University of California, fretting over the decline of incoming Chinese students because of "indignities."[11]

Danger signals were also appearing within the Chinese communities in the United States, but they were viewed mainly by the Bureau of Immigration, which was not inclined to take such matters seriously. On April 30, 1905, Inspector Gardner translated a proclamation by Chung, acting consul general for California, which gave the Chinese Legation's version of treaty negotiations. The proclamation recognized that the exclusion policy was becoming "increasingly severe," and it acknowledged the "oppression, indignity, and general disquietude resulting therefrom."[12] Since the treaty had expired on December 8, 1904, the proclamation announced, the Chinese had a right to claim damages for any restrictions upon their entry in the future. "Furthermore," went Minister Liang's statement, "as your Minister I can no longer bear to see our people unjustly suffering inequities and indignities visited continually upon them, as people who cry but cry in vain."[13] Only two weeks later, in mid-May, the entire explosive situation came to a head for the Chinese in San Francisco. Now convinced that China would be forced to sign the American draft, the merchants sent a frantic cry for help to China's secretary of foreign affairs. As translated by Gardner, the cable read:

> If exclusion treaty is renewed for term of another ten years Chinese in the United States will become extinct. Minister Leong refused to sign treaty. United States sends new Minister to Peking and is to compel the foreign Secretary to sign. Please protest against it for the rescue of us merchants.[14]

This was reinforced by a cable from the General Chinese Club. Both the fear and anger of the San Francisco community were reflected in an article on May 16, 1905, in a Chinese-language daily, *Chung Sai Yat Po*, edited by Ng Poon Chew.

While the alarm of Chinese-Americans over the prospect that their government might approve the American treaty draft was the spark that touched off their cabled appeals, other factors helped to produce the crisis. One was their apprehension at a new digest of laws, which the bureau had developed in May. Especially worrisome was Rule 59, providing for the issuance of a new certificate of identification, to be carried at all times.[15] Rule 59 could be effectively implemented only by a new registration of all Chinese, a course of action the bureau was preparing to take. One other source of anxiety and outrage was the outcome of the *Ju Toy* case of May 8, 1905, facilitating deportations. Also significant in the background was the cumulative effect of the new devices, proudly announced each year in the *Annual Reports* of the commissioner general, to reduce the Chinese population in the United States. In December 1904, writer W. S. Harwood noted a drop in the Chinese population in San Francisco in one year from 15,000 to 10,000. He portrayed the Chinese in America as old, tubercular, and wifeless, and, he predicted, they would become extinct by 1930 or 1940.[16] For the Chinese-Americans the treaty struggle appeared to be a question of survival.

The response in China to these frantic appeals from America was a boycott and demonstrated that the Chinese were ready for action at last and in a manner unique in Chinese history. Certainly, boycotts had formerly been used in China against local officials and had, on one occasion, been employed against a German firm.[17] But a boycott on a national scale had never before been attempted. Although the subject had been discussed for many years, the patience of the Chinese had seemed inexhaustible. "My government," remarked the son of Li Hung-chang in 1892, while he was a diplomat in Japan, "knows how to wait."[18]

For that matter, the government was still being cautious. The decisive response, taking an economic form, came from merchants and patriotic groups. On May 16 in Shanghai, the main commercial center, the *Jen Ching* ("Man Mirror") Literary Society of Shanghai made public the information that Liang would not sign the new treaty and that a United States minister was coming to negotiate in Peking. On the same day the local gentry and merchants met at the Chinese Chamber of Commerce office and confirmed plans made at a May 10 meeting to institute a boycott.

Before adopting resolutions, the Shanghai merchants discussed the exclusion policy at great length. A Mr. Fang, in relating his own personal experience in America, described the mistreatment of Chinese as he had witnessed it. Their circumstances, he said, were "dreadful."[19] Other speakers stressed the importance of national ties, of gaining respect from other nations, and of wiping out a "national shame." Over 200 people were present at the meeting. Great care was taken, in the resolutions adopted, to avoid embroiling the Chinese government in any violation of international law. The merchants resolved not to order or consume goods from the United States. They recommended that servants of Americans ask for higher wages and that the Canton-Hankow railroad concession be withdrawn. A side benefit of a boycott, the report suggested, was that it might stimulate home manufacturing. After deciding to go ahead, the Shanghai meeting took steps to get the movement organized. Practical measures such as finding out what goods were American, and especially which ones were produced by union labor, were taken. In addition, offenders would be ostracized socially, and essays on methods of opposing the exclusion laws were invited. The merchants also resolved to call on friendly missionaries for support.

Mr. Cheng, one of the spokesmen, recommended hiring lawyers to deal with the government of the United States; he also proposed sending telegrams to Peking and to the minister in Washington to urge opposition to the treaty. The point he stressed was getting in touch with other guilds and chambers of commerce and seeking their cooperation.[20] No plans were made to begin the boycott immediately. August 1 was set so that merchants could dispose of American goods by that date. Shanghai also wanted to know how the guilds in other localities felt, and the merchants needed more time to strengthen their local organization. Plans were made for telegrams to be sent to chambers of commerce and leading guilds in 22 ports.[21]

When Canton in South China heard of Shanghai's plans, its response was immediate and enthusiastic. On May 20 eight important Benevolent Societies called a meeting to consider how to prevent approval of the treaty. According to Consul General Julius Lay, they heard speeches and then agreed "to telegraph the Foreign Office at Peking, the Board of Trade, and the Chinese Minister at Washington, against signing the proposed new Treaty, and, unless certain modifications were enacted making the Treaty less restrictive, measures would be taken to boycott American Trade (Imports)."[22]

Lay tried to forestall further moves of this type. He maintained to Chinese officials that it was an internal labor question and that diplomats should be allowed to settle it. In the Russo-Japanese War (still in progress), he emphasized that the president and Secretary Hay were "friends of China."[23] China, he told the secretary of the viceroy, could not afford to be misled by "fallacies." Nevertheless, more meetings were held in Canton, and the planning moved forward. On May 27 several hundred persons gathered at Kwang Chi Hospital and determined to follow the lead of Shanghai. Four resolutions were adopted: 1) a boycott would begin in two months if the United States refused to modify the proposed treaty; 2) members of the literati and guilds would address meetings and manage affairs; 3) regular Sunday meetings would be held at the same location at 12 p.m., and two representatives from each of 72 guilds and from the Benevolent Societies were to attend; and 4) students of colleges and schools were to find out and publish a list of the brands of American goods which were being used for their uniforms; teachers were not to allow students to buy such goods.[24] At that time Lay did not take the movement seriously. He thought that only the leaders — presumably a few merchants and students — were much concerned. However, he informed Washington that one of the smaller schools had already stopped using American goods for its uniforms.

Foochow, on the coast between Shanghai and Canton, was an example of how rapidly the news spread to other cities. Copies of the minutes of the Shanghai meeting of May 16 were distributed widely. Consul Samuel L. Gracey feared "serious results" because of ensuing wild gossip. One rumor, he reported, held that 2,000 coolies had been beheaded in the United States. Gracey, a former Methodist minister who had established an excellent rapport with the local authorities over the years, wrote that, although mob retaliation was a constant danger in China, he was doing his best to calm matters down and was asking the officials to warn the people "not to listen to such wild reports."[25] But, as the general manager of the Pacific Mail Steamship

Company wrote Roosevelt, "after the ball has started rolling downhill it will be difficult to tell when it will stop."[26]

The word spread also to Chinese communities outside China and was greeted with enthusiasm. On June 20 the Chinese in Singapore met and passed a resolution to support the Shanghai action until the United States modified its exclusion policy.[27] A very dramatic display of anti-American rage, coupled with patriotic fervor, was recorded at Yokohama, Japan. On August 6 — a late date to be getting started — Chinese businessmen, led by the Chinese Guild, or "General Guild," agreed not to buy or handle United States goods or to use United States ships. The participants in the meeting were especially aroused by statements of foreigners that Chinese would never work together or show a fighting spirit. One leading merchant, reported Consul General Henry B. Miller, "taking an American gold watch out of his pocket, dashed it upon the floor saying he would use nothing American."[28]

Although the diplomats from the United States were not sitting idly by, their efforts seemed undermined by events which fed the fires of the boycott. Rockhill arrived opportunely in Shanghai on his way to Peking to replace Conger, who had resigned in January. On May 20, immediately upon getting off the ship at Shanghai, he learned from the consul there of the May 10 and 16 meetings and the plans afoot. Vice Consul James Davidson urged him to meet with the heads of the guilds, and he did so on May 21.[29]

Rockhill's speech at Shanghai reviewed the course of negotiations and maintained that their current status was based on the second Chinese draft, not the American draft. He contradicted the impression that China was being forced to accept a treaty draft against its will, and he also denied "categorically and emphatically" that the United States desired to prevent the return of Chinese laborers or "to put burdensome restrictions" on subjects who were not laborers.[30] Although reactions were generally favorable, the Shanghai press still called for the boycott. Rockhill advised Davidson to protest to the local official. When that measure failed also, Rockhill proceeded to Peking to learn that preparations were moving ahead in Foochow, Amoy, Canton, Hankow, Tientsin, and in more remote cities as well.[31]

Rockhill found the mood in Peking about as frigid as at Shanghai. A mass meeting on May 23 vented its wrath on the treaty draft originating with the Department of Commerce and Labor. The adopted statement contained an impassioned plea for national resistance: "We have only a hairsbreadth of time."[32] Rockhill's task was more difficult because of a tactless utterance in the United States by the former minister. In Leavenworth, Kansas, on June 24, Conger was reported to have scoffed at the fear of a Chinese boycott. Chinese merchants, he declared, would not let sentiment interfere with their purchases; moreover, Chinese could not unite on anything. When these remarks reached Shanghai, Tseng Shao-ch'ing, head of the committee on the boycott, set July 20 as the date to begin the operation.[33] Few statements could have played into the hands of the agitators more than Conger's.

If the Bureau of Immigration had shown more sensitivity in June and July, Rockhill might have had more success in heading off trouble, but the bureau was reluctant to soften its position. In a personal letter, Lay in Canton alluded to "the evident desire of Sargent to make a record for the number of Chinamen he excludes."[34] What could he do "when the immigration officials at Frisco, backed up by Sargent, interpret the law, treaty, and the vague regulations in such a way that practically everyone is excluded."[35]

The most tactless move by the bureau at this time happened in Boston in the K'ing family incident. In this affair four students from England, on their way back to China, arrived at the port of Boston in June. They had letters of introduction from Ambassador Joseph Choate in England, but lacked the regular forms prescribed by the bureau for Chinese in transit. The K'ing family was a prominent family in Shanghai; one of the four was the son of the governor of the province of Shanghai.[36] "The students," declared the *Philadelphia Inquirer*, "were detained a whole day on board ship. Then they were compelled to submit to be photographed, and they were not allowed to go on their way until they had given bond not to open laundries or undertake any other kind of manual labor in this free country."[37] Thanks to the bureau, the leaders of the boycott in Shanghai had obtained a vivid example of humiliating treatment to dramatize, and they took full advantage of it.[38] Until then the merchants had been inclined to await the outcome of treaty negotiations. But after the K'ing incident the Shanghai Chamber of Commerce agreed on July 11, under pressure from students in the area, to support the boycott after July 20, "unless satisfactory assurances as to the completion of a liberal treaty were received from Peking."[39] The boycott did indeed become a reality in Shanghai on the date scheduled.

A closer look at Tseng Shao-ch'ing, the official leader of the boycott, and his constituencies is revealing. His most obvious quality was that, as a wealthy merchant, he was representing the merchant class. But he had other ties as well. Since he was from Fukien province, his leadership helped to ensure that the movement was not confined to one region. It is noteworthy also that Fukien was that area which had been embittered and financially damaged by the American acquisition of the Philippines; Tseng himself may have suffered financial loss earlier. He also, having the office of *Taot'ai*, had status within the imperial government. Tseng was also important, as Consul James L. Rodgers detected, because he was in touch with students identified with the K'ang Yu-wei and Liang Ch'i-ch'ao reform elements.[40] Tseng's ties with these students pointed to a thinly disguised partnership between the merchant guilds and the Chinese Empire Reform Association. There were, in fact, some indications that the Reform Association was the senior partner. Indeed, a revealing interview with an editor of a Chinese newspaper in Hawaii suggested that the pro-K'ang people were the earliest organizers and promoters of the boycott. This editor, Ching Yee Om, maintained that he had been advocating a boycott since February 1901.[41] An American reporter, in tracing this story, discovered that in Hawaii the Reform Association was strong and that Liang Ch'i-ch'ao's followers had a newspaper there called *Sun Chung Kwock Bo (Hsin Chung-kuo Pao)*. This same newspaper had printed a long article in February 1904 condemning the discriminatory practices and proposing a boycott to get better treatment. Then the article had been reprinted as a pamphlet and distributed widely in China and elsewhere. Historians accept the substance of the editor's claims.[42] In the same period the Reform Association had raised over $30,000 for laborers who unloaded ships to tide them over the months of trade suspension. Meanwhile, agitation in the press had been continuously carried on in Hawaii.

Not only were the Reform Association's overseas branches, like that in Hawaii, actively promoting the boycott and working with Tseng but its sympathizers in Shanghai, as indicated by Rodgers, were also busily engaged.[43] Gardner had obtained the interesting information that one of K'ang's former students was editor of a large newpaper in Shanghai and was cooperating with K'ang in promoting the operation.[44] This newspaper was probably the *Eastern Times (Shih Pao)*, which journalist Thomas F. Millard pointed to as the pacesetter on boycott matters. The date, July 20, for the beginning of the boycott, as Millard charged in an article in *Scribner's*, was first announced in that paper.[45] He was not aware, however, of the connection between this newspaper and the Reform Association. Rather, he maintained that the paper was Japanese-controlled, and he blamed the Japanese for its propaganda line.

Other elements, in addition to merchants and anti-government factions, supported Tseng. The press, largely as a voice of the Reform Association, but also as a force in its own right, made an important contribution. In Canton, Lay wrote in July of the continuous agitation of the press: "There has been too much of a newspaper flare."[46] As Rockhill analyzed the Chinese press, it was "an uncontrolled press," a badly informed press, and one often bent on stirring up trouble. Nevertheless, he recognized it as "a new force which the Chinese government has now for the first time to contend with."[47]

If the central government had wanted to call a halt to the proceedings in May, it could easily have done so. Two representatives of the Department of Commerce were present at the May 10 meeting.[48] No attempt was made by the boycott leaders to keep their plans hidden from Peking. In Washington, Minister Liang encouraged government support by writing the Foreign Office on May 13 that a boycott would strengthen his hand in the treaty negotiations.[49] The advocates of the boycott too expressed the view that they were trying to help out the government by exerting economic pressure.[50] In May, when the boycott leaders could still have turned back, the Shanghai merchants inquired of the Foreign Office about the progress of treaty negotiations and received a letter from Wu on May 21 to the effect that little headway was being made.[51] The reply could be interpreted as a go-ahead sign and was so taken. Yet the government's position was ambiguous enough to allow for a change in course later or a disclaimer of responsibility — and both of these happened subsequently. For the time being, however, the Powderly stage of the exclusion policy had proved to be a great unifier of the literate classes of China as it brought together Chinese-Americans, reformers, Shanghai merchants, students, gentry, and even the government in a stand of opposition to American policy. The exclusion policy also seemed to be evoking a new set of priorities in China if Minister Liang was to be believed. In a statement in Chicago on May 20, he asserted that the Chinese people "would prefer to pay a huge indemnity or surrender a slice of territory rather than be insulted and menaced as they are by the attitude of the United States."[52]

As the boycott gained momentum in China, a great deal of concerned speculation went on in America as to who or what was behind it, much of which missed the mark by a wide margin. Japan was so

widely suspected of being the real manipulator of events that Baron
Komura, the Japanese foreign minister, had to reassure Lloyd Griscom of the American Legation that his country was not involved. He
promised that Japan would render no assistance to the boycott side.[53]
At that time, when Japan needed friends against Russia, it had little
to gain by antagonizing the United States. The fact that Chinese students and reformers sometimes lived in Japan and looked to that nation for leadership could give the appearance of official support when
such was not the case. In the United States, however, those who were
anti-Japanese anyway seized this occasion to discredit Japan. Germany and other foreign countries were blamed also. But the search
for instigators turned inward upon the United States too. The *San
Francisco Chronicle,* for example, accused the American Asiatic Association of starting the boycott "for the purpose of breaking down our
exclusion laws."[54]

Americans could not understand the origins of the boycott partly because they could not understand what had been happening to
themselves. The exclusion of all Chinese, rather than only laborers,
had evolved as an official policy too gradually and was too well disguised to be comprehended by the general public. Most Americans
were not aware that immigration barriers, starting out as class-based
in nature, had been transformed into discrimination of such a racial-
national type that they could not fail to anger and alienate literate
people and policymakers. Nor did America have any idea how terri-
fied Chinese-Americans had become of the prospect of being driven
out of the United States altogether. In part also, Americans failed to
perceive recent changes in China, especially the growth of a new and
dynamic spirit of nationalism.[55] Implicit in the thinking of most
Americans was a low opinion of China and Chinese.

On December 20, 1904, the businessman H. B. LaRue, an invet-
erate letter writer against the exclusion policy, had written Secretary
Metcalf that "to demand an open door in China and maintain a closed
door here is an outrage on common sense."[56] Most Americans, nevertheless, found it hard to believe that neither Russia nor Japan, nor
any other great and sinister power, had swung the open door shut. In
shocked disbelief, they discovered it was the Chinese themselves.

8

Efforts To Avert the Boycott

From May to July 1905, both Rockhill in Peking and Roosevelt in Washington were being bombarded by distraught merchants, missionaries, and educators, demanding that something be done to stop the boycott from starting. Some believed that a less harsh administration of the existing exclusion policy would solve the problem, but most were convinced that a less restrictive treaty was also necessary.

As usual the American Asiatic Association was among the first to speak out. On May 16 Foord wrote to Roosevelt that he had received a cablegram from the American Association of China in Shanghai that a boycott was scheduled for August. The enclosed cablegram had a note of urgency about it; Foord added a reminder about the vulnerability of the cotton textile industry. He proposed a new treaty that would define *laborer* and admit all other Chinese, mentioning that around the country, commercial organizations, missionary societies, and others had urged the American Asiatic Association to take the lead in pressing for a more moderate treaty.[1]

The president also heard from the Ashcraft Cotton Mills in Alabama, former Senator John L. McLaurin of South Carolina, a tea importer in Boston, the United States Export Association in New York, the Merchants Association of New York, and the Portland Chamber of Commerce. Some clergymen wrote in favor of a more moderate treaty. Articles critical of the exclusion policy appeared in the *New Orleans Daily Statesman*, May 27, 1905; the *Sunday States*, May 28, 1905; and the *San Francisco News Letter*, June 17, 1905.[2] The American members of the Educational Association of China represented an important group in China pressing for action. On June 12 the members wrote Roosevelt to urge better treatment for Chinese students. If this were not done, they emphasized, their own work in

China might be endangered by the antagonisms aroused by the discourteous handling of students. American personnel provided 75 percent of the modern instruction in China, and this American influence through education might well be lost if the current trend were to continue. Not only that. There might also be heavy commercial and political losses.[3]

Even Chinese teachers and students wrote to the president, as in the case of a petition from 350 Chinese teachers and students of the Anglo-Chinese College in Foochow. Notably this communication had a detailed list of student grievances and desires. Consul Gracey, who was also a member of the Board of Trustees of the institution, summarized the requests under ten headings: 1) treat Chinese like other immigrants; 2) avoid the removal of clothing for examinations; 3) provide suitable buildings; 4) process passports in not over a week's time; 5) allow attorneys and friends to be present at hearings; 6) permit students to do part-time work; 7) admit clerks, cooks, miners, laundrymen, assistants of merchants, and skilled mechanics; 8) allow merchants with assets of $1,000 to go and come freely; 9) treat Chinese in the United States fairly; and 10) notify the Chinese consul ahead of time if buildings were to be destroyed for sanitary reasons during a plague.[4]

Another petition from the Chinese of Canton Christian College, while not objecting to the barring of laborers, asked for a less restrictive interpretation of *merchant* and *student*. It also appealed for an end to the harassment of Chinese within the United States. The statement was temperate in tone and lauded the United States for its "leniency" on the Boxer indemnity question and for its aid in neutralizing China during the Russo-Japanese War. It also termed Roosevelt "a friend of the Chinese nation." Nevertheless, the signers made clear that American policies on exclusion were alienating the Chinese people and causing them "to scorn Christianity."[5] In a more outspoken manner the Foochow petition "did not quite understand why your people in China preach the doctrine of Love, while in America you treat Chinese worse than any other nation, nay even the negroes!"[6] The Foochow statement further stressed that the exclusion policy could result in the destruction of the open door policy. Most of these petitions sent to Roosevelt from China were transmitted through Rockhill, who was greatly impressed by them. The one that he forwarded from the American members of the Educational Association of China reflected what he called "the views of the highest class of Americans interested in the student life of China."[7] President O. F.

Wisner of Canton Christian College made clear that the American Protestant missionary community at Canton had helped with the Canton petition and was fully in sympathy with it.

Responding to appeals for action, the American Legation resumed the treaty negotiations which had fared so badly in Washington in 1904. At Shanghai, Vice Consul Davidson assured the American Association of China in May that the new treaty would be liberal and not have unseemly restrictions upon the privileged classes.[8] The responsibility for working out specific terms from May on rested with Rockhill, who soon began to work on a new treaty draft. He was challenged immediately by a Chinese statement that emerged on May 23 from a mass meeting near Peking. It denounced the exclusion rules as pretending to bar only laborers, "but as a matter of fact they exclude all Chinese from the United States."[9] And it proceeded to offer a detailed critique of the exclusion policy. If Wu had not written the document, his keen legal mind and passionate involvement in the question were well expressed by a kindred spirit. The report also analyzed point by point the Department of Commerce and Labor treaty draft. Concluding that the American draft made the existing policy even more restrictive, it declared that China should "most certainly never sign this treaty."[10] If signed, the treaty would hurt China's prestige, disgrace the Chinese people, represent unjust inequality of treatment between two nations, and eliminate the commercial advantage for China derived from the sums of money sent back by Chinese-Americans. Consuls informed Rockhill that the May 23 statement was being widely distributed; in Newchwang in South Manchuria, a circular had appeared in public places with a digest of the charges.[11] Rockhill needed to act swiftly to dispel the doubts and suspicions aroused by these public attacks on the earlier American treaty draft.

On June 1 Rockhill officially assumed charge of the Legation. During the next two weeks he worked on the treaty problem without success. Finally, on June 17 he cabled Washington that he believed the critical point was Article 4 of the Department of Commerce and Labor draft. It would, he maintained, "prove most obnoxious to the Chinese people, and tend to increase the present agitation against us."[12] Article 4 specified which classes of Chinese were allowed to enter the United States. "Can I," he inquired, "agree that all persons proving to our satisfaction that they are not laborers can enter and reside in the United States? All Americans in China," he added, "advocate strongly liberal treatment."[13]

Rockhill's telegram was referred to the Department of Commerce and Labor, which exercised its customary veto power. A lengthy memorandum that traced the history of exclusion from the total exclusionist point of view was prepared for the president's Cabinet meeting of June 20. The account held that an interpretation of November 6, 1880, by the United States commissioners who negotiated the 1880 treaty affirmed the right to exclude all Chinese except those of the specified classes. Under "compulsion," said the memorandum, it would be especially unwise to yield the point. The question was broader, it argued, than protecting American labor; it also had social and political consequences. If a large influx of Chinese occurred, tong wars, prostitution, massacres of Chinese, and separate Chinese communities with their own laws and customs would result. Political corruption was also likely. Furthermore, increased political power, coming with a second generation of voting Chinese, might produce an erosion of the exclusion laws and ultimate triumph of Chinese civilization in the United States.[14] While the opposition of the Department of Commerce and Labor was great enough to keep Rockhill from getting what he sought, Hay's telegram to Rockhill was not altogether discouraging. "Cable draft of a substitute for article four," he requested, "in sense indicated by you, which will be satisfactory to Chinese Government."[15]

In China the tensions were continuing to mount as Rockhill's credentials were officially presented on June 17. On that date he complained to Prince Ch'ing of the Foreign Office about the refusal of the newspaper *Ta Kung Pao* to accept advertisements from American firms, and of its cancellation of one by an "American lawyer in Tientsin." He was "at a loss," he wrote, "to understand why no sufficient action has been taken to put a stop to this foolish movement."[16] As he thus initiated a series of written protests to the Chinese Foreign Office against these early manifestations of boycott activity, he felt the weight of a growing Chinese sentiment in the form of a telegram on June 19 from the "Gentry and people of Nanking": "Please exert your influence to have the Supplementary Exclusion Treaty abrogated so as to secure peace for trade."[17]

During this rising tension Rockhill took up the treaty question on June 22 with His Excellency Na-t'ung, vice president of the Board of Foreign Affairs. He summarized the course of past events, noting that it had been a Chinese decision in January 1904 to terminate the treaty on December 7, 1904, and that this had been done in spite of the urging of the United States to let it run for another ten years. Negotiations for a new treaty had then commenced, and Minister Liang had presented a new draft in August 1904. In September Hay had submitted a counterdraft; in November Liang had produced a second draft. Then, Rockhill continued, he had conferred with both Liang and Metcalf, "because questions affecting immigration come under his jurisdiction."[18] At that point matters had come to a standstill. Although he had now been instructed to seek agreement on a treaty draft, he was "not clothed with full powers."[19] Nevertheless, the exclusion issue was "the only question between us and my Government desires just as far as possible to meet the wishes of China in the matter, and hopes that it may be settled and taken out of the way."[20] Na-t'ung seemed pleased with the remarks of the American minister; therefore, Rockhill proceeded into the areas of agreement and conflict. As he viewed the matter, China assented to the right of the United States to protect its own laborers by shutting out the Chinese working class. Rockhill, however, held out the prospect that workers who had entered the United States illegally at an earlier time might be approved "as having the right to be there."[21] He also stressed the desire of the United States to welcome students, travelers, and other non-laboring Chinese. As for the rights of Chinese in the United States, Rockhill felt that, in broad principle, the United States could accept the Chinese positions.

Two areas of disagreement soon appeared. The American diplomat insisted that visas be issued at only two or three ports in China by United States consular officers, and he refused to consider admitting laborers to the island territories. Despite Na-t'ung's objections, Rockhill remained firm on the latter point, declaring, "Our government is bound to be most cautious in all questions affecting labor."[22] This matter, both agreed, should be reserved for further discussion at a later date. The conference closed on a constructive note.

Exclusion had become the big issue in China, Rockhill reported in late June. A Chinese comprador refused to accept a good job offer from an American, and ads by Americans were rejected by the Chinese press. Foreigners were shocked at the nationalistic spirit in evidence among the Chinese.[23] To curb the organizing activities, Rockhill tried to get the Chinese government to condemn the projected boycott. Consuls at Newchwang, Hankow, Canton, Tientsin, and Shanghai, he wrote Prince Ch'ing on June 24, felt that quick official action was needed. He complained that the timing was most inappropriate, since the treaty was currently under consideration.[24] Peking was slow to respond, however. "Indecision," he wrote Hay on July 1, "and a determination to drift with any current is shown on every side."[25] At length Rockhill's persistence won out. On July 1 the much-desired edict was announced. But first Prince Ch'ing lectured the diplomat on the injustice of the immigration restrictions. Reduce them, he said, and the merchants would have no reason to protest. With much relief and satisfaction Rockhill was able to cable Washington that, after "repeated and urgent representation," the Foreign Office had sent out instructions "to all Viceroys and Governors to stop anti-American agitation and attempted boycott of American goods."[26]

Peking, by having a treaty draft also ready on July 1, made clear that it expected something in return from Rockhill. In this first Chinese draft since negotiations had shifted from Washington to Peking, article 1 defined *laborers* and authorized both countries to prohibit them on a reciprocal basis. It also stipulated that non-laborers should not be excluded from either country; 2 stated that returning laborers should be readmitted with a minimum of red tape and with a simple certificate, which a Chinese consul in the United States could supply upon the departure of the laborer from America; 3 called for the right of transit and for only "just" regulations; 4 held that Chinese in Hawaii and the Philippines should be treated like other Asians and that local authorities should regulate immigration; 5 proposed that non-laborers be admitted upon the presentation of certificates from the Chinese government which had been signed by officials of the United States at the Chinese ports; 6 insisted that Chinese should not be confined if they could provide bail. In addition, they were to have the right to employ counsel, to appeal to a higher court, and to be admitted in cases of irregularity in certificates if no evidence of fraud was present. The same article also banned the molestation of Chinese in the United States; 7 allowed non-laborers to bring their families with them; 8 guaranteed the protection of the lives and property of Chinese subjects in the United States; 9 gave China the right to register laborers of the United States who were in China; 10 gave China the same right to register other citizens of the United States in China; 11 proposed the referral of disputes to the Hague Court or to arbiters; 12 set the time limit at ten years, or longer if neither side gave official notice of its desire to terminate the treaty.[27] The new Chinese draft stated again much that had been said by Liang in Washington. But the emphasis on reciprocity in the treatment of the nationals of the two countries, and the insistence on being treated like other Asians, revealed anew the growing strength of a nationalistic spirit. Instead of proposing revisions of the Chinese draft, Rockhill responded with a draft of his own on July 8. The new American draft prohibited skilled and unskilled Chinese laborers, had ambiguous features in regard to the acceptance of all other Chinese, and omitted any mention of Hawaii and the Philippines. The *Wai-wu Pu* replied with a second Chinese draft on July 19 which made a few minor concessions to Rockhill, but clung to its own definition of laborer ("employed in mining, huckstering, peddling, and laundry work, and in taking, drying or otherwise preserving shell-fish or other fish for home consumption or exportation, and no other person shall be considered a laborer"[28]), requested the admitting of all other Chinese, and specified that local authorities should handle immigration policies for the Philippines and Hawaii and treat all Asians alike. The Chinese draft also preserved a "bill of rights" section for Chinese residents in the United States.

Before the second Chinese draft arrived, Rockhill had become cautiously optimistic. He had received a telegram from the State Department on July 7, inquiring if the July 1 edict would be observed and also informing him that Standard Oil Company believed that the boycott "would be a grave disaster to the petroleum industry of the United States."[29] His reply on July 14 was that Peking and the local authorities were opposing the boycott and that the threat to begin it on August 1 might not be acted upon. In addition, wrote Rockhill, "I hope to have, in the course of a few days, from Foreign Office, final views draft of treaty."[30] Rockhill's optimism lasted only briefly. On July 15 he cabled Washington that the consuls of Shanghai and Canton expected the boycott to take place.[31] The consuls at Tientsin, Newchwang, and Hankow doubted that it would break out in their areas, but those cities were less important to American trade. On July 18 at Amoy a minor but ominous incident occurred when the flag halyards at the consulate had been cut and a man had defecated at the base of the flagpole.[32] The consul had demanded an apology and punishment for the offenders but had found the local officials reluctant to take firm action. Rodgers expected the boycott to begin at Shanghai on July 20 unless a treaty agreement was reached before then. Lay thought the operation would start on August 1 at Canton, where the Standard Oil representative informed Lay that the British-American Tobacco Company had already lost 50 percent in sales.[33]

Although Rockhill realized that he would not be able to produce a treaty in time to stop the movement, he manifested no interest in resorting to military action. The "only way that the question can be handled," he wrote Rodgers, "is by bringing Government pressure to bear on the boycotters and by arguing with them and persuading them unofficially."[34] He outlined for Rodgers and other consuls arguments to use with Chinese merchants: 1) they were going beyond their original objectives; 2) they were hurting their best friends in the United States; 3) they were doing harm to their own financial welfare; and 4) they were antagonizing a friendly nation. To Lay he wrote that he still hoped to have a treaty ready to submit to the Senate before the convening of the next session of Congress.[35]

As the effects of the boycott became evident, the only bright spot for Rockhill was the heavy-handed suppression of agitation in the province containing Peking by Viceroy Yuan Shih-k'ai. To his great delight, the viceroy at Tientsin had issued a proclamation on June 24 prohibiting meetings of over 20 people unless the chief of police was notified in advance. An official who would attend such meetings could seize and punish leaders if an "untruthful topic" were discussed.[36] Unconcerned by this curtailment of freedom of assembly and subsequent freedom of the press by the viceroy, Rockhill pointed to him as an example that other officials should follow. That a man of Yuan's stature took a stand against the boycott was a coup of considerable importance, but he was not joined by the other viceroys. Furthermore, Yuan had indicated earlier that he too was against the exclusion policy. In June he and Viceroy Chang Chih-tung at Wuchang had got in touch with the diplomat John Barrett, then in Panama, and had begged him to exert his influence with the president, which Barrett had done.[37] Yuan, it appeared, shared the feelings of the boycotters but preferred other methods.

On July 20 Rockhill witnessed a significant turn for the worse. Although the original plans for the boycott had set August 1 as the starting date, it began earlier in some places such as Shanghai. On July 18 a mass meeting in that city was attended by 1,500 people. The viceroy, unlike Yuan, made no effort to stop it. Merchants, students from at least 20 schools, members of the Chinese Educational Association, and even 100 women — an unheard-of event — were in attendance.[38] Leaders of powerful guilds were present, and at least one prominent official, *Taot'ai* Ma, addressed the crowd. Patriotic speeches were delivered. As a meeting to demonstrate solidarity and a determination to go ahead, the affair was a spectacular success. Meanwhile, Rockhill was bogged down with his negotiations. The new Chinese draft of July 19 showed the two sides still far apart. The boycott began on July 20 at Shanghai as scheduled and at some of the other treaty ports.

Little help for Rockhill was forthcoming from Washington. In

July, Hay, who had been sick for some time, died, but even when well he had done little about exclusion except wring his hands. Elihu Root would not take over as secretary of state until September 1. Francis B. Loomis served as acting secretary after July 2. Although Roosevelt himself was filling in the void to some extent and taking some important steps, the effects would not be felt for several months. In any case, he was hemmed in by regulations, precedents, court decisions, and confirmatory law pertaining to exclusion — partly of his own making — almost as much as by anything else. And Metcalf seemed immovable. So Rockhill found himself facing great trouble, aware of the need to act, and yet with practically no room to maneuver.

Nevertheless, the drafting charade continued. "I am gratified to note," Rockhill wrote on July 25 to Na-t'ung, concerning the Chinese draft of July 19, "that in most particulars the two drafts are in accord."[39] He did not object, to some of the changes, but others he thought were "unnecessary or impractical." He had therefore prepared another draft, and he hoped for a reply soon so that he could send a final draft to Washington, "at as early a date as possible."[40]

Rockhill's second draft of July 25 barred Chinese skilled and unskilled laborers, but balked at the exclusion of skilled United States laborers from China; furthermore, he rejected the Chinese definition of *laborer.* He also resisted certain procedural requests of the Chinese, and he refused to allow separate consideration of Hawaii and the Philippines. On July 26 he wrote the State Department that he was still not ready with a substitute for Article 4 of the Department of Commerce and Labor treaty. But he hoped "at an early date to be in a position to transmit a satisfactory draft."[41]

While waiting for a reply from the Chinese, Rockhill received word of a new executive order on June 24 by Roosevelt calling on bureau officials to be courteous toward students, merchants, and others.[42] Clutching at this news, Rockhill informed the Foreign Office of it on July 28.[43] This order assured the privileged classes of good treatment, declared Rockhill. Fair words at this point, however, failed to elicit enthusiasm from the Chinese.

On July 31 Na-t'ung sent a polite answer to Rockhill's note and treaty draft on July 25. He thought that differences could be easily adjusted, but there were still "some provisions that are unsuited to the circumstances attending the immigration of Chinese into the United States."[44]Hence, he added, he had a commentary and new draft to present. In Na-t'ung's third draft of July 31, he continued to insist on reciprocity in the policy toward laborers, and he held to the other Chinese positions. As a concession to the United States, China would be willing to list in the treaty those who were not to be classified as laborers:

> Physicans, agents, artists, proprietors of restaurants, proprietors of tobacco shops (includes opium shops E.T.W.), grocery shops, barber shops, whether large or small and proprietors of any sort of shops or stores (includes inns E.T.W.) as well as accountants, shop clerks, cooks, men-of-all work, and the employes of these shops, upper or lower, are not included in the prohibition.[45]

This approach, new though it was, was as unacceptable to the Americans as the previous Chinese positions. Thus, the impasse remained as great as ever.

Rockhill still believed that the solution to the problem was for the United States to admit non-laboring Chinese, and he again asked the State Department on July 28 to allow this.[46] But, as usual, no help came from Washington. Almost two months later, on September 21, 1905, his message finally found its way to Metcalf with Alvey A. Adee's notation of its "showing the situation of the question."[47]

There was always the possibility that the boycott would not last long. Rockhill speculated in late July that it would stop "the day the boycotters begin to lose anything by the movement, until then there will be much talking and agitation."[48] Although the boycott was in effect, reported the *San Francisco Chronicle*, in a dispatch from Shanghai dated July 28, "the Chinese would probably welcome any reassuring indication from America enabling them to withdraw from their position gracefully."[49] Some consuls, notably Gracey at Foochow and Lay at Canton, thought at first that it would not amount to much.[50] Nevertheless, Rockhill saw an unpromising portent in a notification from the Chinese government that no representative of China would attend a meeting in September of the Association of Military Surgeons of the United States.[51]

Indeed, Rockhill soon learned that Peking was making no effort to back up the July 1 proclamation. Viceroy Yuan, he discovered, had been mainly responsible for the edict in the first place; whereas Na-t'ung had vigorously opposed it.[52] As the boycott came into being and spread, he found the government unwilling to issue new proclamations. It was "supine," he complained to Washington. "Movement pleases it," he cabled on August 4, "as effective means to coerce us.

Agitation in American politics confirms belief."[53] He was soon to hear
from Washington that in San Francisco the Foreign Office was denying to the Chinese community there that it was opposed to the boycott
in any way.[54] By August 1 Americans could not sell goods anywhere in
China except Tientsin, where Yuan was in control.

Although Rockhill was contemplating a new approach, he pursued for a while longer the game of trading drafts. His third draft of
August 2, which was the last of the lot, made no concessions to accepting the Chinese definition of *laborer*, to admitting non-laborers, or to
allowing special arrangements for Hawaii and the Philippines. On
less important points he yielded. He agreed, for example, to permit
Chinese consuls to participate in the processing of certificates which
allowed laborers in the United States to visit China and return, and,
by implication, to make legal the status of all Chinese who had entered the United States illegally. But Rockhill's note revealed that his
patience was running out. If his last draft was not acceptable, he concluded, "I shall be obliged to inform my Government that I cannot
reach any arrangement offering a chance for the settlement of the
question, and that I request to be relieved from the further consideration and discussion of it."[55]

The president and ministers of the Board of Foreign Affairs
answered on August 7 that they were sorry to get Rockhill's reply.
They felt that the United States had been "unusually friendly" to
China, and they regretted that the relationship was "disturbed by
acquiescing in the unreasonable views of the Labor Party."[56] But the
Chinese held firmly to their earlier stands. A clear definition of *laborer* was necessary, they insisted, because of the past "ill-treatment" of
non-laboring Chinese, and clarifying language was also needed for
article 4. Moreover, they noted a major reason from their standpoint
for the revision of the treaty was the issue of Hawaii and the Philippines. Special emphasis was placed on the Philippines. It was near
China, the statement observed, and much trade and travel had taken
place. Then the United States had suddenly suspended the inter-
change. "In a word," the Chinese commented indignantly, "the United
States treats the people of all Asiatic and European countries in the
ordinary way excepting the Chinese, against whom strict prohibitions
are enforced."[57]

In those days, William Phillips, second secretary of the Legation, recalled later, Rockhill's sole recreation was to take walks in the
late afternoons. At other times he was in his library either examining
Chinese scholarly writings or preparing official dispatches.[58] Perhaps

it was during one of his strolls that he reluctantly concluded a harder line was necessary. A marked change in policy came early in August. On August 4 Rockhill cabled, "Can I inform Chinese Government that under provision Article 15th, our treaty 1858, we will hold it responsible for any losses sustained by our trade for its failure to stop present organized movement interfering therewith."[59] Roosevelt's quick reply, a notation on the dispatch, was "Confirm all." Rockhill was not only authorized to accuse the Chinese of violating the treaty of 1858 but was advised to "use strong language."[60] Thus, on August 7 he sternly called the Chinese to account. His note interpreted the boycott as a form of "intimidation" at a time when the United States was "seeking to meet with your wishes for a new treaty."[61] The boycott was in effect, he observed, in Shanghai, Canton, Amoy, and elsewhere, and appeared to have the support of officials. Moreover, the July 1 edict seemed to contain some official sympathy for the scheme. In addition, the official title of Tseng Shao-ch'ing, the Shanghai leader, implied further governmental approbation. Therefore, he concluded, "the United States will hold it directly responsible for any loss our interests have sustained or may hereafter have to bear."[62] Article 15 of the 1858 treaty was cited as the basis for future damage claims. While the *Wai-wu Pu* was contemplating how to respond to this new diplomatic offensive, the American minister struck another blow. On August 14 his note was curt and to the point: he had been instructed by his government to end negotiations until after the termination of the disturbances.[63]

Some alarm began to manifest itself in the responses of the Foreign Office. The boycott, Prince Ch'ing wrote on August 26, was the idea of the merchants and not the responsibility of the government. China was sincerely trying to end it; in fact, more telegrams had been sent out to the viceroys to urge them to quiet the people. Tseng was "merely a member of a commercial guild. Severe treatment might excite ... still more trouble and disorder."[64] Prince Ch'ing urged a new treaty as the answer. But so far as Rockhill was concerned, that road had ended. By suspending negotiations until the trouble was over, Rockhill had very neatly got out of his diplomatic cul-de-sac. Whether threats to seek financial restitution from the government would work better than conciliatory words in resolving the boycott issue remained to be seen. But in the short run at least, the tables had been turned so drastically on the Chinese as to transform the boycott into a justification on the American side for refusing to make concessions on the immigration issue.

In a broader sense, however, Rockhill's decision signified a sacrifice of the open door policy for the exclusion policy. The United States was refusing to return to the pre-1898 days, which would have meant the entry of two to four thousand Chinese a year. Exclusion — the new version of it adopted after 1898 — was being given priority over commerce, friendship, missionary, and educational interests, the whole complex of interests that were served by the open door policy. There was nothing extraordinary in this ranking of priorities; rather, it was simply being reaffirmed. But Roosevelt was good at untangling knots. While Rockhill had been working away in Peking, Roosevelt had not been idle in Washington.

9

Roosevelt's Change in Position

While Rockhill journeyed to Peking, and plans for the boycott were becoming known in Washington, Roosevelt in May 1905 was still concentrating on other matters. He had a canal to build, a Dominican Republic to rescue from European creditors, the balance of power to play in Asia during the Russo-Japanese War, and a host of domestic issues to consider as well. But more and more he found himself involved in the problems of China. Americans in general were slow to grasp the fact that the Chinese felt deeply enough about discrimination to take united action against it. One example of such complacency appeared in an *Arena* article in May in which the author reasoned that since the United States had not used "bullying" tactics on China, China's friendship would not be impaired by the "Anti-Chinese legislation of Congress."[1] Events in May were to demonstrate how badly mistaken that writer was.

As news of the impending boycott jolted public indifference, writers in some of the journals tried to put Americans in touch with reality. Chester Holcombe, former diplomat to China, called attention to "the intense racial pride of the Chinese" and the resentment that was bound to arise from discrimination,[2] and an *Outlook* editorial pointed to the choice facing the United States: "either abandon all hope of developing commerce with China or treat Chinamen with respect."[3] Both journals and the press swung in a pro-Chinese direction during the summer of 1905. The boycott was a "perfectly justifiable one," declared the *Independent* in August; its "sympathy" lay with China.[4]

Since Congress was not in session during the summer, legislators could postpone taking public stands, but Roosevelt was faced with a situation that demanded quick action. His commitment to ex-

126

clusion had been extensive in spite of the angry Chinese protests. Now, however, he was besieged by frightened and powerful groups who condemned the exclusionist drift. Among these groups the Harriman interests, Rockefeller interests, Hill-Morgan interests, and the New York business and financial community were important; church and educational leaders joined too in the call for a change in course. Although it was not easy for the president to shift his ground, nevertheless, he began to do so. In June Roosevelt revealed his change of heart to the American Asiatic Association, which had been demanding reforms for some time.[5] On June 12 Foord led a delegation of distinguished businessmen, especially prominent cotton manufacturers, to call on the president and urge him to change his position. The Association's memorial, summarized the *New York Times*, was based on the belief that immigration officials were treating Chinese more severely "than was warranted by either the letter or the spirit of the law" and that this had an adverse effect upon trade.[6] Roosevelt responded by announcing that he favored admitting all Chinese who were not of the laboring class. "But, gentlemen," he cautioned the delegation, "I am not the legislative branch of the Government, and I am only part of the treaty making power."[7]

In his new stand, which signified a sharp break with the exclusionists, he was supported by a wide circle of friends and advisers. Secretary of War William Howard Taft, much closer to Roosevelt than the dignified and humorless Metcalf, had anticipated the president's shift by urging a modification of policy on June 6 at Hot Springs, Virginia.[8] Shortly after the president's statement of June 12, Taft inserted in a commencement address on June 15 at Ohio's Miami University a strong endorsement of the change when he denounced the exclusion policy as it stood as "not only wrong in principle, unjust in operation, but most inexpedient and unwise in policy."[9] Rockhill's cable from Peking on June 7 urged a treaty modification that would admit all Chinese except laborers. Even Lodge, who had so vigorously supported the exclusionist Mitchell-Kahn bill in 1902, wrote from Italy on the need to "treat the Chinese more civilly."[10]

Without waiting for Congress Roosevelt prodded the immigration bureaucracy into a change in course. On June 14 Roosevelt sent word to Metcalf to issue "rigid instructions" to officials to be courteous; he sharply criticized H. H. North, the official in charge in San Francisco, for a recent instance of classifying merchants as laborers and then threatening deportation: he "should be strongly rebuked for what he did."[11] Roosevelt, writing Metcalf again on June 19, used an inquiry from Minister Lloyd Griscom in Japan as to how members of the Japanese peace delegation would be treated by immigration officials to point out the bad reputation of the bureau among Asians. He informed Metcalf that he wanted to join with him in working out a set of instructions "sufficiently drastic to prevent the continuance of the very oppressive conduct of many of our officials toward Chinese gentlemen, merchants, travelers, students, and so forth."[12] On this same day the dying secretary of state received visits from the president and then from Taft. "The President," Hay wrote in his diary as his final entry, "is determined to put a stop to the barbarous methods of the Immigration Bureau."[13]

Roosevelt found Metcalf annoyingly inflexible, however. To the press Metcalf expatiated on the "bogus certificates" which were easily obtained in China and pointed to the need for a tighter law to remedy this problem.[14] Metcalf also prepared a racist-oriented defense of exclusion, based on long range social and political grounds, for presentation at a Cabinet meeting scheduled for June 20.[15] Bitter words were exchanged at the two Cabinet meetings that covered the subject. According to the *New York Times*, the main division of opinion was between Taft and Metcalf,[16] but in reality the entire Cabinet was arrayed against Metcalf. The critics of exclusion at the second Cabinet meeting on June 23 were encouraged by a telegram that day from the Portland Chamber of Commerce. To the surprise of many this west coast group called for more liberal regulations and modifications in the laws.[17] Eventually the Cabinet overruled Metcalf, relaxed the enforcement measures, and recommended to Congress that it modify the laws when it reconvened. Hay would notify Peking of the new policy.[18]

Metcalf, who considered his authority on this issue to be from Congress, remained stubbornly opposed despite the changes proposed by the Cabinet. This was made clear in a public exchange between him and Taft immediately following the June 23 meeting. Taft, who at this time was filling in for the ailing Hay,[19] bluntly charged that the bureau was to blame for the troubles with China. Metcalf immediately rejected the allegation and denied that the law had been "harshly administered."[20] Metcalf was sure that he would lose out politically in California if he gave in to the president,[21] but neither could he defy the president too openly. On June 24 he conceded to Roosevelt that "officers may have been overzealous."[22] He was preparing, Metcalf wrote, a circular for immigration officials and was instructing them to extend the "widest and heartiest courtesy" toward members of the privileged classes. The press would be informed of these policy changes on June 26. He indicated also that, if careful checks were made by consuls, the bureau would not question the certificates of Chinese arriving at American ports. By using a broad interpretation of the treaty privilege of transit, he offered tentatively to admit doctors, lawyers, clergymen, and other non-laboring Chinese. These statements represented a significant reversal of much of the earlier Powderly policy. When the press reported these measures to liberalize regulations, the anti-Chinese forces spoke out angrily. The "Chinese, Japanese, Corean [Korean] Exclusion League of Alameda County" in California, purporting to number 10,000 members, denounced Taft. As for the regulations, "they have never," asserted one member, "been too stringent for the laboring classes."[23] The *Chronicle* saw the administration as being duped. On the other hand, the American Asiatic Association hailed the new trend and foresaw a chance to get a better treaty and improved domestic legislation.[24]

Although the moves of late June to moderate the regulations were significant, Roosevelt pressed for even more sweeping changes, guided by one of the keenest pro-Chinese legal minds, Max J. Kohler. Kohler's ideas, conveyed by letter to Roosevelt on June 26, were an attack upon Metcalf's form letter reply to critics. Metcalf's standard defense of the bureau maintained that it was forced to take stern measures because the laws required it to do so. Kohler argued that, contrary to the bureau's claims, its regulations and actions were often violations of the law — not implementations. Among the many cases cited by Kohler one concerned rule 23 of July 27, 1903, which directed port officials to retain the certificates of arriving non-laboring Chinese, illegally deprived visitors of proof of their right to be in the United States, and was in "absolute violation of Section 6 of the act of 1884."[25] Kohler maintained that Metcalf could easily liberalize the exclusion policy without new legislation by changing the prescriptions of his own department to bring them into line with current laws. Metcalf, finding his position undermined, tried a new tack; he would set up a commission to study and recommend changes in the regulations.[26]

If more ammunition were needed to indict the departmental regulations — though ammunition had never been the main problem — it was available within the Department of Commerce and Labor itself. The ingratiating James R. Garfield, son of former President Garfield and head of the Bureau of Corporations, had participated in efforts to harmonize the views of the department and the Chinese government and had won the confidence of John E. Gardner, the scholarly Chinese inspector at San Francisco. Garfiesd's reward was the receipt of a perceptive critique of the immigration policy. Gardner condemned the Griggs opinion of 1898, which had served as the basis for many of the restrictive rules. Perhaps the most significant point among his criticisms was that the English version of the 1894 treaty varied greatly from the Chinese version and was "both wrong and mischievous."[27] According to the Chinese text, non-laborers were clearly entitled to enter the United States whenever they wished. The gist of Gardner's report reenforced Kohler's position that the bureau's rules were often illegal.

Bowing to the intense pressure of the moment, Metcalf proceeded to appoint his commission. Friends of exclusion, notably Campbell, who was the law officer of the bureau, were selected; but Sargent was not among the three from the department who composed it. The commission's assignment was to examine and revise the departmental regulations.[28] The bureau may well have thought that by making a few more administrative changes it could forestall a more sweeping revision of the basic exclusion laws. Whether the Chinese would be mollified remained to be seen. This flurry of activity to soften the exclusion policy by executive action in late June was obviously designed to persuade the Chinese to call off the boycott, which had been set to begin on August 1. Would the Chinese respond by doing so?

The Chinese response to the president's initiatives was bound to occur on several levels: Chinese-Americans represented a significant but unofficial position on the matter; official reactions on local and regional levels might differ from Peking's; and responses fluctuated in accord with certain specific stages in the complicated evolution of the boycott — before July 1, July 1 to July 20, July 20 to August 1, and after August 1 when the boycott was at last in effect to its fullest extent.

Since Chinese-Americans were a major factor in instigating the boycott, their reactions to the president's moves were specially important. Roosevelt was aware of the need to influence these people, but he arrived late on the scene. Before he had become actively involved, Chinese-Americans had effected a united front in the General Society of Chinese Residing in the United States for the Opposing of the Exclusion Treaty. Reflecting a new national spirit that transcended the usual class and cultural barriers, the San Francisco section drew support from "The Chinese Mercantile Associations, the Chinese Christian Societies, the Chee Kung Tong, a high-binder Society . . . the Chinese Empire Reform Association, the Publisher of the Chung Sai Yat Bo, the Man Hing, and the Wah Kee newspapers."[29] A poster in San Francisco on June 20 announced that the General Society would collect a dollar from each Chinese in the United States to finance the movement.[30]

A similar pattern was evident in various overseas communities. Leading Chinese merchants in Penang, for example, agreed on June 28 to join with Singapore and Shanghai in the boycott, "pending the withdrawal of the Chinese Exclusion act."[31] In Havana, Cuba, $10,000 was being raised to help with the effort.[32] From Victoria, British Columbia, came the news that 6,000 Chinese were contributing to a fund to compensate any coolies who refused to unload American ships in Chinese ports.[33] Hawaiian Chinese notified boycott leaders in Canton that if money were needed they would be happy to contribute.[34] In the Philippines Chinese were also raising funds.[35] Before the episode was over the boycott had also spread to Japan, Thailand, and Singapore. The main coordinators were the Reform Association and the merchant guilds.

Roosevelt, searching for a way to halt this organizing activity, directed his attention to various segments of the American coalition, especially the Chinese Empire Reform Association. One of its leaders, Liang Ch'i-ch'ao, had written a pamphlet criticizing the exclusion policy.[36] In late June, Roosevelt scheduled several conferences in Washington with K'ang Yu-wei, its most important leader, who was in the United States. At first, K'ang seemed to respond favorably and described the president to a reporter as "one of the best and most strenuous rulers he ever knew,"[37] and again, in an interview with the press at the Waldorf, K'ang quoted the president as promising to do his "utmost for the Chinese in regard to the modification of the Chinese Exclusion Act."[38] But Roosevelt, even with K'ang's favorable remarks, found himself unable to win the support of the Reform Association. Unlike the officials and merchants who in the past had reluctantly accepted a class-based policy, the Reform faction opposed any discrimination against Chinese as a nationality group. The "whole nation of China," maintained K'ang, had become "indignant" over the unfairness of the Exclusion policy; the boycott was to "prevent the exclusion of any Chinaman from the United States."[39]

Roosevelt's failure to influence the Reform Association became increasingly evident throughout the summer of 1905 as the Association's leaders made speeches in support of the boycott and continued to collect money for it. Quan Yick Nam, enemy of the Association and friend of Roosevelt, urged him to suppress the speech-making and the sending of money to China.[40] But Roosevelt lacked the authority either to dissolve the Association or to make enough concessions to conciliate it; he could only keep the channels of communication open and hope for a more favorable turn of events later. While Roosevelt was trying to sway the Reform Association, he and others in his administration were also appealing to another important group, the merchants; without their support, the boycott would have remained on paper. In late June, Sargent was in Hawaii urging the merchants to be calm and reasonable while negotiations for a new treaty were taking place,[41] but as subsequent developments indicated, he had failed to impress them.

Other efforts by Roosevelt and his advisers to head off the boycott similarly failed. Although the boycott was not scheduled to begin until August 1, news arrived before the end of June that it had already started in some places. An indication of this, as Taft learned from Schwerin on June 25, was that Chinese businessmen in Hong Kong were already purchasing Australian flour. "Hong Kong," the telegram noted, "is the great flour port of China."[42] In Canton the gambling houses were abandoning the free distribution of an American brand of cigarette in favor of a Macao brand. "Habitual gamblers," observed a Hong Kong newspaper, "who seldom trouble themselves about anything, have come to look upon the Americans as an enemy to their race."[43] Students and teachers in government academies in China were also reported to be no longer using American products.

Between July 1 and July 20, as more evidence appeared that the boycott threat was turning into a reality, Roosevelt took further steps to appease Chinese-Americans, especially the merchants. On July 9, for example, the creation of Metcalf's commission to revise the regulations was publicized. On July 14 the Chinese in San Francisco were informed of a significant step by local immigration officials to speed up the landing of returning merchants: if white witnesses appeared one month before the merchants were due to arrive and gave testimony to the bureau, they could be landed almost immediately.[44] But even the merchants could not be dissuaded at this point. The united front on the Chinese side remained firm. Thus, on July 20 the American people learned that the boycott had now spread to the five ports of Shanghai, Canton, Tientsin, Hankow, and Newchwang.[45]

During this time, July 1 to 20, Roosevelt seemed more successful with the Chinese government than with the boycotting factions. On July 1 Rockhill had procured an edict from Peking to the provincial officials requesting them to discourage the movement.[46] Even without American prodding, Peking might well have had misgivings about an agitation that could take an anti-dynastic turn at any moment. If the edict were vigorously enforced, the boycott had little chance of surviving. Nevertheless, Roosevelt and Rockhill soon discovered that the edict was not being enforced and that Peking was resisting American pressures for more action. Even if the Manchu dynasty had had anti-boycott leanings, it could not ignore the telegrams and cables, pouring in from within and without China, to do something to end American discrimination.[47] Most regional officials seemed inclined to allow the boycott to continue. Moreover, Minister Liang in Washington, reflecting another layer of government, was friendly to and perhaps secretly allied with the leaders of the movement.[48]

The San Francisco Chinese apparently played an important part in getting Peking to change course again. When the boycott leaders there first heard of the anti-boycott July 1 edict, they reacted in a fit of rage by threatening to hire an assassin to murder the head of the Foreign Office. The violent outcry led Consul General Chung in San Francisco to deny that the Foreign Office had ever "prohibited or obstructed" the boycott.[49] Reassured by this statement, the *Chinese Free Press (Tai Tung Yat Bo)*, one of the four Chinese newspapers in the city at that time, asserted that "all officials in China are of one mind in encouraging and aiding merchants in the matter of retaliation."[50] But it also advised that if the head of the Foreign Office had temporarily lost his nerve, "he should wake up, be penitent, and set himself right."[51] The entire episode of the edict and then the backtracking revealed that the Chinese government from May to August was being subjected to heavy pressure from all sides. And for the time being, Chinese public opinion was strong enough for the boycott to override the protests of American officials.

The next development occurred between July 20 and August 1 and was short but significant. Despite the premature outbreaks of late June and the spread to five ports on July 20, there was still time for negotiations before the final date set for a full-scale boycott, and some were tried. At this point the boycotters believed themselves to be in a good bargaining position. A circular in San Francisco on July 24 called attention to the amelioration of the regulations and attitudes of the Immigration Bureau and also noted the more courteous treatment displayed toward passengers on the last two ships. All of this was "proof of the efficacy of the measure."[52]

The Chinese merchants of San Francisco on July 28 took the initiative in approaching Gardner and proposing to stop the boycott if the United States would return to the policies prior to the Griggs opinion of 1898.[53] This was tantamount to a request to admit all nonlaboring Chinese and differed markedly from the stand of the Reform Association against all discrimination. But could the boycott be terminated at that point, even if the merchants gained what they sought? In Gardner's opinion they had the power to do so through their ties with merchants in China and with the diplomats Wu and Liang. But nothing came of this last minute foray. Instead, shortly thereafter on July 29 the Chinese held a mass demonstration in San Francisco and affirmed their support for the enterprise. On August 1 the boycott, which had already started in some places, took effect officially in many additional areas. Roosevelt had lost another round.

Schwerin, a leading pessimist, on August 1 wrote Sargent from San Francisco to impress on him the hardships accompanying the boycott. Chinese merchants had cancelled their orders with the Del Monte Milling Company and were placing no others; this was a severe blow to that company. Furthermore, Chinese bankers, through their guilds, had agreed not to do business in the future with the International Banking Corporation of America.[54] An observer in China, the Reverend J. M. W. Farnham, missionary of the American Presbyterian Church in Shanghai, who was concerned about the missionary as well as the business impact of the boycott, pointed out to Roosevelt the bleakest prospect of all: "This boycott, if carried out to its logical sequence will drive out every American and subsequently every other foreigner."[55] The bargaining position of the Chinese seemed strong.

In San Francisco the Chinese kept telling Gardner what their terms were, and he in turn relayed this information to Sargent.[56] Gardner thought that even the leaders of the Reform Association would be willing to end the boycott if the United States would return to a class-based policy. He had disucssed the matters with the Conservative party, which was loyal to the empress dowager, and the Reform party, which favored the emperor. The Conservatives, mainly merchants, could work through Minister Liang, who could send back dispatches stating that the United States was now correctly interpreting the treaties. The Reform group could get K'ang's former student in Shanghai, an influential newspaper editor, to spread the word that the United States was changing its policy. As a result the boycott might soon fade out and obviate the need for a treaty. Roosevelt could solve the problem easily, thought Gardner, by an improved administration and interpretation of existing laws and treaties — that is, by admitting non-laboring Chinese, as had been the policy prior to 1898.[57] Gardner, an excellent source of intelligence, supplied information also on how the money was being used. On July 18, $2,000 had been sent to Shanghai; another $1,000 had gone to Hong Kong. Fans depicting Americans abusing Chinese were to be given away in large quantities in the Canton area. Pamphlets citing examples of mistreatment of Chinese were being prepared for use in the Shanghai area. Gardner pointed to "the wisdom of putting an early stop to the spread of this kind of literature."[58]

Roosevelt found his powers too limited to meet the demands even of the conservative merchants. The boycott leaders had predicted optimistically in June that within six months all exclusion laws would be repealed.[59] By August they were less certain, but they were determined to continue. "We . . . are thoroughly aroused," proclaimed the *Chinese Free Press* on August 7, "in this matter of opposing the exclusion treaty."[60] The president's reform measures had been a sham to date, declared a Chinese manager of the Russo-Chinese bank in an interview in San Francisco on August 5: bureau officials were still questioning certificates; moreover, in Canton the consul had become so cautious that no certificates were being approved at all.[61] Money and cables kept flowing from Chinese-Americans to China. One cablegram to Shanghai cost $136.40.[62]

Although the effort was painful for them, Chinese-Americans seemed willing to hold out for a long time. Undoubtedly the rival factions found cooperation difficult. Nevertheless, the revulsion against the exclusion policy had evoked enough of a national feeling to keep them welded together. As late as March 1906 an immigration official remarked on "the tenacity of purpose exhibited . . . to secure the kind of legislation which they consider fair."[63] Not until natural calamity struck — the San Francisco earthquake of April 18, 1906 — was the fighting spirit of the San Francisco Chinese crushed. If a minimum of one dollar per Chinese-American went to China during the boycott period — and there is every reason to believe that $90,000 or more was sent — a substantial amount of the financing of the effort in China must have been carried out by the overseas Chinese, particularly those in the United States.

Apparently the only way the president could break this united front was to appease the upper-class Chinese by limiting exclusion to laborers only. His reforms through executive action, significant though they were, still failed to achieve this end. Thus, the boycott continued. The President could, of course, increase his pressure on Peking. Such an approach had its drawbacks, however, for the securing of the imperial edict of July 1 had accomplished little. Moreover, Roosevelt had to exercise restraint in making demands, since, as Rockhill reminded him, the Chinese government was weak and unstable.[64] A revolution, Minister Liang hinted, might result from too swift and harsh government action against the boycott.[65]

Roosevelt, in spite of the risks, began in August to insist that Peking act more vigorously. When Rockhill requested permission to charge the Chinese with violating the treaty of 1858, Roosevelt not only approved but instructed him to "use strong language."[66] Roosevelt had another grievance against Peking in its recent cancellation of the Canton-Hankow railroad concession; hence, on August 15 the president's secretary notified the State Department to convey his displeasure to China's foreign office. "The Chinese government," wrote Alvey A. Adee to Rockhill, "must be made to understand the gravity of the situation."[67] For a time in August Roosevelt seemed unsure about pressing harder. Until Elihu Root took over as secretary of state on September 1, he was largely on his own. The *New York Daily Tribune* counseled him to abandon the exclusion policy for the sake of the open door policy.[68] But his thinking was moving in another direction. Although the president is "puzzled," wrote Adee to Rockhill, nevertheless he is "inclined to think this Government must take a stand."[69] In late August Roosevelt called on Rockhill to go to Shanghai and query the guilds about their plans, but the trip did not materialize.[70] Rockhill, however, could point to dividends from this harder line. Viceroy Yuan Shih-k'ai had shut down a newspaper in Tientsin which had printed an article in support of the boycott, and on August 31 the imperial government was to issue a new edict against the boycott.[71]

Peking was evidently shaken by Roosevelt's sharp words, yet it had to contend with the continued outcry against the exclusion policy. Wu surfaced briefly in Peking to explain this once again to Americans: a new national spirit was emerging in China; people were reacting against the insulting attitudes of port authorities and were uniting to express their resentment; an educational test might be an acceptable substitute to Chinese for the existing system and yet be as effective in barring the laboring class.[72] He also insisted that, while laborers might be barred from the United States proper, they should be allowed into Hawaii and the Philippines. But these new proposals emanating from Peking were ignored in Washington.

In September, Roosevelt, Peking, and the boycott leaders still held stubbornly to their former positions; however, some new developments encouraged Roosevelt to think he could make additional demands of Peking. On August 29 he had signed the final papers allowing China, after the high price of $6,750,000 had been paid to the American China Development Company, to recover control of its railroad line,[73] thus, making him less dependent on the good will of China; but the loss of the concession was deplored by many, especially Consul Lay at Canton.[74] Negotiations terminating the Russo-Japanese War were also drawing to a close; the United States had supported China's interests and could ask for return favors. It was also to Roosevelt's advantage to have a strong new secretary of state in Root, who, incidentally, respected Chinese civilization and disliked the exclusion policy.[75]

While the president pondered what measure to take next, frightened American businessmen persuaded him in September to bypass Peking and see what he could do on the regional level. George C. Perkins, California senator, was one of those who, in late August, urged that Taft — then on a trip to Asia — try out this experiment. The merchants, he explained, believed Canton and its viceroy to be the center of the trouble. Taft's visit should be made an "official affair with immediate authority."[76] Telegrams in the same vein arrived from the Portland Chamber of Commerce, San Francisco merchants, and the British-American Tobacco Company;[77] a representative of Standard Oil called on Loomis at the State Department to add its endorsement.[78] Although Roosevelt rejected Perkins' request at first, on September 2 he had a telegram of authorization sent out to Taft. On September 4 the secretary of war cabled that he was in Canton.[79]

The Taft mission had a number of curious features. Originally intended as a junket to persuade reluctant congressmen to accept the Roosevelt-Taft policies on the Philippines, the party had a romantic side with the presence of the president's charming daughter, Alice, and her suitor and future husband, Nicholas Longworth.[80] In Japan the mission, combining business with pleasure, undertook some diplomatic chores. Now, in addition, Taft found he was expected to settle a complicated situation by applying the carrot and stick in Canton.

Taft had a difficult task ahead of him, since the most hostile feeling was, by all odds, in the Canton area. Consul General Lay had become a target of abuse. And since the viceroy was making only token moves against demonstrations, anti-exclusion meetings — as well as anti-American placards in public places — had been building up tension for several months. On August 16 Lay wrote of the loss in sales of 10,000 cases of oil by Standard Oil and of the failure to sell any flour at a time when 500,000 bags would normally have been sold.[81] At the time the Taft party arrived, the city of Canton was calm; but a picture intended as an insult to the daughter of the president was posted in public places; coolies shook their fists at members of the group.[82] Taft, afraid to allow the women to land in the city, took only close associates to meet with Chinese officials.

According to the brief instructions from Roosevelt, Taft was to meet with the viceroy and other influential Chinese and avoid making "definite promises . . . but make them realize that we intend to do what is right and that we cannot submit to what is now being done by them."[83] Dutifully and tactfully, with reminders of how much the United States had done for China, Taft delivered the veiled threat at a public banquet.[84] If Chinese officials allowed the use of force to prevent the purchase of American goods, he was careful to mention, this was a treaty violation.

While Taft was meeting with officials at Canton, Representative Duncan E. McKinlay, member of the party from California, received an invitation to meet in Hong Kong with merchants who were brought together by Liu Kan, an importer. Senator Patterson and other Americans joined him in a meeting with 25 Chinese merchants. The Chinese expressed their willingness to accept the exclusion law if they were not subjected to delays and sojourns in the detention shed. They would be perfectly willing to supply a bond of $2,000 pending the checking of their papers.[85] The McKinlay contact appeared to be with the most conservative and conciliatory element in the Chinese boycott spectrum. Taft agreed to transmit the Hong Kong merchants' proposals to the president.

After visiting Canton Taft offered without enthusiasm to come to Peking to exert more pressure there, but Rockhill discouraged him, and Roosevelt did not press him.[86] Thereupon the Taft entourage split. The president's daughter with her friends traveled to Peking, but Taft and the remaining members of the group returned to the United States. In Canton the immediate results of the visit were disappointing. Indeed, on September 12 Lay reported that "the agitation has taken a new lease of life and instead of subsiding is growing."[87] The American merchants, who had held such high hopes for the Taft trip, discovered to their sorrow that Taft had no magic wand to wave. The viceroy showed no inclination to yield to American wishes.

The only benefit from the trip was Taft's ability to supply Roosevelt with the latest information on the attitudes of interested groups overseas. When Taft met with Americans in Hong Kong representing companies such as Hammond Milling, Singer Manufacturing, Standard Oil, and British-American Tobacco, he was advised that the president should resort to force if necessary to get the Chinese government to suppress the movement.[88] In meeting with Chinese merchants he learned that they would settle for a more liberal interpretation of the existing law with regard to admitting non-laborers; an acceptance of the consular certificate issued in China as binding; and an end to the detention sheds.

When Taft made his formal report to the Cabinet on October 3, Roosevelt used the occasion to review the entire problem. He had to recognize that many of the irritants which had produced the boycott were still present. Immigration officials at San Francisco, for example, were still deporting members of the privileged classes. And Rockhill in Peking was complaining that his office could not possibly carry out the thorough investigation demanded by Metcalf.[89] Meanwhile Metcalf, who was too ill to attend the session, denied to the press on the next day that the regulations were in any way at fault nor was his department's administration of them.[90]

Roosevelt was now faced with more dangerous developments in China. The merchants in some places were losing control of the boycott to more extreme elements, as Lay indicated in his dispatches from Canton in September. Patriotic groups in China voiced the same aspirations as the Empire Reform Association in the United States that all forms of discrimination against Chinese should cease. Furthermore, an anti-foreign feeling was growing in intensity; perhaps another Boxer Rebellion was in the offing. The *New York Daily Tribune* suggested another aspect of the problem to haunt Roosevelt: "the greatest significance of the boycott is the possibility of future use of this method of coercion if the first attempt succeeds."[91] The Chinese government also seemed defiant over the charges that it was violating treaty obligations. To demonstrate that two could play that game, the Chinese Legation threatened to seek compensation for damages in cases of unwarranted deportations. If the charges were turned down in American courts, the Chinese suggested taking the question to the Hague Tribunal.[92]

In early October a good case could be made for either of two courses: a harder line or more concessions. The Cabinet concluded, after weighing the information supplied by Taft, that the president should use his executive powers to secure further modifications in the regulations. Metcalf, however, whose cooperation was essential, remained unconvinced.[93] And the fact remained that, despite all of the conciliatory moves the president had made to date, he was getting nowhere with the Chinese. A difficult summer had come to an end without a solution. Roosevelt had negotiated with the Reform Association and the merchants; he had also dealt with Peking and a regional official; but he had met with failure at every turn. The maximum demand of the Chinese was the termination of all discrimination; the minimal demand was to admit non-laboring Chinese. He was willing to grant the minimal demand, but his presidential powers had proved insufficient. He had to turn to Congress for new legislation.

Before Congress would adopt a more liberal policy, public opinion must first be reshaped. Keenly aware of this, the inner circle of the administration went to work. On October 19 Taft allowed a carefully prepared statement to go to the *Churchman*. In it he discussed specific points that might be included in a new exclusion treaty to placate the educated classes for past mistreatment.[94] On the next day Roosevelt made some pointed remarks in a speech given in Atlanta: American attitudes toward Chinese had been responsible for the boycott which was injuring cotton manufacturers; more courtesy should be shown; and, Congress ought to take action both because of self-interest and to do "what is just and right."[95]

The president directed his attention to west coast businessmen as well. One example was his reply to a letter from T. C. Friedlander, secretary of the San Francisco Merchants' Exchange, who had suggested that the Japanese might be behind the boycott, since they seemed to be profiting from the shift in orders.[96] Not at all, responded Roosevelt; the blame rested with the United States government and public opinion behind it. In particular, the Bureau of Immigration had "acted with the utmost harshness toward the Chinese."[97] The merchants of San Francisco should support his reform of the bureau and favor less restrictive legislation. "If you," he wrote, "and all the other American merchants who are injured by the boycott will urge your representatives in Congress to do away with the cause of the boycott, you will probably succeed."[98]

The Chinese minister, working along parallel lines, sought advice from both Root and Taft on an address that he was scheduled to deliver in Chicago in November. In his speech Liang would state that the president's order in June had improved the situation and that the Chinese government had issued an imperial decree against the boycott, "pending action of Congress to relieve the situation."[99] The minister would propose the admitting of all Chinese except laborers. Trade, he would make clear, would not improve without an abandonment of the past exclusion policy. Taft, who received the draft before Root, responded warmly to its contents,[100] while Root, although more reserved, was also encouraging.[101] Liang pressed his point again in an article in the December *Harper's Weekly*. While hailing the open door policy, he condemned exclusion. Future trade was dependent on revising the exclusion policy.[102] Nickerson, the Chinese consul at Boston, was also writing vigorous pro-Chinese articles.[103]

These pressures for moderate exclusion were building toward the president's annual message to Congress to be delivered in December. By September 23, the president had prepared the first draft of an immigration section calling for the acceptance of upper-class Chinese.[104] But trends in China were threatening to undo Roosevelt's careful preparation. The Chinese Students Federation, taking a nationalistic position, had cabled the president on October 9 to request "general immigration laws irrespective of nationality."[105] The murder of five missionaries on October 28 at an American Presbyterian Mission at Lienchow in South China raised the even more alarming question of whether Chinese authorities could control the anti-American sentiment which had become so pronounced in the southern areas.[106] Roosevelt was worried enough to order a naval force into the Chinese coastal area on November 15.[107]

The many crosscurrents did not deter Roosevelt from making his appeal to Congress on schedule. In his message of December 5 he made a special effort to avoid antagonizing American labor: the working class of China represented unfair competition and should not be admitted. But he urged a revision of laws and treaties so that all Chinese except laborers could be admitted. The examinations should be held in China, and the consular service — not the bureau — should be strengthened to perform this task efficiently. The president also pointed to the need to resolve the conflict with the open door policy. "As a people, we have talked much of the open door in China, and we expect, and quite rightly intend to insist upon, justice being shown us by the Chinese. But we cannot ask the Chinese to do to us what we are unwilling to do to them."[108] These statements by the president in 1905 stood in sharp contrast to his position of 1901, when he had called for tighter legislation.

There were indications, however, that this formula of admitting non-laboring Chinese would meet with a great deal of resistance. The

Chinese would have been satisfied the year before with this stand, as Foord noted, but now they were demanding more.[109] Nor were the anti-Chinese likely to acquiesce meekly in the president's views.

But the course of events had led to a marked shift from the offensive to the defensive by the exclusionists. About the time the boycott began, anti-Chinese on the west coast were preparing to launch a drive to bar Japanese and other Asians also. The Japanese and Korean Exclusion League, which held a meeting in San Francisco on May 7, 1905, at which, it claimed, 40,000 people were present,[110] headed this effort. On May 15 O.A. Tveitmoe became the president of this new organization. Other prominent leaders included the battle-scarred Chinese exclusionists, Livernash and Furuseth, who, assuming that they had won the battle for Chinese exclusion with the law of 1904, demanded the extension of the policy to all Asians. Resolutions by the California legislature, an anti-Japanese campaign by the *San Francisco Chronicle,* and a move by the San Francisco Board of Education to assign Japanese children to a segregated school were all manifestations of the vitality of the new movement.[111] But the Chinese boycott soon became a major distraction.

The *Chronicle* at first adopted the line that the boycott was a conspiracy to undermine the exclusion act with Wu as the "prime agent in the movement."[112] Harshness at American ports toward Chinese was a consequence of lies by the Chinese as to their real status.[113] It felt "genuine sorrow" at the critical remarks by Taft at the Miami University commencement.[114] The administration had allowed "itself to become the victim of . . . a worked-up movement to break down the exclusion laws."[115] For a number of months the *Chronicle* carried on an anti-Japanese harangue and also argued against changing policy on the Chinese because, wrote Barrett to Roosevelt, the editor, M. H. deYoung, wanted the support of labor to get into the Senate, and Livernash wanted to get back into the House.[116] Whatever the motives, the newspaper and the League promoted their cause with vigor and determination.

In Washington Metcalf was trying to stem the pro-Chinese tide,[117] and Sargent was urging that no concessions be made to the Chinese under pressure. These men, however, were being forced to bend to the president's will. Garfield was for a while deluded into thinking that Sargent had been won over to the new policy.[118] Nevertheless, no permanent change of heart was displayed in the public statements of the Department of Commerce and Labor: exaggerated reports of cases of fraud and perjury continued; American consuls and Chinese officials were regularly portrayed as hopelessly corrupt; and all Chinese entering the United States were presumed to be laborers in disguise.

In these trying times for the anti-Chinese side, a boost to morale came in the form of a court decision on the constitutionality of the exclusion act of April 27, 1904. The judge in a deportation case said, "The sovereign may, through legislation, nullify a treaty."[119] After such a victory the bureau could more easily shrug off sharp attacks by the pro-Chinese. What did it matter that the *New York Times* spelled out an unpleasant fact? "That is what we did. We violated a treaty by statute."[120]

At the November 1904 annual convention of the AFL, which was still in the forefront of the defenders of the exclusion laws, a committee had warned the executive council to stay on its guard "and to resist to the utmost any so-called liberalization of the exclusion laws."[121] With Gompers as president the injunction was not really necessary. When the boycott became a public issue in June 1905, the executive council decided to send a committee to see Roosevelt about various labor matters including the "attempt . . . to nullify the Chinese exclusion laws."[122] After meeting with the president on July 12 at Oyster Bay, Gompers expressed dissatisfaction with Roosevelt's assurances that he intended to keep out Chinese laborers and only admit the upper classes.[123] In July Powderly joined the effort to prevent liberalization. Since 1902, when Roosevelt had forced Powderly to resign, the two had become friends again. This friendship, however, did not deter Powderly from disparaging the boycott as insignificant and primarily a device to bring large numbers of Chinese laborers into the country.[124]

Meanwhile, Gompers was telling labor audiences to hold fast despite the boycott. At a union meeting in New York City on July 21, he denounced it as a scheme by Wu to get "the issuance of the President's recent order."[125] Any trade lost was inconsequential, he argued, in terms of other costs to American civilization. Gompers also spoke out against using Chinese labor on the Panama Canal — a major issue for labor at that time. On various occasions he lashed out at those favoring modifications. Churchmen ought to devote their misplaced energies to the "uplift of the workers of our own country."[126] At the AFL annual convention of November 13-25, 1905, Gompers labeled the boycott a "bugaboo for the weak-minded."[127] The delegates endorsed his determination to resist changes in the Chinese exclusion laws, and a committee commended the work of the Japanese and Korean Exclusion League.[128]

The exclusionists found it difficult to head off pro-Chinese resolutions by prestigious organizations. A meeting of the Trans-Mississippi Commercial Congress at Portland on August 16-18 was such an occasion. Here pro-Chinese spokesmen presented a strong case for modifying the exclusion laws in the interest of promoting trade and getting in step with the open door policy.[129] Judge J. E. Raker of California led the opposition in a bitter attack upon what he and others termed a move to admit "coolies" but failed to block a resolution calling on Roosevelt 1) to secure better treatment for the exempt classes; 2) to set up an investigating commission; and 3) to work for comprehensive immigration laws.[130]

At the Immigration Conference, called by the National Civic Federation and held in New York City on December 6-8, 1905, Gompers took violent exception to a resolution approving the president's recommendation to admit all Chinese except laborers. As clergymen and others defended the resolution, Gompers received support from Senator W. A. Clark and Powderly. Although the exclusionists did weaken the original resolution, they could not hinder the passage of a final statement which emphasized the need to admit students and merchants, and also "bankers, doctors, manufacturers, professors and travellers."[131] The exclusionists lost again when the San Francisco Merchants' Exchange, on December 15, fully endorsed Roosevelt's position.[132] Even the president of Harvard, Charles W. Eliot, spoke out in a public address in Boston on December 16 against the racial theories of the "labor orators."[133]

The California congressmen, disregarding the new pro-Chinese atmosphere, decided to press for the extension of exclusion to Japanese and Koreans. Although urging them on, the *Chronicle* confessed that this would be "no easy task."[134] Livernash, Furuseth, and other Exclusion League members made plans to go to Washington and lobby. When the congressmen arrived in Washington, they called on the president on December 6, but their reception was a cold one. "Do you suppose," Roosevelt asked, "I would approve a bill that would be in violation of a treaty and an affront to Japan?"[135] His honeymoon of 1902 with Livernash, they learned, had long since ended. Indeed, to the great delight of the Japanese, who publicized the interview both in Japan and in Japanese-occupied areas of Manchuria, the president pounded on the table, denounced the Exclusion League, and threatened to deport Livernash.[136]

But the exclusionist side was still powerful, even though it had suffered some setbacks. Congressmen felt a need for some kind of bargain. In a remark to Loud of California, Speaker Joseph G. Cannon made a compromise proposal that came from the heart of a master politician. "Are you trying to stir up things," he asked, "so that we will fight Chinese exclusion? You'd better leave well enough alone."[137] A political deal in which the exclusionists would abandon their demands for Japanese exclusion in exchange for preserving the status quo for the Chinese made a great deal of sense to congressmen caught in the middle. For the Chinese, however, such a settlement would have been incredibly ironic. It would also have prolonged the boycott. Prospects, however, looked brighter for the Chinese than they had in years. With Roosevelt on their side, and with the open door forces working hard for them, they seemed in a strong position to extract concessions from a reluctant Congress. "There is quite a sentiment," conceded the *Chronicle*, "in favor of tinkering with the Chinese exclusion laws."[138]

10

American Diplomatic
Efforts To Pry the Door Open

As Roosevelt announced his support for a more liberal exclusion law, and as Congress braced for a new donnybrook on the subject, Rockhill worked in Peking with grim determination to bring the boycott to an early end. He had his choice of trying persuasion or threats. Roosevelt in August 1905 felt a harder line was necessary. In his instructions to Rockhill he explained that he was also planning to advocate the admitting of all Chinese except laborers — the point that Rockhill had been urging since June — and that he would take "a far stiffer tone with my own people than any President has ever yet taken."[1] But he made it clear that he expected Rockhill also to take a firmer tone with the Chinese: "Unless I misread them entirely, they despise weakness even more than they prize justice."[2] In the communication Rockhill could hardly miss the implication that the president thought him too gentle with the Chinese.

Rockhill was not eager to resort to methods of intimidation, but early in August he had already taken a harder line, such as his suspension of further discussions about a new exclusion treaty and his threat to collect damages from the Chinese government, under provisions in the treaty of 1858, for all losses resulting from the cessation of trade. By August 31 he had extracted another imperial decree condemning the boycott. Thus, he had anticipated Roosevelt whose instructions were out-of-date before they arrived in Peking.

Nevertheless, the situation confronting Rockhill remained grave. If the boycott could be settled by the mere issuance of a decree, his problem would have been quickly solved with the pronouncement of August 31. To be sure, some historians — Morse and Griswold, for example — have dated the boycott from May to September.[3] The dispatches of Rockhill, however, contain reports of boycott activity until

146

May 1906, as do the consular dispatches and the trade reports.[4] Although any fixed date for its end has to be arbitrary, a realistic time period would seem to be from July 20, 1905, to May 1, 1906. Since the official position of the United States was to belittle the boycott's effects and to pretend that the episode was over long before it really was, the official records can be misleading.

In early September, while the boycott dilemma continued to plague Rockhill, he had to cope with another problem which he did not relish. This was the arrival September 12 of the Taft party which included Alice Roosevelt. The presence of the Americans had some value, however, in testing the attitude of the empress dowager, who showed official goodwill by receiving the president's daughter in a gracious manner. Wu, as translator, was a man in the middle, sometimes caught between western customs and Chinese court etiquette. "It was a curious experience," Alice Roosevelt Longworth wrote later, "to see the same man who enjoyed making blandly insolvent (*sic*) remarks at dinner parties in Washington and invidious comments on America in press interviews, kotowing at one's feet."[5] The occasion was also notable because for the first time foreign men and women were received together by a Chinese ruler.[6] After this high point and more sightseeing, the 45 Americans went on their way, to the great relief of the Legation.[7]

Now Rockhill could again concentrate on the problem at hand. The question of how much pressure he should bring to bear on the Chinese was a serious one. If he forced the dynasty to bend too far in his direction, it might then be challenged by rising nationalistic forces that expected Peking to stand up to foreigners. If the government were toppled, the United States might lose more in the process than it gained. "In Washington," wrote a member of the Legation in a private letter, "they don't seem to understand how feeble the Chinese government is."[8] Although pressing harder, Rockhill believed that conciliatory measures were appropriate on his side too. In fact, on September 5 he was seeking permission from Washington to resume treaty negotiations. The Chinese government, he pointed out, was "holding out hopes" in the edict of getting a treaty in the near future, and it would be in an "awkward position" if no action followed.[9] He also stressed that he had received only "oral instructions" from Hay regarding negotiating terms "and with the knowledge of the Secretary of Commerce and Labor."[10] While promising to obtain as much of the treaty draft of the Department of Commerce and Labor as he could, he requested written instructions. On September 8, pressed by the *Wai-wu*

Pu to resume negotiations, he again sought clearance from Washington, but without success. He also urged congressional action to modify the exclusion policy. The boycott was dying out gradually, he wrote on September 27, but it was likely to revive "with increased intensity" if Congress did not take action.[11] Late in 1905 and early in 1906 Rockhill coordinated the efforts of consuls throughout China as they encountered different types of problems. He found the movement formidable and frustrating as it spread outward from the treaty ports and created a heavily charged, anti-American atmosphere.

The boycott has received much attention from historians and has been examined from many viewpoints: as a stage in the development of Chinese national consciousness, as a test of the effectiveness of the boycott technique, as an incitement to imperialistic tendencies in President Roosevelt, as a device by the national bourgeois class in China to eliminate competition with home industrialization, and as an added source of internal disenchantment with the Ch'ing government.[12] Therefore, only a brief summary is necessary. The boycott will be viewed here, in contrast to other studies, as a backlash to the specific Powderly stage in the exclusion policy. Thus, particular emphasis will be placed on the participation of individuals who had experienced discrimination in America, on the damage to American interests, on the open door policy as a counterpoise, on Rockhill's responses to the boycott as a bargaining device, and on the types of tensions and interactions found at Canton — the greatest trouble spot.

Chinese-Americans, facing their crisis in May, activated a complicated chain reaction by their outcries, and the Chinese Empire Reform Association responded by advocating a boycott and organizing it. In China, the merchants — with Peking's cooperation and encouragement — adopted a plan in May and invited merchant guilds of other port cities to join, with favorable reactions. Tseng Shao-ch'ing became the leader of a loosely organized committee.[13] The committee decided to give the United States two months in which to drop its discriminatory practices and treat Chinese people as equals.[14] Rockhill asked for a six-month postponement, but this was refused. The boycott began officially on July 20, 1905.[15] Merchants were to stop buying American products. If they violated this rule, they could be punished by public condemnation, fines, and expulsion from their guilds.[16]

The public support needed for the success of this venture was forthcoming. At this time in China's history a newly articulate and activist public opinion — namely, merchants, students, and journalists — was endeavoring to influence government policy.[17] Mass meetings, pamphlets, placards, and newspaper editorials helped to rally support for the boycott cause.[18] Enthusiasm rose to a high point. One man in Shanghai saw the "beginning of a new era. . . . If we succeed in getting justice from America now, we may then boycott the nation that forces opium down our throats, and the others that grab our provinces."[19]

Despite such optimistic predictions, troubles soon began to plague the movement, which had seemed effective in August, but lost ground in September.[20] A principal problem was the emergence of factions in the Shanghai boycott committee. Su Pao-sen, a merchant handling textiles, challenged the leadership of Tseng and argued in July that the boycott should mean only the stoppage of all new orders of American goods.[21] Although the Tseng group wished to prohibit the sale and distribution of all American goods, the more narrowly defined approach of the Su group won out on July 20. This same moderate group on July 30 extracted the agreement that businessmen could sell any American goods ordered before July 20, regardless of when they arrived in China.[22] Other divisive issues arose in August and September.

A second problem for the boycotters was the decision of Peking to withdraw its support. From the beginning leaders in the government had not been unanimously in favor of it. Indeed, Viceroy Yuan Shih-k'ai had opposed it so vigorously in June that he had awakened some doubts in the mind of the empress dowager, Tz'u Hsi.[23] Rockhill's threats and powers of persuasion began to carry some weight.[24] Advisers to the empress dowager counseled her on August 31 that the movement might be getting out of hand and that Chinese trade might be adversely affected.[25] An edict intended to discourage the boycott followed on the same day. Another on March 5, 1906, was more sharply condemnatory and effective.

The energetic measures taken by Viceroy Yuan in Chihli Province were especially crippling to the movement — measures he perhaps would not have dared to take if the merchants in his area of Tientsin had not been out of sympathy with the trade restrictions.[26] He prohibited the boycott in his section and forbade newspapers or public meetings from discussing the subject; he thus kept trade open and enabled Shanghai merchants to divert their American goods northward for sale.[27]

As merchant enthusiasm declined, student elements — prominent from the first and represented by Ku Chung in Shanghai — tried to keep the effort going,[28] but this was difficult in the face of official hostility. Rockhill and Rodgers thought that the United States was helped in Shanghai by American support for the Chinese position in a jurisdictional dispute with the British involving a complicated and explosive court case. Before the matter was settled, a serious anti-for-eigner riot erupted on December 18.[29] But the United States did not alter its official position. A significant development in Shanghai was the merchants' declaration of a conditional truce. In a polite letter to Rockhill on October 1, Hang Shen-hsiu and over a thousand other Chinese merchants, claiming to represent every province, announced that they would suspend the boycott until Congress had a chance to act. If Congress did nothing, they would resume the boycott, perhaps by agreeing among themselves not to buy American goods. Oaths had been taken, the letter affirmed, and fathers would instruct their sons not to buy from the United States.[30] They were not being anti-Ameri-can but were reacting against the insulting treatment of immigration authorities. Rockhill took the letter seriously and informed Washing-ton that a change for the worse might follow if Congress failed to act "in a conciliatory manner."[31] Although the merchants had declared their truce in October, Rodgers was aware of continuing "nervous ten-sion" in January 1906 and blamed students for keeping some agitation going in Shanghai.[32] In spite of the restlessness of the students, the city gradually quieted down.

In the meantime, the movement was evident in various coastal cities, such as Foochow, Amoy, and even as far north as Newchwang in Manchuria. It also spread up the Yangtze River to such cities as Nanking and Hankow, but by May 1906 it had failed to penetrate Chungking.[33] Boycott attempts were also made by some Chinese communities in Southeast Asia, as in Bangkok and Singapore. The pattern everywhere was similar to that in Shanghai, but had distinc-tive local variations too. Americans received most of their informa-tion from Shanghai, however, and tended to think of the whole affair in terms of that particular location.

Direct links can be easily discovered between the active partici-pants in the boycott and the prejudice they had personally encoun-tered in America. A prominent Shanghai merchant, Mr. Sun, manag-er of flour mills and brother of the vice chairman of the Shanghai Chamber of Commerce, for example, had visited his two brothers in schools in the United States and while there, according to an Ameri-can businessman of Shanghai, "he thought he was treated as a dog."[34]

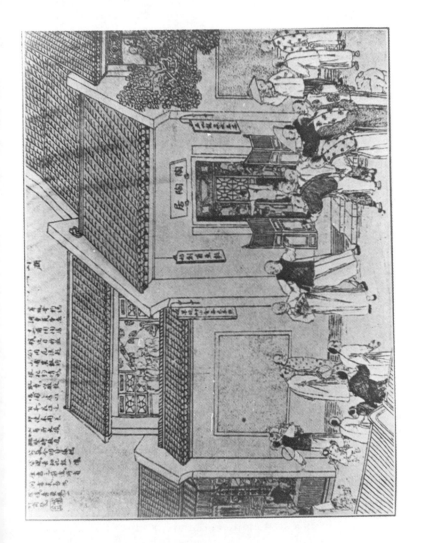

Boycott of a Shop Selling American Flour. (*Outlook* 82 [March 24, 1906].)

He subsequently became one of the promoters of the boycott. Another example is the participation of the K'ing family after the incident mentioned above involving tactless handling of the four young people in Boston in July 1905.[35] While Tseng Shao-ch'ing, the boycott leader, had never visited America, it is noteworthy that Ku Chung, who tried to continue the movement in Shanghai as Tseng lost enthusiasm, had received his education in the United States. Consul General Rodgers found him bitter and determined.[36]

Another type of backlash to American policy is the case of Palanca (Chen Kang), boycott leader at Amoy, whose ties were with the Philippines like those of many others at Amoy. He had become embittered over the application of the exclusion laws to the Philippines,[37] where he was born and where he was believed to have personally experienced mistreatment at American hands. Teng Hu Lee, Yale graduate, headed the Chinese Students Federation founded in Shanghai on July 1, 1905.[38] He, as mentioned earlier, had been refused readmittance to the United States in 1903 to do graduate study at Columbia. The organization Teng headed was active in the boycott.

The Boston police raid of 1903 had its bitter heritage carried to China in the person of Feng Hsia-wei (Fung Ha-wai, Fernando Ruiz). This young man came originally from South China; he had gone to the United States, and had been angered by being caught up in the police raid. He spent some time in the Philippines, then returned to China and wrote a book about his unhappy experiences in America; he finally committed suicide by taking poison on July 16, 1905, near the American consulate in Shanghai. The note near his body explained that he was protesting against the American policy and that he wished the Chinese people to unite behind the protest movement.[39] These cases and others suggest that those groups — such as merchants and students — and individuals who were victims of the Powderly stage of the exclusion policy supplied the emotional base for the boycott movement.

Any attempt to assess the damage to American interests from the boycott encounters the problem of which yardstick to use. Should one generalize, for example, from statistics on sales to China? The official figures in round numbers for exports to China in 1905 stood at 57 million dollars, in 1906 at 44 million dollars, and in 1907 at 26 million dollars.[40] Since exports from America were high in 1905, did that mean the boycott was a failure? Consul General Rodgers was inclined to think so.[41] On the other hand, since exports dropped drastically in 1906, did that mean the boycott had significantly harmed American trade? Charles Denby, Jr., in the State Department thought one should look for the effects of the boycott in the 1906 figures.[42] But can the 1906 drop in exports be fully accepted as confirmation of commercial losses from the boycott? How can the impact of the end of the Russo-Japanese War, natural fluctuations in international trade, or changes in competitive positions be ruled out?

With so many imponderables to consider, differing conclusions on the extent of commercial damage can be reached. Chang Ts'un-wu is an historian who holds that the decline in exports in 1906 was a result of excessive exports to China in 1905 and that other foreign countries had similar experiences.[43] He discounts the amount of damage suffered by Americans and adjudges the boycott a failure. While Chang's reasoning is persuasive, a case for rather severe losses can be made from the statistics. Certainly American businessmen trading in China at that time thought they were being hurt, and their testimony at hearings conducted in the spring of 1906 offered supporting statistical evidence. Moreover, in the assessment of damage to American interests in China, it might be well to go beyond the commercial side and consider missionary, educational, and diplomatic aspects too. Perhaps the term *boycott* is misleading because the movement was never limited in scope to the commercial.

Missionaries had anticipated the movement with alarm and were further dismayed to discover a growing disenchantment with American missionaries. Consul Samuel L. Gracey had once inquired of a local Chinese minister what people were saying as they looked at a display of anti-American posters at Yenping in the Foochow area. Their remarks were: "Mr. Main, Miss Hartford, Miss Linum have appeared to be good people, but their goodness is false goodness."[44] Many firms at Foochow refused to cash the drafts of missionaries.[45] In Shanghai an attempt was made to establish a national Christian church and have all foreign missionaries leave the country.[46] In some districts Chinese would no longer buy bibles and religious tracts.[47] Bishop D. H. Moore of the Missionary Society of the Methodist Episcopal Church observed that in the section around Hankow on the Yangtze River "this commercial disturbance is reaching out into the lines of operations upon which we have been working, namely, educational and religious and semi-religious development of institutional work. . . . furthermore . . . this commercial unrest seems to trace itself back to this exclusion law of our country."[48]

American educators in China encountered their share of difficulties too. Unrest and criticism of Americans, for example, produced some tense times at Anglo-Chinese College, a Methodist school at Foochow founded in 1885. Before the boycott began, students were disturbed because three of them had recently been held at an American port for nearly three months before being allowed to enter the country. Then they read the anti-American boycott literature and heard exaggerated rumors, such as that 2,000 coolies had been beheaded in the United States.[49] The student body, however, followed a course of moderation in adopting a ten-point statement calling for changes in the exclusion policy to be forwarded to Washington by Consul S. L. Gracey.[50]

Students at American schools were urged by boycott committees to leave their schools, not to buy American goods, and to boycott places where American supplies were used or instructors employed.[51] Fortunately for the schools, no mass migration from them took place, but, at the same time, the boycott ferment was troublesome. An example of an extreme reaction by a student was the case of a young man in South China who obtained his parents' permission to destroy his American-made record player. While his family watched as he broke it up with a hatchet, others made a pile of articles of American origin in the home and burned them.[52]

Even Viceroy Yuan took a step damaging to American educational interests in China by stripping Dr. Charles D. Tenney, president of Tientsin University and superintendent of the Chihli Provincial Schools, of his positions. Rockhill, who was greatly upset by this, viewed the event as "a subject of great importance to our interests in North China."[53] Yuan had to remove him, reported the press, because Chinese educators refused to work any longer with an American.[54] As a sop to the United States Yuan soon shifted the distinguished educator to the newly created position of superintendent of all Chinese students in America and England. But this was small comfort. To astute observers the Tenney affair made clear that American influence in Chinese educational development had been dealt a sharp blow.

In measuring the injury to American interests, the factor of good-will is not easy to define in precise terms but should not be overlooked either. Before the boycott, consuls were attesting to being placed on the defensive over exclusion. One case is that of Vice Consul Wilbur T. Gracey, son of the consul at Foochow, who wrote from his post at Nanking on November 29, 1904, that the exclusion laws were "one of the greatest points against which he have to contend in endeavoring to promote American trade and good feeling."[55] When the boycott commenced a few months later, it was accompanied by placards, songs, and plays denouncing the United States. Surely some long range adverse effects on American interests in China may be presumed from this. "The damage, already done to American trade," observed S. L. Gracey, "and the unfriendly feeling engendered against Americans especially, cannot be estimated."[56]

The boycott movement, therefore, cannot be seen in exclusively commercial terms. It was a much more broadly-based, protest effort — motivated by the Powderly stage of the exclusion policy — that threatened the entire gamut of American interests in China — economic, religious, cultural, and political. But in this generally bleak picture, the United States had one asset of great value: the open door policy, although these retaliatory measures by the Chinese had brought the open door interests in China under direct attack. While the exclusion policy was — as a historian describes it —"a Stumbling Block" for the open door policy,[57] a reverse logic can be used to characterize the open door policy as a shield and deflector for the exclusion policy.

Support for this hypothesis can be found in examining the arguments used by Yuan against the boycott movement. On June 21, 1905, he asked the Foreign Ministry to issue orders to the viceroys to bring the boycott to an end on the grounds that the open door policy had been useful to China, that the United States had favored China's neutrality in the Russo-Japanese War, that American help was needed in the peace negotiations, and that the United States would help to uphold the territorial integrity of China.[58] With the territorial integrity of China — primarily Manchuria — as the common bond, Rockhill received invaluable assistance from Yuan in fighting the boycott.[59]

The open door policy was also a major talking point for consuls to persuade local officials to protect American interests. Thomas Sammons in Newchwang, for example, called on leading Chinese and pointed to "America's service on behalf of preserving the integrity of the Chinese Empire."[60] And William Martin at Hankow told the *Taot'ai* that Americans had "done everything that they could to be a friend of your country, refusing to absorb any of your territory."[61]

If the open door policy can be seen as a counterweight to the exclusion policy, one can discern in China a mirror reflection of the division in America's China policy. Yuan, in the north, concerned with Manchurian problems and seeking American cooperation, could be called a symbol of the appeal of the open door. His political enemy in the south, Viceroy Ts'en Ch'un-hsuan of Kwangtung and Kwangsi, who was sympathetic to the boycott and anti-American, might be viewed as a symbol of the hostility aroused by the exclusion policy.[62] However, there is danger here of oversimplification.

Rockhill needed Yuan's help and any other offsetting factors he could find in the fall and winter of 1905-1906. He was also aided by the innate preference for stability of the Ch'ing officials, the financial losses of Chinese merchants, and factionalism among the boycotters. Rockhill continued to cajole and threaten. In August he was unsuccessful in securing the removal of Tseng.[63] However, he could take great satisfaction from the edict of August 31 against the boycott. Armed with this, the minister and consuls could then complain if local officials failed to suppress anti-American activities. Viceroy Ts'en in the south became a special target for criticism after October, and, as will be noted later, the viceroy's actions thereafter indicated some sensitivity to this pressure.

Rockhill also sought help from foreign nations with influence in China. Although they were critical of the United States at first, when they began to fear that the boycott would spread to their goods too, they came over to the American side.[64] At Tsingtao, for example, the German minister cooperated with the United States.[65] And at Newchwang, when Chinese workers refused to unload a shop carrying American kerosene and cotton goods, Japanese authorities intervened and saw that the cargo was unloaded and moved to a storage area.[66] At Hong Kong British officials refused to permit public meetings on the boycott. Outside of China, foreign powers such as the British in Singapore also promised to help. While it is true that the boycott continued there in a spirited manner for about a year, Lord Lansdowne promised to "do everything possible" to slow it down.[67]

Nonetheless, Rockhill and the consuls in China were faced with an anti-American display that had a great deal of vitality and vehemence about it. To account for this, historians — such as Chang Ts'un-wu, Betty Field, Shih-shan Henry Tsai, and Akira Iriye — have regarded the boycott as an expression of a Chinese national feeling. The point is not to be gainsaid, but it can be overemphasized. One should not overlook the possibility that this national sentiment might have focused on another issue and against another country if the American exclusion policy — especially the post-1900 stage — had not offered itself as a ready target for attack. Thus, it took the exclusion policy as well as a nascent Chinese nationalism to produce the potent combination. As Rockhill observed, the new national spirit had "been coming," and it "only required a vent." But he also perceived that the "American exclusion law afforded that vent."[68]

There was always an obvious answer to Rockhill's predicament, as the head of the Foreign Office told him: with alterations in the exclusion treaty "the Chinese will not have any grievance with regard to harsh treatment and everybody will be pleased and glad to submit."[69] But the Department of Commerce and Labor would not allow that. Instead, American interests in China would have to suffer — and they did.

While public expressions about the boycott had died away in most of China by the end of 1905, the movement remained active in Canton, which offers an excellent illustration of the bad feeling stirred up in China over the exclusion policy and of the difficulties American diplomats encountered in coping with it.

Many factors might be mentioned to account for the high pitch of anti-American sentiment at Canton and the continuation of the boycott there long after it had lost its effectiveness elsewhere. Among these might be named the long anti-foreign tradition, the anti-dynastic tradition, the presence of business interests engaged in smuggling persons into the United States, the slowness of the United States in paying compensation to the family of a man who drowned in an incident in 1904 involving drunken American sailors, some earlier friction between an American consul and the viceroy, and local hostility toward the American company that had started building the proposed Canton-Hankow railroad.

But not one of these reasons is as fundamental as the exclusion policy — especially in its post-1900 form; it was by all odds the most obvious source of frustration and anger. Chinese-Americans were largely from the Canton area and could write of their unhappy experiences to their relatives. In addition, Chinese individuals deported from the United States or denied admittance were frequently from this section and had returned to live in their original districts.

If the United States had had a tactful, knowledgeable man on the scene in 1905, matters might have proceeded more smoothly; but the American consular system did not work in that manner at that time. Consular appointments were political plums. Julius Lay, who arrived in March 1905, although not lacking in ability or experience, was hardly the right man for Canton at such a critical time.[70] His abrupt, impatient, and aggressive approach to problems was not well calculated to appeal to Viceroy Ts'en Ch'un-hsuan. Nor did Lay, fresh from a post in Spain, have a background for understanding the problems he encountered. The rising tide of Chinese patriotic sentiment, the most dynamic force in Chinese affairs by 1905, escaped his notice for many months.

But even the best of American consuls might have failed in an

Anti-American Placard. (Enclosure in Consul James L. Rodgers to Acting Secretary James L. Loomis, April 20, 1906, Consular Dispatches, Shanghai. Library of Congress.) The text which originally accompanied the placard was translated in the dispatch as follows: "There was a certain merchant's wife who went to America to seek her husband, but because she spoke in a frightened and embarassed manner, and her words were confused, the American officials shut her up in the wooden detention shed by the sea, and set a day for further examination. Would you believe that she was detained several months. Suddenly her appearance changed and she became a lunatic. Her husband in the past had been very fond of her, and could not curb his anger and grief, so at once he headstrongly sold his effects, so that he might take his wife away from America. He accompanied her home to China and never went to America any more."

atmosphere in which the exclusion policy remained a constant irritant throughout the course of the boycott. Lay, expressing his frustration in a private letter to Rockhill, wrote: "what can we do when the immigration officials at Frisco backed up by Sargent interpret the law, treaty, and the vague regulations in such a way that practically everyone is excluded?"[71] Hints of growing tension appeared in April 1905 in an article in a Canton newspaper denouncing the United States for not acting fairly in the case of the drowned compradore. Criticizing the Chinese government for weakness, it excoriated foreigners for their cavalier handling of Chinese and called on the Chinese people not to let themselves "be treated like Jews, Indians or Negroes."[72]

No hesitation was manifested in Canton when word urging the boycott came from Shanghai. May 20 saw the first of a series of meetings to plan a course of action. Lay suggested to the viceroy's secretary that Chinese merchants avoid "hasty action."[73] Nevertheless, the first meeting produced telegrams to the Foreign Office, the Board of Trade, and the Chinese minister in Washington in opposition to the American draft of the exclusion treaty. Unless modifications were made in the policy, announced the Cantonese, they were determined to go ahead with their plans.[74]

The Eight Benevolent Societies assumed leadership. Weekly meetings were held on Sundays at Kwang Chi Hospital. On May 27 the leaders provided for the attendance thereafter of two representatives of each of the 72 guilds. Although they decided to wait two months before triggering the boycott officially, they resolved to get students and teachers at schools using American cotton goods for uniforms to stop the purchase of such goods at once. In this respect then the operation was to begin immediately, with the action at this early stage suggesting a commercial-academic coalition. Indeed, reported Lay, some students had already decided not to use American products for their uniforms. He attributed their interest in the treaty to their fear "that under the terms thereof, they may be excluded from going to the United States."[75]

At first, Lay did not take the whole thing seriously. It was ridiculous, he wrote Rockhill unofficially, "for the Chinese to talk about boycotting American goods, but these meetings stir up bad feelings."[76] When $1,500 arrived in June to pay the widow of the compradore, he was hopeful that the merchants would then withdraw their support.[77] To the secretary of the viceroy he suggested that the issue should be left in the hands of diplomats, and that any drastic action should await the final terms of the treaty.[78] Nevertheless, the meetings continued, and the plans went forward. Throughout June the Canton press enthusiastically endorsed the effort and printed anti-American articles.[79] Fleming D. Cheshire, the former consul, still in Canton, was now showing concern. On July 1 a mass meeting on the exclusion question attracted a crowd of 20,000. Chinese Christians prepared a petition to be sent to Roosevelt; placards appeared in the city with the appeal, "Let us with one heart boycott American goods!"[80] But Lay still believed that in the showdown Chinese merchants would not be willing to suffer financial loss to themselves.[81]

On July 2 a Chinese newspaper announced that the boycott would commence in Canton on August 1.[82] Steps were taken to identify American products by publicizing trademark information and the names of American firms. "We must not deal with the Americans until the Exclusion Treaty is no longer enforced,"[83] proclaimed a public statement which boldly set the unrestricted emigration of Chinese to America as the goal. By July 10 trade was already suffering, even though the official date had not yet arrived. Washington still hoped that Canton would be the only place involved and expected the Chinese government to take countermeasures.[84] Lay believed that the effort would not last long, yet one year later it had not entirely disappeared from Canton. The meetings in late July were attended not only by merchants and students but also by "common ignorant men whose sympathies are not only anti-American, but anti-foreign."[85] His statements indicated that a reform or revolutionary element, possibly supporters of K'ang Yu-wei or Sun Yat-sen, was moving in and taking over.

In July the temper of the American business community of Canton, as reflected by Lay, was adamant. Any concessions to the Chinese on the treaty issue, he warned Washington, might be viewed by them as a victory for the boycott; they might then "employ this means of trying to coerce not only Americans, but all foreigners whenever a question arises with any western nation."[86] In a July 21 letter to the viceroy, he was referring to apparent treaty violations. He pointed out to the State Department the declared intention of the boycotters to print in the press the names of Chinese merchants who were ignoring the venture. If the affair spread to outlying areas, he cautioned, attacks on missionaries might occur.[87]

Meanwhile, on the Chinese side ambitious and carefully laid plans were nearing completion by the end of July. An article in a July 24 Canton paper stated that the organization which had previously taken the name Opposing Exclusion Treaty Society was daringly changing it to incorporate the boycott concept. Unlike the emphasis placed elsewhere on the welfare of the privileged classes, the new name was stressing retaliation "against the maltreatment of Chinese laborers."[88] The boycott would continue as long as the exclusion treaty remained in effect. Printed notices and speakers were provided; literature in support of the embargo would be distributed throughout China and other parts of the world. If more money became available than was needed for the boycott effort directly, it would be used to establish a factory in Canton and a nationalistic newspaper. All of this, on paper at least, turned Canton into a propaganda center for denouncing the United States.

Although merchants and the more conservative elements had been in control at first, the new departure in July, in name and spirit, revealed that a much more fiery brand of leadership had gained the ascendancy. To Lay the new resolutions added up to coercion of Chinese merchants and therefore violations of article 15 of the 1844 treaty, article 15 of the 1858 treaty, and article 1 of the 1880 treaty — all providing for unrestricted trade between the United States and China. On the same day that the resolutions were made public, Lay sent a scorching letter of protest to Viceroy Ts'en.[89]

On August 1, the boycott date, Lay was still hopeful that those merchants most directly affected would not join in, but by August 9 he reported a decline in sales of oil and flour. Moreover, the British-American Tobacco Company had suffered a drop of 50 percent in sales.[90] The news in Canton of the president's order of June 26, which was that American officials show more respect, came too late to shake the will of the demonstrators. Placards and literature continued to be disseminated; weekly meetings were still held. During August, Lay watched with dismay the end of trade in American oil, flour, and other goods, not only in Canton, which was the distribution center for South China, but in the neighboring districts as well. At Wuchow, up the Pearl River from Canton, the Chinese agent for Standard Oil reacted to threats upon his life by fleeing to Hong Kong.[91] Oil junks were delayed at *likin* (tax) stations while cases were punctured.[92] A boat woman, believing a box to contain American goods, refused to ferry it across the river. A missionary reported that several Chinese students had left Christian College in Canton, a Presbyterian college, "because it is an American institution."[93] Newspapers refused to print advertisements of American firms or statements in defense of the American position.

Throughout August Lay pressed the viceroy constantly for action; their thinking, however, was so far apart that communication was difficult. Lay presumed the boycott to be for better treatment of the upper classes; he therefore argued that the president's order to the immigration authorities in June had solved the problem;[94] for the viceroy the entire movement was in retaliation for the exclusion of laborers and could only be terminated when they were no longer barred. After Lay informed the viceroy that only Congress could effect such extensive changes, Ts'en demanded that the consul "cable the President to convene Congress at once to pass a modified Exclusion act."[95] These exchanges make evident that Canton demanded far more than Shanghai.

Although Ts'en called the boycott a voluntary movement and refused to interfere with it unless violence occurred, he finally issued a proclamation against it on August 10, which Lay promptly labeled "a perfunctory document."[96] While arguing that in Canton an inflamed public restricted him more than other viceroys had been, Viceroy Ts'en released a second proclamation on August 24. Lay had to confess at this point that "the fair-minded foreigners believe the viceroy has gone as far as he can."[97] The principal argument used by the viceroy with his people, however, was that further action should be suspended until December when Congress would meet and have an opportunity to act. He warned Lay that then something would have to be done.

By September, after one month of the embargo, the anguished cries of the oil and flour interests in Canton had reached Washington. Reluctantly, Roosevelt had sent his secretary of war to Canton to deliver the warning that the United States would not tolerate the cutting off of its trade; even this visit brought no improvement in the tense and embittered atmosphere of the city. If anything it became worse. The Chinese employees of the American consulate received anonymous letters warning them to quit or risk being shot. Lay also received an anonymous letter threatening him with death. The consul turned in the names of agitators to the viceroy, who arrested them. But then, Lay learned (incorrectly, as he later discovered), he released them. Lay was convinced that the viceroy had let it be known that he would not enforce his proclamations. The consul, tersely explaining his problems in a cable to the State Department on September 12, predicted that violence might break out and requested a gunboat.[98] This was promptly sent.

A show of military power at Canton raised the crisis to a more serious level. The next question was, how far would the United States go in upholding its trading privileges? For Rockhill, who had been expressing the view that the Chinese government was solving the problem, the turn of events at Canton was deeply upsetting. He complained, in a wire to Lay on September 15, of having been bypassed in the gunboat request and instructed: "Make no threat Viceroy. In principal *(sic)* I am strongly opposed to calling for the navy when not absolutely necessary for the protection of life and property."[99] He feared, Rockhill informed Washington, that asking for a vessel might get to be a habit with consuls lacking experience. He deplored a return to the "old 'gunboat policy' of twenty years ago."[100] But the American businessmen at Canton, Lay wrote Rockhill, were "regular wild indians."[101] At least, Rockhill now realized more clearly the dimensions of the Canton problem. Preoccupied before with the Shanghai situation, which was closer at hand and more important in terms of volume of trade, he now tried to get Peking to be firmer with the viceroy. The boycott still continued at Canton, Rockhill informed Prince Ch'ing on September 13, and the employees of the consulate had been threatened. He requested "more efficient measures."[102]

But Peking showed no enthusiasm for sterner measures. Throughout the Canton area tension remained high during September, and trading languished. According to Lay, in his district American trade was "suffering a half a million dollars gold, a month."[103] Control was in the hands of a "rough coolie element."[104] A Chinese agent of the British-American Tobacco Company was beaten at Wuchow; nearby, the same fate befell the agent for the New York Life Insurance Company.[105] At Swatow, a city on the coast to the north of Canton, Standard Oil could find no one who would transport its oil, provide pilot service, or load and unload cargoes. The branch stores of the Canton merchants observed the boycott in Kong Moon, a city of 300,000. In Sun Ning, a city of 500,000, where there were laborers who had been in the United States and had been refused reentry, the feeling was decidedly unfriendly. Along with Canton the Sun Ning boycott leaders were demanding an end to any discrimination against Chinese in American immigration policy.[106] P.S. Heintzleman, vice consul, found on his travels outside Canton that his interpreter was being ridiculed for associating with an American. Anti-American literature was plentiful; and as Chinese travelers left Canton by boat for trips up the river, they received free copies of newspapers filled with boycott information. During the ride, literate passengers would read the anti-American material to the others. Money for these activities seemed to be no problem.

With time, new and increasingly ingenious devices were developed by the inventive boycotters to dramatize their cause. Among them the most striking was the holding of a series of memorial services for the martyr Feng-Hsia-wei, who had committed suicide on July 16, 1905, in protest against the exclusion policy. American diplomats were slow to understand what had happened and to grasp the full import of this event. Rockhill's dispatch described a Filipino, Fernando Ruiz, who had drunk from a bottle across from the Shanghai consulate and had died before Americans could get him to a hospital. Americans had paid for his burial, but in August the Shanghai *Taot'ai* had requested his body for a Chinese relative. It had been turned over to him with other remains, including a note stating "that he was glad to die for his country."[107] Even if the story had been pure fabrication — which was not the case — it would not have mattered to those who capitalized on the incident. Memorial services were held in November. At Fatshan, ten miles from Canton, thousands of people turned out on November 26. At Wuchow, 300 miles away, the excitement at a service on November 19 was so great that 20 missionaries sent a worried telegram; the USS *Callao* hurried up the river to protect them.[108] Missionaries reported that the people in Kwangsi province, and even in remote Yunnan province, had heard of the martyr. The services in themselves had a dramatic impact; even more important was the ability to keep the anti-American movement alive without violating official proclamations against boycott meetings and anti-American literature.

Lay had already decided that Viceroy Ts'en must be removed. September had not gone well in Canton; October was no better. Lay remained distinctly uncomfortable about the threat on his life. While he was ill in October in Hong Kong, the rumor spread that he had been poisoned and was dying. He was, he wrote Rockhill, "sorry to disappoint them."[109] On October 30 a jeweler refused to serve his wife. "My chair coolies are hooted in the streets," he wrote, "and I would not be surprised if my servants left me."[110] Although the viceroy issued proclamations, they were so worded that they revealed Lay had forced him to do so. To Ts'en, maintained the consul, imperial edicts were nothing more than "waste paper."[111]

Rockhill stuck with his moderate position, however. Aware that the removal of a viceroy, especially this one who was a close friend of the empress dowager, was no easy task, he contented himself with more notes of protest. Thus, on October 30 he informed the Foreign Office that trade in Kwangtung province suggested either the viceroy's "utter incapacity or his unwillingness to deal with the question."[112] In that same context he delivered the gist of Taft's message to Canton from Roosevelt that "the American Government desires to act justly toward China, but at the same time can not tolerate any injustice from China."[113] Not until an act of violence occurred in South China did official attitudes shift. On October 28 the tragic slaying of missionaries at Lienchow (Lian Chou, Lien Chau) occurred. The Americans, from Roosevelt to Lay, adopted a harder line. The viceroy, thrown on the defensive, had to bend but did not by any means capitulate entirely.

The Lienchow massacre, the one instance during the boycott period when American lives were lost, deserves special attention. For some time missionaries in the Canton district had indicated that the exclusion policy was interfering with their work. Chinese Christians had made a statement on July 15, forwarded by O.F. Wisner, president of Canton Christian College, to Rockhill for transmission to Roosevelt, in which the American missionary community in Canton had warmly endorsed the call for treaty modifications favoring the exempt classes.[114] It was with dismay that the Reverend William Ashmore of the American Baptist Missionary Union revealed in the *Missionary Review of the World* for October that the boycott was embracing the mission schools also, "and there is no reason why they may not come to affect missionaries generally, and even affect the well-being of the missionaries personally."[115]

Nevertheless, it proved difficult to determine subsequently whether the anti-American spirit had been a significant factor in that specific incident. On October 28, at a small village of 300 inhabitants 300 miles up the river from Canton, five Presbyterian missionaries were killed. The crisis developed from a protest made by Dr. Edward C. Machle because a local feast was being held on property claimed by the mission. When his protest was ignored, he seized a small cannon used to set off fireworks, but later returned it. Not realizing this, a rowdy, partly-drunk element entered the mission buildings to find the cannon and to loot. Discovering a human fetus in alcohol, the infuriated mob of some 2,000 dashed off in search of the missionaries, who had taken refuge in a cave. While some were able to escape detection, including Dr. Machle, his wife and child were killed. Others slain were Dr. Eleanor Chestnut and the Reverend and Mrs. John R. Peale.[116]

The boycott center in Canton quickly disavowed any connection with the trouble, and pointed out that it had no branch in that village. Lay noted, however, that prominent gentry at Lienchow had sent to

Canton for literature and that posters were reported to have been up in that area. Furthermore, he stressed, the first news of the murders had gone to the boycott headquarters in Canton.[117] Dr. Machle reenforced Lay's suspicions with his early telegram on the night of October 28: "The boycott has much to do with it."[118]

The Chinese built up a strong case later to show that the episode was a spontaneous local affair precipitated by the tactless handling of the villagers by the missionaries. Implying that the explanations were incomplete, the Reverend Herman O. T. Burkwell, missionary for the British and Foreign Bible Society, pointed to three earlier reasons for anti-foreign feeling in the Lienchow area: the ending of the traditional examinations for government office; the conversion of temples into schools for western studies; and the proclamation ending the Taoist ceremony called *ta tsiu*. The inflammatory boycott literature then came into this already disturbed area. He had found on his trip to the district that "everywhere you went all that was sung into our faces and hissed into our ears was 'kill them, kill them.' "[119] The matter was eventually settled with a money payment by Chinese authorities to the relatives of those murdered and the punishment of some of the local people.

No matter where the blame rested, the Lienchow case rang alarm bells. Roosevelt hurried to strengthen American naval power along the coast of China. Missionary societies seriously discussed withdrawing their missionaries from the more remote sections. Lay again urged Rockhill to seek the removal of the viceroy.[120] And Rockhill increased the pressure on the Foreign Office.[121] Over Lay's protests Root sent Cheshire to Canton to assist the beleaguered consul. The viceroy, sensitive to charges that he had not been doing enough to protect foreigners, now showed a stronger inclination to quiet the agitation. More conservative Chinese were also alarmed over the reports of violence in the interior. The fact that Chinese merchants had sought out McKinlay and arranged for a meeting with members of the Taft party in September was evidence that a merchant element in Canton and Hong Kong was eager to extricate itself from the financially burdensome impasse. American businessmen in Canton too had learned some lessons over the previous months. Moderate elements on both sides looked for a way out.

Thus, on December 4, Vice Consul Heintzleman reported that there was a meeting "some weeks ago" between representatives of Standard Oil Company, Sperry Flour Company, Hammond Milling Company, Stockton Milling, Singer Sewing Machine Company, British-American Tobacco Company, and other American businessmen with approximately 50 "members of the local boycott committee and delegates from the Hong Kong merchant guilds."[122] At the meeting the American merchants agreed to work for a modification of the exclusion act and for the better treatment of Chinese at the ports of entry with the understanding that initiating these steps would pave the way for a resumption of trade.

But a split now appeared on the Chinese side between moderates who professed to be satisfied with the admitting of upper-class Chinese and the extremists who insisted on the termination of all restrictions. The San Francisco Chinese, when informed of these new developments by the Canton negotiators, took a negative view and cabled: "the Exclusion Act must be repealed; nothing short of this will give satisfaction."[123] Not giving up yet, however, Chinese leaders, meeting at Kwang Chi (or "Chai" in some records) hospital on December 3, produced a 15-point list of demands. In substance this list, less demanding than San Francisco's, followed the lines of Minister Liang's draft of 1904 in acquiescing in the exclusion of laborers, in insisting on the acceptance of non-laboring Chinese, and in calling for the free entry of Chinese into the island territories. Then 50 Chinese merchants, including representatives from Shanghai, took the 15 points to Dr. Ho Kai, a Chinese lawyer in Hong Kong who was also brother-in-law of Wu T'ing-fang and friend of Sun Yat-sen, and with his assistance on December 9 worked out a revised 12-point statement.[124] For Canton the new design was the most restrained ever to be seriously considered. Its main thrust was to guarantee the free entry and respectful treatment of non-laboring Chinese. As for Hawaii and the Philippines, all Chinese were to be let in, "provided that the legislature or local authorities of such Islands are willing to admit such laborers."[125]

The moderates in Canton failed to carry the day, however. At a meeting at the hospital on December 17, the majority of those present signed a statement repudiating the 12-point program; instead, the group cabled Liang, "Please insist that no Exclusion Treaty will be negotiated and enforced, so as to satisfy the desires of the Chinese people."[126] Thus spoke the extremists, the laboring class, and the overseas Chinese who were determined to resist any treaty that assigned Chinese a position under that of other nationality groups. Canton, it should be noted, had never observed the merchants' truce declared in Shanghai in October. The boycott had continued there without let-up since July, and now as the principal center of agitation Canton showed no inclination to yield.

During the negotiations of November and December, the viceroy threw his support behind the moderates. Prior to December his public statements, much to the annoyance of Lay, gave the impression that Congress would soon liberalize the laws to admit laborers as well as members of the upper classes. Rockhill pointed this out to Prince Ch'ing on December 4, and condemned the "unwarranted and mischievous statements of the Viceroy."[127] The United States, he asserted, had never considered admitting laborers; nor had the Chinese government ever requested it in the current treaty negotiations. But the viceroy, in contrast to his public pronouncements, cabled the Chinese minister in Washington on December 20 that he supported the 12 points and that he would attempt to bring the boycott to an end if the United States adopted them.[128]

In December the American and Chinese positions were closer than they had ever been. Roosevelt's recommendations to Congress for new legislation were reasonably similar to the formula contained in the Canton program endorsed by the viceroy. Ts'en, however, insisted upon affirmative action right away.[129] But it was April before a Senate committee considered the Canton plan — and then not seriously. When Congress failed to act in December, the moderates in Canton lost out to the extreme wing. A common front behind the boycott was reestablished in Canton and some other places. Consuls at Foochow, Hangchow, and elsewhere remarked about the revival of agitation. Americans were astonished at the continued show of unity. No one, declared Cheshire, "could have dreamt how it has brought merchants, compradores, brokers, and others together for the mutual support."[130]

Although the atmosphere remained sullen and hostile in Canton, the viceroy was under too much pressure from his own government and from the United States to permit any more meetings or the distribution of literature. He also took special pains to prevent or punish acts of violence against foreigners. Thus when the house of the Reverend Andrew Beattie, Presbyterian missionary, was robbed on February 3, 1906, he responded immediately to Lay's loud calls for action. Authorities soon caught the thieves, and the *San Francisco Chronicle* could report with satisfaction that four of the bandits had been beheaded on March 12.[131] Such swift and punitive justice did not seem likely to promote the sale of American goods, however, nor to speed up the rate of conversions to Christianity. Quite the contrary.

In addition, the United States was in an explosive predicament. K'ang Yu-wei and Sun Yat-sen had deep roots in South China. Reform and revolutionary elements flourished in the area and grappled with the problem of how to turn this anti-American patriotic movement into a full-fledged uprising. One faction speculated that the murder of

Lay could touch off a revolution. After he was assassinated, the plotters reasoned, "the American gunboats would open fire on the city — then it would be naturally easy for them to murder Mr. Ts'en and other officials."[132] Indeed, internal revolution was more likely than war between China and the United States; nevertheless, the consul at Chefoo thought war "not at all improbable."[133] Although Peking wanted no part of either, there was always the prospect that the central government might lose control of events. China was restless. The trend, as Cheshire noted on January 6, was away from being anti-American and "becoming anti-foreign and . . . anti-dynastic."[134] Both Cheshire and Lay recommended that naval strength be maintained not far from Canton. Meanwhile, gunboats were also being sought by Shanghai, Chefoo, and Newchwang.

As for the original source of friction, the discriminatory immigration policy, it remained nearly as troublesome as ever. From the viceroy's standpoint, the issuance of certificates was at first treated primarily as a means of raising revenue. His charge was $96.00 (Mexican). Lay's more careful screening, however, often led to the rejection of applicants approved by the viceroy. When the viceroy tried reluctantly to raise his standards, he found American definitions incomprehensible. To the viceroy, for example, a student was one who passed his Chinese examinations; to the consulate, however, a student, to meet the requirements of the Immigration Bureau, had to speak English, prove that he could finance his education, and supply an outline of the program to be pursued on the university level.[135] When the viceroy urged Lay to accept his interpretation, the consul relayed the question to the State Department; but the Bureau of Immigration refused to give ground, and Lay had no choice but to be uncompromising on this point.[136]

Nevertheless, with time the boycott gradually weakened in Canton too. By March 1906 the continued suppression of anti-American literature was having some effect. Public opinion was now diverted by a new tax set by the viceroy to finance the construction of the Canton-Hankow railroad. "I think we can now," wrote Lay on March 5, "look for the end of this dangerous movement."[137] Some Chinese merchants, even though they had been able to shift their purchases to Australian flour and Sumatran oil, yearned for the day when they could once again buy American products. The earthquake in San Francisco in April which, Lay reported, "had a salutary effect in cutting off for a while, and possibly forever, the regular remittances . . . of money,"[138] was another reason for its decline.

In July 1906 Lay summed up the commercial losses in Canton.

From July 1, 1905, the boycott had gripped the entire province. Revenues for Canton in 1905 amounted to $2,220,000 gold, or $36,000 above 1904. But the increase was misleading, he explained. Figures did not take into account "national feeling." Shipments had continued to flow to Canton as usual, but the goods did not sell. Standard Oil Company estimated its loss at $350,000 gold; losses in flour were not quite so serious. Future figures would show the effects better than those for 1905. He was of the opinion "that the end is not yet in sight,"[139] nor would it be so long as the exclusion laws remained unchanged.

Thus, the record at Canton as elsewhere was one of damage to trade and to American missionary and educational interests. And the disaffection was greater than elsewhere. But throughout South China, according to Burkwell, the non-commercial impact was far-reaching. His testimony at the investigation of the Lienchow trouble included the following exchange:

> *Burkwell:* A year ago America was the favorite nation among any nation you like.
> *Q.* All through the country?
> *A.* Yes, all through the country. . . . people welcomed us everywhere.
> *Q.* Now we are the best hated?
> *A.* Yes, it is everywhere the same.[140]

In many areas of China the anti-American wave had confirmed that the exclusion policy — in its post-1900 stage — presented a threat to American interests in that country. A churchman, writing on the boycott in the *Missionary Review of the World*, did not mince words:

> Our amazement at the Chinese boycott tells the story of our national sensitiveness, and of theirs. With blundering fatuity, for nearly twenty years, we have shut the doors of this republic to the people of China . . . and during the same period we have been prating about the Open Door over there, as if it was a special graciousness on our part, to keep that door open while we closed our own.[141]

11

Congress and the Foster Bill

Congress continued to receive reminders that it could either be a help or hindrance in solving the distressing diplomatic problems of 1905 and 1906. Since its inaction was undermining the efforts of diplomats in China, some of them began to point this out and discreetly urge that some of China's demands on exclusion be met. Rockhill, for example, had written Washington on several occasions that Congress should relax the exclusion laws. Former Minister Conger told the *New York Times* that, while the Chinese government could use "methods of repression," the "remedy largely rested with this country."[1] Consul Walter T. Griffin, from Limoges, France, told the Men's Association of Trinity Reformed Church in Plainfield, New Jersey, that he could not understand "why a man should be barred because of his color, the slant of his eyes or the way he wears his hair."[2]

In China the consuls took varying stands but in general looked to Congress for some type of remedial legislation. Sammons favored a literacy test; Lay favored a better definition of terms. Consul General Edward S. Bragg of Hong Kong was in a class by himself. This old Civil War general, who was eighty years old in 1905, was convinced that the exclusion laws were in conflict with treaties; in harsh terms he lashed out at the Bureau of Immigration for waging "war upon the Chinese."[3] Nevertheless, legislators were still not eager to reexamine priorities on the exclusion issue. Nothing might have been done if the president had not also spoken out firmly. His call for revised legislation in his message to Congress in December was a prodding that Congress could not easily ignore. Indeed, when the Foster bill appeared in the House it was an early reminder that the legislative branch had to face the issue whether it wanted to or not. If Congress, however, had the key to the boycott, as Conger implied, legislators seemed more intent on losing it than on unlocking doors with it. In May Representative Champ Clark, powerful House Democrat, was asking what had happened to the bill.[4] If even this astute political veteran was confused about its whereabouts, it was exceedingly well hidden.

The bill, HR 12973, introduced by David J. Foster of Vermont on January 24, 1906, appeared in the House and was referred to the Committee on Foreign Affairs. It had originated with the president of the American Asiatic Association, who had organized a subcommittee to prepare the bill. Since it followed the president's recommendations, Foord expected the administration to support it. He assured the readers of the *Journal* that the secretary of state was "in complete accord with the Association in the work which it has undertaken."[5] Furthermore, business organizations would back the bill, and churches and missionary societies would "exert all possible influence in securing the passage of such a measure of justice to China."[6] The Foster bill, in essence, prohibited laborers and admitted all other Chinese; it also tried to ensure that the credentials issued in China would not be questioned at the American ports of entry. But since it contained a broad definition of *laborer*, Foord thought the draft should also satisfy "the most exacting of labor agitators or Pacific Coast politicians."[7] The State Department helped to create the right atmosphere for action by Congress by lauding a new imperial decree in January against the boycott. The *San Francisco Chronicle* saw this decree as indicating "an earnest desire on the part of the imperial government to meet our wishes."[8] Secretary Root, too, the *Chronicle* observed, hoped that Congress would enact an exclusion law that would be more acceptable to China.

Commercial organizations and church groups rallied behind the Foster bill with petitions to the House Committee on Foreign Affairs. The Trades League of Philadelphia, the Altruistic Association of Hillsboro, Ohio, the Pittsburgh Chamber of Commerce, the Merchants' Exchange of San Francisco, the New York Produce Exchange, and the New York Chamber of Commerce all urged some form of liberalization.[9] Presbyterian churchmen in the St. Paul area, Congregational ministers of the Minnesota Congregational Club, and Presbyterian ministers at Troy, New York, joined the other petitioners. A typical rationale was supplied by the Troy Group: "Both we and they are suffering, commercially, educationally and religiously, from flagrant errors on our part which we trust the new legislation now pending on Congress will promptly, fully and honorably correct."[10] While a few petitioners opposed all discrimination, most took care to note that the Foster bill provided "safeguards against the landing of Chinese of the Coolie class."[11]

China's official, though not unqualified, blessing of the Foster bill came at a breakfast (at 1:00 p.m.), sponsored by the American Asiatic Association, for the Imperial Chinese Commission, on February 3, 1906. At this breakfast Minister Liang singled out Foster for praise. He thought that the spirit of the bill would "go far toward settling the present disturbed mind of the Chinese in the Orient."[12] In the same vein Foord proclaimed that the bill would eliminate the contradiction in American policy toward China.[13] Foster, in justifying his bill, maintained that the United States should conduct itself "as a great nation toward all the nations of the earth."[14] The building of the Panama Canal created a need for businessmen to seek closer and more friendly relations with China. Throughout the meal Foster was acclaimed; indeed, the "breakfast" turned into little less than a rally in support of his bill. Foord openly appealed for political agitation by businessmen and religious groups.[15] Chairman Hitt of the House Foreign Affairs committee was in the audience.

Among businessmen who spoke out in the following days for more relaxed legislation, none did so more loudly than Schwerin, the vice president of the Harriman controlled Pacific Mail Steamship Company. "The complete destruction of what has been built up," he asserted, "is now threatened."[16] He warned of danger to missionaries, possibly "wholesale massacre," and of major commercial losses. His statements, appearing in the press on the eve of public hearings on the Foster bill, February 13, were well timed to impress legislators. If the powerful Harriman interests had any influence in Congress, prompt action seemed certain to follow.

In February Congress seemed to be responding favorably to these urgent pleas. An attempt on February 14 by the House Committee on Immigration, stronghold of the exclusionists, to gain control of the bill was beaten back.[17] Instead, on February 15 a subcommittee headed by James B. Perkins of New York started hearings on behalf of the Committee on Foreign Affairs. The hearings offered a propaganda platform to the interests promoting the Foster bill; these ranged from State Department personnel to business and church representatives. Chinese diplomats hovered attentively nearby. Pro-Chinese articles appeared in influential journals.[18]

At the hearings Charles Denby, Jr., chief clerk, testified for the State Department. Son of a former minister to China, holder of business and diplomatic posts in China, adviser to Viceroy Yuan Shih-k'ai, Denby had impeccable credentials. He had been in China until March 28, 1905. In a lengthy statement he interpreted the boycott as at first a protest movement by the privileged classes with the limited aim of obtaining better treatment for themselves; the effort had later been transformed into a nationalistic drive to erase all discrimination against Chinese. In responding to friendly leading questions from the chairman, Denby endorsed the point in the Foster bill that designated China as the location for customs examinations rather than the American ports of entry. Also he regretted that fewer Chinese students were coming to the United States; increasingly they were going to Japan, Belgium, and elsewhere. Thus the drift of his testimony favored the Foster bill. To please the exclusionists, Denby also suggested limiting the ports of debarkation to two: Shanghai and Hong Kong.[19] There was close questioning by unfriendly congressmen, especially by Duncan McKinlay, the Representative from California who had earlier seemed an ally of Taft's.[20] McKinlay asked Denby if trade benefits, great though they might be, would be worth the dropping of the exclusion laws. No, agreed the trapped Denby, "perhaps the game would not be worth the candle."[21] In addition to McKinlay, Everis A. Hayes and Kahn were also members of the California delegation to watch out for state interests at the hearings.

It was clear the Foster bill was in for a hard time. Yet the chairman revealed his sympathy toward it in his questioning, and the second member of the three man subcommittee exposed his support also in remarks on February 15. This was William H. Howard of Georgia, who, as a member of the Taft group touring Asia at the time of the boycott, had learned firsthand of the loss of sales by the American Tobacco Company, by cotton goods manufacturers, and by life insurance companies.[22] Although the third member, Jacob S. Fassett, New York Republican, followed a more neutral course, the general composition of the subcommittee indicated widespread geographical support and some bipartisan backing for the bill.

At the same hearings, Mrs. Lucia Ames Mead of Boston, author of a 1905 *Boston Transcript* article entitled "The Yellow Peril," shifted attention away from the trade issue to the importance of the educational stake and the long-range advantage of friendly relations. Going well beyond the Foster bill, she proposed that Chinese students be offered American scholarships. Then, after completing courses in western science and culture, those students would return to China to serve as teachers.

The February hearings lasted for only one day and closed in an atmosphere favoring pro-Chinese legislation. The backing of businessmen for the Foster bill remained strong. On February 18 the Board of the National Association of Manufacturers called on Congress "to correct present evils and restore friendly relations with China."[23] D. M. Parry, the Board president, blamed labor for the boycott, the loss of trade, and the threat of war. He declared that the "whole weight" of his organization would be "thrown into the cause for the correction of present evils by the enactment of proper laws by Congress."[24] During the month before the hearings resumed, frightening reports of Chinese unrest appeared in the press. Public attention also focused on Roosevelt's dispatching of troops to the Philippines. Despite the assurances of the Chinese minister that China was quiet, some people feared a sudden attack on missionaries and businessmen. "The scenes of 1900," pledged Liang, "will never be repeated."[25]

At the reopening of the hearings on March 14, support for the Foster bill reached its highest point. A delegation of 26 businessmen and churchmen, headed by Foord, appeared before the House committee. The group included spokesmen for the New England Cotton Manufacturers' Association, the Southern Manufacturers' Association, the Chamber of Commerce of New York, the Boston Chamber of Commerce, the Boston Merchants' Association, the Cincinnati Chamber of Commerce, the Manufacturers' Association, the Pacific Mail Steamship Company, and the National Association of Manufacturers. In addition, representatives from the Protestant Episcopal Board of Missions, the Missionary Board of the Methodist Episcopal Church, and the American Board of Foreign Missions were also there. The organizations represented gave an impressive show of strength. Familiar faces — from the hearings of 1902 — reappeared. Hamlin and Evarts, two of the most eloquent, were there. About half of the delegation did not belong to the American Asiatic Association, but Foord was the catalyst and had carefully coached the members to speak on specific points. D. A. Tompkins, for example, representing the National Association of Manufacturers from Charlotte, North Carolina, stressed the southern interest and pointed out to labor the advantage of selling cotton goods to China.[26] Foord announced at the outset that the entire group was "possessed of only one voice" which declared "in favor of the House bill 12973."[27]

Foord's strategy stressed the positive — that concessions should be made to China as a matter of justice, national honor, and American self-interest. He did not want it to appear that the United States was yielding to boycott pressure, but the tactics of the anti-Chinese side forced a change in plans. Businessmen began to emphasize the harmful effects of the boycott and the need for relief. Ellison A. Smyth, a large cotton manufacturer from South Carolina, testified that orders had reached zero six or seven months earlier and that they were "still dead."[28] His case was typical of mills in his region, he maintained. Silas D. Webb, president of the China and Japan Trading Company, exporter of locomotives and various other items, estimated that his sales were down to about a tenth of what they had been. More statistical data on trade losses were supplied at a later meeting of the hearings. The most important information was that given by W. H. Libby of Standard Oil. Blaming losses directly on the boycott, Libby revealed that sales from October to December 1904 had been 2,052,000 cases but in the corresponding months of 1905 had been only 315,000.[29] Murray Warner, a Shanghai importer, held that his imports had dropped to 10 percent of what they had been previously.[30] Even this remaining trickle of trade would have vanished, he contended, if Viceroy Yuan had not taken stern measures in his area. Both Libby and Warner urged Congress to admit the privileged classes of Chinese.

At the March 14 meeting, clergymen emphasized the undermining effect of the boycott on missionary activities as a reason for new immigration laws. Bishop D. H. Moore of the Methodist Church observed that, according to letters from missionaries, "this commercial unrest and excitement and boycott, directly and indirectly, have a tendency to block our work out through the country."[31] American missionaries, noted Samuel B. Capon, president of the American Board of Foreign Missions, had been well regarded after the formulation of the open door policy, but more recently "the influence of this unrest . . . has disturbed this good feeling."[32]

A boost to the pro-Chinese cause came from an unexpected source when Sun Yat-sen, still an unknown to most non-Chinese in the United States, appeared before a committee to present his views as a Chinese visitor who had personally undergone an insulting experience. His remarks, forcefully stated, led one California congressman to seek rebuttal information from Sargent.[33] The bureau responded with the news that Sun was a political refugee and regarded by the Chinese government as an anarchist and revolutionary; the bureau denied having mistreated him.[34] Sun's statements were probably of greater value to himself in his bid for leadership among Chinese-Americans, however, than in influencing legislation.

The attitude of the hearings had taken a negative turn by April, despite eloquent assaults on the exclusion policy. On April 9, 1906, the bureau came out against the Foster bill. Instead, Sargent urged that Congress keep the existing law "as your foundation" and amend it.[35] He was agreeable to enlarging the list of privileged Chinese and expanding the policy of readmitting Chinese who had previously been in the country. But he also sought a new registration of Chinese and the right to deport all who had not been previously registered. Campbell, the law officer, was flexible also. Indeed, he held that, if the existing law was retained, the provision for "travelers for curiosity or pleasure" was a category broad enough to admit all non-laborers. The bureau, he assured the subcommittee, already considered a "banker" to be a "merchant."[36] Further revelations of lawmaking by the Bureau — which had been regularly enacting its own anti-Chinese laws — were checked by the timely intervention of McKinlay. It was clear, nonetheless, that the bureau was fighting a rearguard action against the Foster bill, even though that bill had originally been strongly backed by the administration.

Gompers, who made an impassioned appeal to preserve the existing law, was far more outspoken in opposing the Foster bill. His views were reinforced by Furuseth of the Japanese and Korean Exclusion League. The most detailed and skillful probing of the pro-Chinese positions, however, came from McKinlay on behalf, he said, of California, Washington, Utah, Nevada, and Oregon. Since McKinlay had been an assistant United States attorney in San Francisco and a member of the Taft party which had visited China, he could speak with some authority on Chinese affairs. McKinlay and his fellow Californians even challenged the basic assumptions of the supporters of the Foster bill. Was there really a boycott? Did it have any connection with the exclusion policy? Was not missionary activity the real cause — if there actually was a boycott? Were not foreign competitors, the Japanese especially, the real troublemakers in inciting the Chinese? Was not the unrest in China mainly a phenomenon of the times? If a boycott did indeed exist, and if it was a product of the exclusion policy, were not changes in immigration regulations — those already made — sufficient to allay the unrest? Was not the source of pressure to liberalize the policy really a group plotting to bring coolie labor into the United States? Would not harmless concessions to the Chinese lead to further demands and an end to the exclusion policy? "Is this boycott," asked McKinlay, "for the purpose of removing the restrictions against the coolies or for better regulations? If for better regulations, we have them now. If it is for the purpose of entirely removing the exclusion law, that is another matter."[37] To McKinlay the boycott was a plot originated by the San Francisco Chinese.

Finding the labor-west coast combination growing in power, Roosevelt made an effort to soften the opposition of the AFL in a meeting with its executive committee, nearly 100 in number, on March 21. At this conference requested by Gompers, the committee argued that the exclusion law was already too weak and therefore should be strengthened. Roosevelt appealed to the labor leaders to help him ensure good treatment for businessmen, professionals, students, and visiting Chinese. "I have," he declared, "a right to challenge you as good American citizens to support that policy."[38] The president's attempt to sway labor, however, ended in failure. To Gompers the existing law was "the most effective law for the exclusion of Chinese that we can develop."[39]

Realizing by late March that the Foster bill was in danger, Roosevelt cast about for a more acceptable formula. On April 2 Metcalf sent Perkins a letter purporting to reflect the views of the president and proposing amendments to the existing law.[40] The new provisions included stationing immigration officials in China, allowing laborers to return to the United States without restrictions other than the holding of a certificate, permitting Chinese immigrants to be free on bail while awaiting appeal decisions, and requiring a new registration of Chinese in the United States. A spokesman for the Foreign Affairs committee hinted that the committee might give priority to the Metcalf amendments over the Foster bill. But the California delegation immediately voiced opposition to the bail provisions and the simplified arrangement for readmitting laborers. Reacting negatively to all four proposals, the *San Francisco Chronicle* concluded: "The only change required in our exclusion laws is to extend their operation to all Asiatic coolies."[41] With such criticism mounting, it appeared that even these mild revisions, which actually contained important anti-Chinese features desired by the bureau, were going nowhere.

Another try at compromise, also doomed to failure, was a bill offered on April 11 by Representative Edwin Denby, son of the former minister to China and brother of the chief clerk in the State Department, Charles Denby, Jr. As a representative from Michigan, Denby had been following the hearings carefully and considered himself also an authority on China. His bill (HR 18022), he explained, although still barring laborers, was intended to reduce friction with China.[42]

In his catch-all bill, which tried to give something to both sides, Denby excluded all Chinese except certain designated classes, and increased the exempt classes to include bankers, editors, bookkeepers, and others. It also offered legal concessions to Chinese within the United States and proposed a clearer and more liberal definition of *student*. On the other hand, for the benefit of the bureau the bill called for limiting the number of ports of debarkation from China and for re-registering Chinese in the United States. The bill had the earmarks of close collaboration with the State Department, and further evidence of State Department backing showed up in an effort by Root later to interest China in the measure.[43] By April 12, however, the bills and liberalizing amendments all appeared doomed. California congressmen had extracted a promise from House committee members that they would report no bill at all during the current session of Congress.[44] "The House and Congressional Committee leaders have been told," reported the *San Francisco Chronicle*, "that if the exclusion matter is let alone California will send a solid Republican delegation to the sixtieth Congress."[45] Only a few days later, on April 18, the San Francisco earthquake, with its destruction of property and with deaths running up to 700, proved to be a diversion of major proportions. Its net effect weakened the pro-Chinese side.

The entire effort, once so formidable, had collapsed by May; neither did a decent burial await the Foster bill. On May 26 Clark of Missouri asked on the House floor what had happened to it. Perkins professed to be considering the Foster and Denby bills and also the proposals of the Department of Commerce and Labor. "From them all," he said, "we hope to evolve something that may ameliorate the service in a way that will meet the approval even of the gentleman from Missouri."[46] As the session drew to a close the Foster bill's demise took place behind the closed doors of the committee chambers: the Foreign Affairs committee simply failed to produce a new bill.

Some variations appeared in the Senate, but the end result was the same. One significant innovation was the bold initiative taken by the Democratic south. A resolution by the Georgia legislature called on the Senate "to repeal or so modify what is known as the 'Chinese-exclusion act' as will not only restore friendly relations, but extend our commerce with that country."[47] On January 25 and again on January 29 South Carolina's Democratic Senator Benjamin Tillman introduced a resolution calling on the Senate Committee on Immigration to investigate the boycott situation and propose remedies.[48] "The people down my way," explained Tillman, "are very deeply interested. . . . We have a large market . . . for our manufactured cotton goods . . . and the trade was growing rapidly. . . . But since this agitation . . . broke out there is a kind of shiver of dissatisfaction in China."[49] Although west coast Senators opposed the bill, charging that the south was seeking cheap Chinese labor to avoid being so deeply dependent on Negro labor, the resolution passed. It was probably no accident that members of the imposing Imperial Chinese Commission were in the Senate gallery at the time the resolution was first introduced.

Although the pro-Chinese had scored a victory with the Tillman resolution, a less auspicious trend appeared a few weeks later in the form of new bills in the House to extend exclusion to Japanese and Koreans. The bills expressed the wishes of nearly all of the people in his district, Representative Hayes of California contended, "if not 95 percent of all the people of the State of California."[50]

The Senate hearings did not begin until April 17, after the House committee had completed its public deliberations. Senator Dillingham was now chairman of the Senate Committee on Immigration. In the files of the committee were urgent requests for relief from affected business interests. "The present situation in China," wrote the vice president of the Oliver Machinery Company of Michigan, "means the loss of our entire business there."[51] Also in the Sente committee files were requests for action from some of the largest Protestant denominations: from the Presbyterian Church on December 18, 1905; the Protestant Episcopal Church on January 15, 1906; the Reformed Church on February 23. The correspondence added up to an imposing array of business and religious sentiment calling for a more relaxed exclusion policy.

By April, however, the administration had retreated from the December proposal to admit all but laborers. Indeed, it had seemingly deserted the pro-Chinese side altogether. "If we are going to adhere to our policy of not letting in Chinese labor," declared Denby, "the present law, properly administered, should meet all demands, I think."[52] He suggested one administrative change: the shifting of examinations to China, where immigration officials, working from consulates, could check on the qualifications of Chinese. He also favored limiting this processing to two Chinese ports. All of his recommendations fitted the prescriptions emanating from the Department of Commerce and Labor. Denby discussed the Canton Chinese demands of December 3, 1905, as revised on December 9, but dismissed them as impossible. He advised against yielding to China under pressure. In any case, the boycott was now about over, "but it is latent and could be stirred up again very easily."[53] The gist of his remarks could easily be interpreted by the anti-Chinese side as meaning that, since the crisis was over, there was no need for quick action or major changes.

Since the State Department had made an about-face on April 17, the resumption of hearings on May 1 seemed anti-climactic. No businessmen were present to complain of continuing losses; no observers from Canton appeared to testify of the bitterness and lengthy duration of the ordeal there. Churchmen from the less antagonistic Shanghai and Tientsin areas presented the boycott as a thing of the past which never seriously damaged American interests anyway. The scholarly ex-college president Bishop James W. Bashford, however, made a case for enacting the Foster bill, or for at least some symbolic legislative gesture, "so that it could be reported back in China that America had changed the exclusion act and adopted a new bill."[54] Robert R. Gailey, former general secretary of the YMCA in Tientsin, supporting Bashford, also urged the making of at least token revisions as a concession to the new nationalistic spirit.[55] But the Senators seemed more impressed with the counter-argument that Congress should not yield to Chinese pressure.

When the Senate hearings of May 1 terminated open sessions, Foord still did not admit defeat. He was sure that a report would come from the House committee within two weeks. It would probably be a "composite production," he speculated in the *Journal*, "framed on the lines of the Foster Bill but differing from it in some essential particulars." The Senate was moving along parallel lines, he explained; and in the middle of May friends of the Foster bill might need to make "another demonstration in its favor before the Senate Committee on Immigration."[56] The May issue of the *Journal* was filled with the official record of the hearings, but, by then, the pressure in the Senate to undo the exclusion policy had slackened off markedly. That it was not entirely dead was evidenced by a letter on May 19 from the chancellor and six deans of the University of Nebraska to Senator E. J. Burkett, which, reflecting the interests of educators, urged action to reverse the shifting of Chinese students from American to European universities.[57] On the day before, May 18, a lengthy statement that persuasively summarized the pro-Chinese position arrived from Chauncey R. Burr of Portland, Maine. "An offended nation," he postulated, "can very easily become an angry nation, and an angry nation the size of China may suddenly blossom into a world power. It behooves us, therefore, to treat her seriously."[58] The letter was printed as a Senate Document. But the Burr letter was the last gasp of a dying cause in the Senate. Once again, as with the Foster bill in the House, quiet execution behind closed committee doors was the fate of all efforts to liberalize exclusion legislation.

Although reasons can easily be found for the failure of the drive to modify the exclusion policy, the outcome is still surprising. Many powerful moneyed interests were behind the effort, and the support of leading churchmen, distinguished university heads, and a dynamic president, it would seem, should have produced more dramatic results. Yet the entire movement collapsed in a matter of months. One important factor in its defeat was the reduction of tension in China by the spring of 1906. When overt anti-American demonstrations ceased, the sense of urgency vanished in Washington. Moreover, Roosevelt as well as members of Congress worried over the possibility that China might consider conciliatory moves as signs of weakness and demand more. Root complained to Liang of "a natural tendency among men to revolt against coercion. . . . Such had been the effect in the American Congress of the course pursued by China."[59] To be sure, it was a natural posture for nationalistic legislators to assume in view of their prior racial antipathies.

But especially significant was the rallying behind the status quo of labor, west coast congressmen, the influential *San Francisco Chronicle,* and the Department of Commerce and Labor. This combination was victorious in 1902 and 1904 and again in 1906. Many techniques which had worked before were used again, especially the sending of petitions by AFL locals. These petitions against the Foster bill poured in overwhelming numbers upon the key House and Senate committees.

A distinctive feature of the exclusionist activities of 1905-1906, which has been overlooked, was the leadership by the Japanese and Korean Exclusion League. Because it was thought the anti-Chinese battles were over, the League was formed in May 1905 in California to carry the banner against other Asians. Its leaders, Tveitmoe, Livernash, and Furuseth, planned in December 1905 to go to Washington to seek new exclusionist legislation.[60] Instead, the League found itself in the middle of the struggle to liberalize Chinese policy, and it thereupon shifted temporarily from the offensive to the defensive. Although the name implied that the League had nothing to do with Chinese matters, it was made up of west coast labor leaders and racist-minded individuals who had been involved for years in the Chinese question. The League became very active and influential in the drive to destroy the Foster bill, and the scope of its activities can be demonstrated by some of its stands. When the Imperial Chinese Commission arrived in San Francisco in January 1906, the League protested to congressmen that Jeremiah W. Jenks, representing the president, had made statements that were "a complete reversal of the present policy of Chinese Exclusion."[61] On February 4, 1906, the League adopted a resolution that both condemned the Foster bill in principle and attacked such specific parts as a provision allowing Chinese appeals to courts from rulings by the bureau. On February 14, 1906, it joined with the City Front Federation of San Francisco in a resolution that again denounced the Foster bill.[62] Printed petitions against the bill, numbering in the hundreds, then began flowing to Congress from San Francisco, San Jose, and elsewhere in California. Nevertheless, the League in a statement on March 9, 1906, opposed the use of force against China, a position which was also adopted by the San Francisco Labor Council.[63] China, it held, had a right to control its domestic affairs, just as the United States had that same right. Furuseth, a west coast labor leader and its spokesman at the House hearings in April, asserted, "The question . . . is, What is the West going to be — yellow or white?"[64]

The League was a vital link between the labor movement and racists. Gompers and the AFL worked along lines parallel with it in opposing the Foster bill. The AFL, at its 1905 annual convention, commended the entire effort of the League, while Gompers announced that he would direct much energy toward maintaining the exclusion policy.[65] Unstintingly, in the following months he fought against all proposed changes. At the hearings he was asked if he would not at least allow Chinese preachers to come to the United States. His reply was: "We have an overproduction of them here."[66] These labor and League elements were angry over the apparent wavering of the Bureau of Immigration which, caught between Roosevelt's policy and its exclusionist constituency, had to keep twisting and turning. On February 5, 1906, Metcalf announced the adoption of new regulations which abandoned the Bertillon system, provided for quicker processing, ensured that Chinese who had been rejected knew of their right of appeal, reduced the red tape for returning Chinese residents, and dropped the restrictive definition of *student*.[67] In effect, these changes sloughed off a number of provisions that had so antagonized Chinese-Americans and upper-class Chinese. Even without these public alterations there was evidence that the bureau had tempered its methods: for example, in contrast to 1905, when 29 percent of the certificates visaed by consuls had been rejected by immigration officials, in 1906 the number dropped to 6 percent.[68]

But the bureau maneuvered constantly to forestall basic modifications in the immigration laws. It went to great length to defend its past policies in a detailed statement to the Committee on Foreign Affairs on May 25, 1906.[69] Metcalf also warned in his departmental report of June 30, 1906, that, although trade with China might seem attractive, if "the price to be paid . . . is the unrestricted immigration of Chinese of all classes, then, in the interest of American labor and American citizenship, we had better forego entirely that trade."[70] As Metcalf clung to the exclusionist side, Roosevelt made a decision. The president, in shuffling Cabinet posts, in October made Metcalf the new secretary of the navy. He did not touch Sargent, however.

As the exclusionist forces held firm and Congress adjourned without acting, Foord paid sorrowful tribute to the power of the labor-California coalition. The labor vote was important to the Republican party, especially in California, he told his readers. Little more could be done for the time being,[71] but friends of the Foster bill should keep promoting it. When Congress reconvened in December, the bill might then be reported and subsequently passed. Such an outcome was never to be.

If the Chinese were encouraged by these words of Foord, they must have been incurable optimists. No evidence of a change in priorities had emerged from the deliberations of Congress. Rather, when the Republican party, the dominant party at the time, chose to kill the Foster bill, it was conceding a point that had been made by Gompers at the hearings. At the moment he was being questioned by Representative Fassett, who wondered whether "the severity of the administration of the laws might result in shutting us out of the markets of China." If so, that was "regrettable," responded Gompers, "but not one-half or one tithe as dangerous as the possibility of the Chinese coming here."[72]

Not only was the trade issue involved in this exchange but also missionary and educational interests, and peace and friendship with China. Gompers' answer applied to them all and was the same answer which, at one time or another, the Department of Commerce and Labor, the *San Francisco Chronicle,* and the Japanese and Korean Exclusion League had given. The vitality of the exclusionist movement was as great as ever. In 1906, as in 1902 and 1904, exclusion — of an extreme type — took first place over any other considerations.

12

Roosevelt's Techniques in 1906

By April 3, 1906, the president had given up hope of getting Congress to ameliorate exclusion. "I do not think Congress will act," he wrote Root on that date, "and therefore you and I will have to do the best we can . . . to partially offset the effects of the inaction of Congress."[1] Not only was the general import of the observation significant; the "I" in the equation was also meaningful: Roosevelt, it was clear, would continue to give his personal attention to the China problem for, it is a matter of record, he had not been waiting for Congress to act anyway. He had been using for sometime various weapons from the presidential arsenal. His most drastic measure, beginning in January, had been to initiate plans for the possible military seizure of Canton. The entire episode, in addition to illustrating the gravity of the exclusion-boycott issue, might be interpreted by some scholars as evidence that both racism and imperialism influenced Roosevelt's policies at this juncture. The latter point is debatable, however; although Beale makes a good case for the imperialistic orientation of Roosevelt, it can also be argued that the president was less an imperialist than a pragmatic politican searching for any kind of solution that worked.

Before looking into the facts of the proposed military operation, one might consider briefly the interesting subject of Roosevelt and racism. In 1906, it should be noted, the President was not taking racist positions. On the issue of Chinese exclusion, for example, he was urging Congress to return to a class-based policy — the barring of laborers — and to move away from an openly racist posture. He was also worried that Congress might extend its exclusion policies to the Japanese, and he spent a great deal of time pulling political levers to kill bills aimed in that direction. The United States had to be careful about the Japanese, Roosevelt cautioned Gompers, since they "had shown themselves to be great fighters and sailors."[2] In the crisis that arose in 1906 over the decision of the San Francisco school board to assign Japanese children to segregated schools, he worked unstintingly to get the San Franciscans to moderate their stand.[3] In all of these instances his positions were anti-racist. Whatever his personal beliefs might have been, he was certainly being pragmatic in these matters.

When Roosevelt considered military action, he again seemed to be pursuing a pragmatic course. Much of his thinking was defensive rather than aggressive in an imperialistic sense. He was genuinely concerned about the safety and welfare of American citizens in China and fearful of being caught off guard. Was the Lienchow massacre of late October 1905 a harbinger of things to come? Missionaries in remote areas were in exposed positions. A rescue operation carried out by American military forces would not be easy. In December the Shanghai riot awakened new fears. Any president, faced with these circumstances, might have taken military precautions. Roosevelt was convinced by January that American military power had to be increased in Asia — even though the boycott was supposed to be over except in Canton. After a Cabinet meeting on January 2, Taft notified General Leonard Wood in the Philippines that reinforcements were coming.[4] Roosevelt suggested to Taft that 15,000 men be sent out immediately, and 5,000 more in a month's time. "We ought not to take any chances," he wrote Taft on January 11; "we cannot afford a disaster."[5] If fighting broke out in China, the seizure of Canton would be the first step. The president was urged on by such close associates as Wood, who pressed for the "big stick" approach.[6]

Alarming developments in February seemed to confirm the wisdom of the American military build-up. On February 4 came the news that the home of Dr. Andrew Beattie, Presbyterian missionary at Fati, near Canton, had been looted.[7] Rockhill reported on February 14 that English and Catholic missions at Changpoo (p'u) had been destroyed on February 9 but that Americans had not been harmed.[8] There was also word from Peking of the removal of Dr. Tenney from his position as president of Tientsin University. Rumors spread that the Chinese government might also discharge E. B. Drew, the American commissioner of customs at Foochow.[9] The Presbyterian Church was said to be seriously considering withdrawing its 75 missionaries in China to the treaty ports.[10] Among the young Chinese who had received military training under the auspices of the Chinese Empire Reform Association and were returning to China was the nephew of editor Ng Poon Chew.[11] Experienced observers continued to predict greater trouble. Consul Martin in Hankow urged on February 8 that the United States have the strength to "compel with power ample protection."[12] At Chefoo, Consul John Fowler had become a prophet of doom. Bishop J. C. Hoare of Hong Kong characterized the situation in the south as more serious "than before the Boxer rising."[13] Dr. A. H. Smith was reported to have told a Congregational Church rally in the United States on February 15 that he expected tensions to mount.[14] Roosevelt could not take these admonitions lightly.

An especially ominous telegram in February was publicized by Wong Fong in Cincinnati: "I received word yesterday that the order has been sent out to the subordinate circles of the Chinese reform association to throw-off all the foreign elements in our country, starting February 24."[15] He urged his American friends in Los Angeles, San Francisco, and Seattle to cable their acquaintances in China "to seek protection of Germany temporarily," and "to get out of the country before February 24."[16] This man, formerly secretary of the Six Companies in San Francisco, sounded sincere and knowledgeable. His warning had to be taken seriously.

Although later events proved these alarms were groundless, the fears of Americans in both China and America were real and widespread in January and February. War between the United States and China was conceivable at that time. But then the tensions eased quickly. Representatives of eight foreign missions convened on February 17 at the headquarters of the Presbyterian Board and discussed the China problem at length with Dr. Arthur H. Smith, Dr. Hunter Corbett, and the Reverend H. W. Luce. They concluded that their missionaries were in no immediate danger and should remain at their posts.[17] Reassuring statements came from various quarters. On February 23, General William S. Shafter, Spanish-American War celebrity, discounted the prospects of an uprising,[18] and Washington released Rockhill's dispatch asserting that he saw no cause for alarm and that the Chinese government wished no harm to come to foreigners.[19] In Peking Wu T'ing-fang insisted that the boycott was not basically antiforeign; it was "retaliation" against "arbitrary discrimination."[20]

Roosevelt was slow to drop his guard, however, and remained ready for military action until April. He finally wrote Wood in the Philippines that he did not think there would be "any expedition to China."[21] Still, he remembered the Boxer experience. Up to 15,000 men would have been needed this time, he speculated. "It would be an act of utter folly," he wrote, "to underestimate our foes, who would beyond all comparison be more formidable than they showed themselves in 1900."[22] Thus, the records indicate that the president was primarily concerned with strengthening the American military position in China for the protection of American citizens there. At the same time, it must be added that Roosevelt was not averse to using military power to worry the Chinese government and induce it to give in to his terms. Indeed, some strong statements accompanied his military maneuvers between January and April. Roosevelt did not in this instance fully follow the script, "Speak softly and carry a big stick"; he carried the "big stick," but he also chose to speak loudly rather than softly.

Behind Roosevelt's tough diplomatic stance were two important assumptions. One was his conviction that the Chinese government was not seriously attempting to stamp out the boycott. The other was his belief that Peking had lied to him in July 1905 when it pretended officially to be opposed to the boycott while, at the same time, assuring the San Francisco Chinese that it approved of their activities. In a note from Root to the Chinese Legation on February 14, the secretary of state raised the question of this apparent double-dealing and asked for an explanation.[23]

The hard line of the administration became even sterner on February 21, when the State Department instructed Rockhill in Peking to demand that the former consul general at San Francisco deny publicly the authenticity of his July 1905 proclamation endorsing the boycott.[24] Proceeding next to open intimidation, Roosevelt on February 26 abruptly ordered Peking to terminate the boycott and other anti-American expressions. "Unlawful combinations," went the message to Rockhill, "in restraint of . . . free commerce . . . thrive unchecked."[25] The Chinese government, it noted menacingly, had seemed to forget the lessons of the Boxer Rebellion. The statement of February 26, sounding like an ultimatum, was delivered to Prince Ch'ing by Rockhill on March 1 in writing.[26] It elicited a prompt affirmative reply. On the four specific demands, Ch'ing largely capitulated; the government had no desire to allow a repetition of the Boxer disturbance since it might well destroy the dynasty. He also pledged firm action to suppress anti-foreign agitators. Although he hedged on the boycott issue, he nonetheless maintained that conditions were improving: "Nothing had ever disturbed these relations as had the ill-feeling aroused last year in connection with the negotiations looking to a new Immigration Treaty."[27]

Without delay Peking carried out its promise to act against the anti-foreign movement. On March 5, 1906, an imperial edict denounced anti-foreign rumors and stressed the wisdom of cooperating with the foreign powers. It lectured students on the needs for self-control and loyalty. The edict further directed officials to maintain order and protect foreigners. And it warned that if they failed they would be held accountable.[28] But as for the boycott, which Peking tried to separate from the anti-foreign issue, the Chinese insisted to Rockhill that earlier edicts had already dealt with that subject. Merchants had only been meeting to try to secure amendments to the exclusion treaty. Conditions in China were peaceful. The Foreign Office urged Rockhill to telegraph Roosevelt and "dispel his suspicions."[29] The Chinese government, while denying that Roosevelt had reason to be alarmed, went to even greater lengths to pacify him. In the Beattie case, for example, local authorities quickly tracked down the robbers and severely punished them. They also had a guard of thirty men stationed around Beattie's mission.[30] Then, after the furor over Beattie, Rockhill discovered with embarrassment that the missionary was a British subject.[31]

Other steps by Peking in March, April, and May demonstrated an anxious desire by Peking to appease the irate Roosevelt. When Rockhill complained on March 10 that anti-American placards were reappearing in Hankow, the Foreign Office at once sent out orders to local officials to stop the agitation.[32] In April, when news of the San Francisco earthquake reached Peking, the empress dowager donated 100,000 taels for general aid and 40,000 more for the specific relief of Chinese-Americans.[33] Another gesture of symbolic importance was the appointment by the Foreign Office of an American architect and engineer to design and build new quarters for the Foreign Office.[34] On April 28 Rockhill learned that in June Tenney would leave China with forty Chinese students to be placed in American schools at China's expense.[35] Wu, who had departed from the Foreign Office in November, was reported to have left Peking by June in a manner which suggested that the dynasty was displeased with him.[36] By June 1906 a dispute in Nanking involving Standard Oil was finally settled.[37] Such gestures represented a significant reversal of Chinese official policy of only a few months earlier, when Chinese students had been withdrawn from the University of California, when the government had found an excuse not to be represented at the annual meeting of the Association of Military Surgeons, and when Tenney had been forced to resign his post. Not all questions were resolved, however. The refusal of local officials to use the word *American* in stamping the deeds of property purchased by missionary societies remained an issue.[38]

And the recalcitrant viceroy at Canton retained his post. Nevertheless, by the summer of 1906 the Chinese government had gone far
toward appeasing the United States.

While Roosevelt was adopting a peremptory tone toward Peking, Rockhill expressed concern over the weakness of the Chinese
government and its growing unpopularity. The dispatches he sent
back in the spring of 1906 were intended to calm Roosevelt, who, he
feared, would go too far. "The country is quiet," he remarked on
March 8, "and there is no such thing as anti-foreign movements."[39] As
for the boycott, "the Government took stringent and prompt action
forbidding it from the first, and as a result the situation for some time
past has been quiet."[40] With satisfaction he reported on the quick action of the government in suppressing anti-American placards in
Hankow in April, in its early apprehension in the same month of bandits in the Beattie incident, and in the punishment of local officials
who had allowed rioting to occur at Nanchang. Whether Rockhill's
reporting in the early months of 1906 influenced Roosevelt is unclear.
Much of it was perceptive and accurate, but in his desire to discourage
the president from using military power, he gave an overly optimistic
view of the boycott. Nevertheless, his deliberately misleading reports
may have played a significant part in pacifying Roosevelt. In the
short run, at least, Roosevelt's determination to appear strong had
paid off. He had secured more official Chinese protection for American citizens in China and a further dampening down of the boycott.

To examine the military and diplomatic aspects of the Roosevelt
policies alone, however, is to miss at least half of his total program.
The two sides to his policy, as he had revealed it to Rockhill on August
22, 1905, were not to let the Chinese think the United States was
weak, and to do justice to the Chinese. We must "make it evident," he
wrote, "both that we intend to do what is right and that we do not intend for a moment to suffer what is wrong."[41] Although his conscience
appeared to be waiting for the propitious political moment, nonetheless, Roosevelt did much during the early months of 1906 to meet the
complaints and demands of the Chinese.

His basic position, as contained in his annual message to Congress in December 1905, was that congressional legislation should
make possible a friendly welcome to all Chinese except laborers. But
while he went to great pains to secure favorable action from Congress,
he was also maneuvering elsewhere. In January, for example, he was

planning an impressive reception for the Imperial Chinese Commission. This commission, of some importance in Chinese history, was traveling to various countries to study their governmental structures before recommending fundamental changes in the Chinese system. The president realized the significance of the event and sent Jenks to California to represent him. Plans for the welcome included the firing of a salute, a troop escort, and the decoration of war vessels. The commission was to be given "unusual honors," explained the *Chronicle*, "in an effort to impress the Chinese Government of the friendly attitude of the United States and to mitigate the boycott sentiment in China."[42] For a brief time the anti-Chinese element remained silent while banner headlines extended warm greetings, bands played, and friendly crowds gathered. Leaders in the Chinese community participated in the reception and banquet. Guests at the dinner on the night of January 13 included two generals, an admiral, and the chief justice of the State Supreme Court. The presidents of the University of California and of Stanford University were also present. Friedlander and Schwerin were prominent representatives of the business community. Even North, head of the immigration office in San Francisco, attended.

At the banquet most of the speakers emphasized the need for good relations between the two countries and for more trade. Judge W. H. Beatty saw the meeting as a "memorable event," likely to lead to more friendly ties and, most important, to "commercial amity."[43] University presidents Jordan and Wheeler stressed the richness of Chinese civilization and the value of mutual exchange. Naval Officer John P. Irish hoped for the day "when this country will achieve its true dignity by treating China on a basis of perfect equality with all the other nations of the earth."[44] The presence of approximately ninety San Francisco Chinese represented an unprecedented degree of recognition for that community. To editor Ng Poon Chew the meeting was a "red letter day" for the Chinese. Indeed, for a brief moment San Francisco seemed to undergo a miraculous change of heart.

The Imperial Commissioners were received warmly as they toured eastward, and were greeted cordially by the president on January 24 in the Blue Room of the White House. Here one of them addressed the president as "the staunchest friend of China" and heard him in turn speak of the common interests of the two countries "tending to mutual advantage."[45] Yet even as these warm exchanges took place, Roosevelt was seriously contemplating an attack on Canton, and in Peking a missionary — not a military expert, of course —

thought he detected unusual military activity by the Chinese.[46] As the commissioners continued on their way they were repeatedly told by churchmen and business groups of the determination of Americans to treat Chinese better. Richard Olney, former secretary of state for Cleveland, supporting Roosevelt's policy from the Democratic side, mentioned in a speech in Boston on February 12 the need for the president to protect American citizens and insisted that the president's statements to Congress favoring the better treatment of Chinese reflected the thinking of a majority of the American people.[47]

Still another conciliatory measure by Roosevelt at this time was the public announcement on February 5 of changes in immigration procedures agreed upon by Metcalf's commission. These changes included the termination of delays in landing and the use of the Bertillon system for Chinese immigrants. Roosevelt considered these reforms inadequate, and on February 24 appointed a new three-man commission to look into the operations of the bureau, "especially as regards its influence in connection with the Chinese boycott of American goods."[48] Made up of Ralph M. Easley of the National Civic Federation, Jenks, the Cornell economist, and James B. Reynolds, a social worker, this body did not give promise of doing any whitewashing. The new commission was authorized to get records, talk to employees, report to the president on its work, and keep its investigation entirely confidential.

In the early part of 1906 Roosevelt was also encouraging more liberal legislation through Perkins and the subcommittee of the House Foreign Affairs committee.[49] Root was speaking out as well. Chinese of high position, Root told leaders of the House of Representatives, had "been subjected to gross indignity and gross hardships in many cases, and I do not wonder they are indignant at it."[50] He stressed the need to admit all Chinese except laborers. Meanwhile, Roosevelt also tried to sell his program to labor leaders, but in vain.

An unusual opportunity for the president to allay the bitterness of the San Francisco Chinese occurred unexpectedly with the earthquake disaster of April 1906. Roosevelt, whose humanitarian instincts might have come to the fore anyway, was quick to take advantage of it. Chinatown had been wiped out, and the Chinese community, left destitute and homeless, was forced to take refuge in empty lots and parks. Even here looting and mistreatment followed the refugees and compounded their misery. In a note of special solicitude, Roosevelt wrote on April 23 to his secretary of war:

According to the newspaper reports the suffering and destruction are peculiarly great among the Chinese. I need hardly say that the Red Cross work must be done wholly without regard to persons and just as much for the Chinese as for any others. Please wire Dr. Devine at once to see that this is done. Would it not be well also to wire to General Funston to the same effect? I know nothing of the matter beyond what appears in the daily press.[51]

Taft took care of the suggestion immediately. An official response of gratitude to the president came in a few days from the Chinese consul general in New York, who praised Roosevelt for taking "it upon himself to see that everyone shared alike in the relief."[52] The Roosevelt administration also decided to allow supplies for the stricken Chinese to enter the country from China and Vancouver without payment of the normal duty charges.[53]

With Roosevelt setting the example, special attention was given to the plight of the Chinese as the work of rebuilding commenced. On May 22, when Minister Liang visited San Francisco, "he expressed himself," reported the *Chronicle*, "as well pleased with what has been done for his countrymen since the fire."[54] Taft commissioned the Army to help build a camp for Chinese refugees in Oakland. The refugees in turn, as an exchange of letters between Liang and the secretary of war show, became warmly attached to the major in charge.[55] Nevertheless, the recovery was slow and painful and hampered by local anti-Chinese prejudice. There was, of course, no money or extra energy to support the boycott, and the San Francisco Chinese ceased to be a significant factor in continuing the enterprise. Roosevelt's positive measures in this time of crisis may have counted too in disengaging the Chinese-Americans from further boycott efforts.

No such generalization applied to other overseas Chinese communities. The Hawaiian Chinese, until April 13 at least, were still eager to promote the boycott financially. Indeed, a significant exchange took place between Honolulu and Shanghai. Honolulu had $12,000 to give Shanghai for the boycott, but Shanghai answered that it needed no more money, that it had plenty on hand.[56] Thus Shanghai indicated its withdrawal from the movement — in any open, organized way at any rate.

Although Roosevelt made headway by a combination of threats and conciliatory moves, he faced a major obstacle in the uncompromising attitude of the Chinese students. No group had been more active or more hostile throughout the entire period of the boycott. Roosevelt and members of his administration were especially concerned over the prospect that the next generation of Chinese might be so bitter and alienated as to jeopardize future trade, missionary interests, and even diplomatic relations.

By June 1905 the president was already disturbed about the zealous involvement of students in the Canton area in the boycott.[57] He was also worried about the large number of students who had chosen to study in Japan. Rockhill's explanation that Japan was closer geographically and also less expensive failed to satisfy him.[58] In a letter on August 10 Jenks painted a dark picture of the growing defection of students: Japan was getting 3,000 Chinese students, while Germany, Belgium, and France had up to 500 apiece; only about 50 were then in the United States.[59] Something special must be done about this problem, he cautioned.

On January 3, 1906, Francis M. Huntington Wilson, chargé d'affaires in Japan, again reminded the administration of the growing appeal of Japan. He estimated that 5,000 students were in that country, 2,000 of them there at the expense of the Chinese government. The number had grown so large "as to promise to have some effect upon the relations of these two peoples."[60] The report was well designed to arouse the competitive instincts of the president. Other interested Americans with long memories could wonder what had gone wrong since the day in 1872 when China had chosen the United States, out of all the nations in the world, to educate its first group of students.

This decline in the number of Chinese students studying in America was not the only problem area; the possible withdrawal of Chinese students from American-operated schools in China was another. At that time over 20,000 students were enrolled in American schools and colleges in China. In 1905, 77 percent of the foreign teachers in China, based upon membership in the Educational Association of China, were Americans.[61] American educators in China held great hopes for the future. "We are ambitious," wrote the president of Canton Christian College and 32 other Americans to Roosevelt, "to see our country acting as head master."[62] In the current transitional period especially, they stressed, it was "desirable that we should cultivate the acquaintance and good-will of the students who are to be the moulders of the new China."[63] If Chinese students were to drop out of these institutions, as some boycott resolutions advocated, the impact would be disastrous in both the short and long run.

Educators like President Wisner of Canton Christian College

might cry: "The opportunity for Americans to lead China, education-ally, is unprecedented,"[64] yet many students were becoming anti-American. They were leaders in mass protest meetings, in preparing and distributing placards and resolutions against the exclusion policy, and in making a national hero of the young protester who had com-mitted suicide in Shanghai. American consuls in nearly every part of China — in such widely separated areas as Canton, Foochow, Shang-hai, Tientsin, and Hankow — reported on the leadership of students in the boycott. Students, wrote the head of the American Association of China at Shanghai, had "educational associations in nearly every important city, and they continue to meet and pass resolutions con-demnatory of our Government, and making excitable speeches in denunciation of nearly everything that the Americans have done."[65] Merchants would resume trading, the writer maintained, if only the students would allow them to do so. Some positive action by Roosevelt seemed to be needed. Students indicated their demands in a telegram sent by the Chinese Students Federation in October 1905 urging the enactment of general immigration laws in place of a law that specifi-cally discriminated against China.[66] But this request was something that Roosevelt would not have granted in all probability even if the power had been his. As this student antagonism continued to persist, there were, nevertheless, some developments cheering to the presi-dent. One was a flare-up over attempts by the Japanese government to regulate student affairs.[67] Angry students, leaving that country by the hundreds early in 1906, were so busy berating Japan that they temporarily forgot their grievances against the United States. In ad-dition, the anti-boycott imperial edict of March 5 admonished stu-dents to exercise more restraint and directed them "not to interfere with the foreign relations of the Government."[68]

Roosevelt was still pressed by educators and others, however, to formulate a specific program to win back the students. President Eliot of Harvard, for example, maintained that the boycott would come to an early end if scholarships at Harvard could be made avail-able to Chinese students.[69] President Edmund J. James of the Uni-versity of Illinois also proposed that Roosevelt organize an education-al commission to visit China and formally invite the Chinese govern-ment to send students to the United States.[70] Dr. A. H. Smith of the missionary community besought the president to adopt this or a simi-lar plan on the grounds that investing in young Chinese would yield "the largest possible return in moral, intellectual, and commercial in-fluence."[71]

In one way or another most of these schemes turned to the Boxer indemnity funds for financing. This was not a new idea; Rockhill had earlier discussed the notion with Hay.[72] Altogether, China was committed to pay the United States $24,440,778.81. Since the administration calculated that all claims could be settled at the lower figure of $13,655,492.69 and interest, a substantial amount remained either to be returned to China or to be used in some other way.[73] As was to be expected, this bonanza had a hypnotic appeal for some people. Influential individuals proposed a range of projects, such as establishing a gold reserve fund, investing in the economic development of China, and building a railroad in China.[74] One congressman, who opposed Rockhill about returning the money to China, advocated using the fund to build battleships.[75]

Within the administration, Jeremiah Jenks, formerly an educator, lobbied to retain the money for educational purposes. Since his plan contained a monetary feature, he could attract the endorsement of politicians and financiers as well as educators. In a letter to the president on August 10, 1905, he revealed that he had gained the support of Hugh Hanna, Charles Conant, A. D. White, and Albert Shaw.[76] In seeking an appointment with Root on October 2, he claimed that Senators Aldrich and Allison were also "very much interested."[77] Later he wrote Root that his project had the approval of the most astute bankers in China as well.[78] But Jenks and others were frustrated by changes in Roosevelt's attitude. At one time the president was inclined to favor simply returning the surplus monies to China; but when the boycott became effective, he abruptly reversed his position.[79] His negative attitude was especially evident in October 1905, when he instructed Jenks to draft a statement on China but to omit all references to returning any of the money.[80] At that time he was furious over both the boycott and the Chinese decision to cancel the Canton-Hankow railroad concession.[81]

Although various alternatives remained under consideration, the idea of using the funds so as somehow to recover the goodwill of Chinese students did not die. Indeed, new plans appeared from unexpected sources. A. W. Bash, for example, a railroad man who hoped to salvage something in the way of railroad business from China, consulted members of the faculty of the University of Washington in preparing a bill that provided for the expenditure of 20 million dollars of the indemnity to finance the educating of Chinese students in the United States. Senator Samuel H. Piles was reported in January 1906 to be ready to introduce this bill. Meanwhile, in Tacoma, Bash was on hand to welcome the Chinese commission on behalf of the president and secretary of state. Even the *Chronicle* endorsed the Bash plan in the hope that China would thereupon terminate the boycott.[82] But Roosevelt, although not hostile to the project, still hesitated.[83] While he marked time, the *Outlook* began pushing its own versions. On March 31, 1906, it proposed that, to allay Chinese resentment over past mistreatment, the United States use part of the indemnity funds for scholarships for Chinese students.[84] Repeating these views on June 2, it added that some of the money should also be used to promote western studies in China.[85]

While such recommendations were being discussed here, steps to restore the flow of students were also being taken in China, and in the summer of 1906 a group of forty Chinese students arrived under the escort of Dr. Tenney. These students, recruited and turned over to Tenney by Yuan, were scheduled to enter the Harvard Summer School.[86] Rockhill, greatly concerned that they be well received, gave advance notice of their coming.[87] With the distinguished and knowledgeable Dr. Tenney as supervisor and chaperon of the group, the prospect of embarrassing encounters with immigration officials was remote.

Not until 1908, however, about a year after a presidential recommendation, did the plans to assign some of the indemnity funds for educational purposes receive congressional approval. In the interim, further efforts were made to divert the money into other channels.[88] But Roosevelt was aware of continuing student enmity.[89] He was also unhappy with the renewed drift of Chinese students to Japan. His decision at long last to take positive action on this matter was eloquent testimony of the major role which students had played in the boycott movement and of the special importance the Roosevelt administration attached to regaining their favor. Although the fact that the money was eventually used to educate young Chinese has been interpreted by some historians as primarily a humanitarian gesture, the surrounding circumstances support Beale's inference and Michael Hunt's findings that self-interest was the principal motivating factor.[90]

When this measure to help Chinese students is added to Roosevelt's other actions, they add up to an intricate pattern, hidden behind a militant facade, of separating and appeasing the various groups and classes of Chinese who had joined the common effort to maintain the boycott. He offered something to the government, to anti-Manchu reformers and nationalists, to merchants, and to Chinese-Americans — as well as to students. The government, for example, could not overlook his support for the territorial integrity of China during the Russo-Japanese War and in the peace settlement. Reformers and nationalists found the United States a place of refuge; furthermore, one of their leading spokesmen, K'ang Yu-wei, had been received at the White House courteously. Merchants knew that Roosevelt had issued orders to immigration officials to extend polite treatment to Chinese at the ports of entry. And Chinese-Americans now found that immigration agents were leaving them alone. However, the remedial steps which Roosevelt took still fell far short of eliminating discrimination against Chinese, and the treaty question remained an important piece of unfinished business.

13
The Treaty Problem:
Striking a New Balance

The realization that domestic legislation by the United States would permanently replace the treaty relationship on immigration which had been in effect from 1868 to 1904 was not altogether apparent to either side at the end of 1906. Nor was the changeover a simple and easy process as it unfolded. But even as treaty negotiations continued, disengagement gradually took place. The General Deficiency Appropriation Act of April 29, 1904, which had severed domestic legislation from treaty obligations, and confirmed and added to the exclusion policy, was the major step taken in the new direction. When the treaty of 1894 ended on December 7, 1904, the State Department, temporarily at a loss on how to react, sent instructions to consular officers on April 15, 1905, to use section 6 of the 1884 law and pretend that the policy, now based upon domestic legislation exclusively, was continuing under an "amended treaty."[1]

From the Chinese standpoint the termination of the 1894 treaty had resurrected the Burlingame treaty of 1868, resulting in a court case concerning the Chinese interpretation. In a circuit court of appeals in Cincinnati on January 9, 1906, the federal court ruled in the *Hong Wing* case that the 1904 law was constitutional and that Hong Wing and six other Chinese were subject to deportation.[2] In addition to losing out on the key issue by this decision, the Chinese government lost its right to claim damages stemming from the deportation of Chinese in violation of the Burlingame treaty. The decision rendered meaningless, therefore, the efforts of the Chinese Legation since April 1905 to assemble a record of such claims.[3] Nevertheless, on January 12, 1906, the Chinese Legation insisted that it would not abandon its plans but would take its case to the International Court to press for compensation which now amounted to one million dollars. At the same time, however, the Legation, by ending its statement with the observation that it would not take further action until it could ascertain the trend in Congress on exclusion, showed it was mainly intent on influencing legislators.[4] The realities of the situation left the Chinese little recourse but to acquiesce in the American immigration policy which by then was based exclusively upon domestic legislation.

To be sure, a new and more liberal treaty was still theoretically possible, but the course of negotiations over the months and years from 1904 to 1906 did not offer much encouragement. For the Chinese a new treaty was pointless unless they could secure one that excluded only laborers, but the Department of Commerce and Labor continued to insist on one that either expanded exclusion or at least confirmed the status quo in terms of the legislation of 1902 and 1904. Compromise between two such divergent viewpoints was impossible. Nevertheless, negotiations dragged on into the summer of 1906, after Congress adjourned without acting.

Before tracing the course of treaty negotiations in 1906 to their indecisive close, the chronological steps which preceded them are as follows. On December 10, 1901, Wu had sent a note to Hay requesting treaty revision. Two years went by. On January 24, 1904, Conger in Peking cabled the State Department that China had formally notified him that it wished to terminate the treaty on December 7 of that same year; after that, in spite of the urging of Hay to continue the existing treaty, China held to its position. On April 29, 1904, before the expiration date of the treaty, Congress eliminated the treaty stipulations from the exclusion legislation and extended the law indefinitely. In Washington, on August 12, 1904, Chinese minister Liang submitted the draft of a new treaty which requested better treatment of Chinese-Americans and of Chinese of the privileged classes visiting the United States. Although the State Department was willing to accept most of the Chinese draft, it found the Department of Commerce and Labor adamantly opposed. Eventually it bowed to the wishes of that department and submitted to the Chinese Legation on November 29, 1904, a Commerce and Labor draft, which upheld the old restrictions and added new ones. A few days later, on December 7, 1904, the treaty of 1894 ended. Thus, domestic legislation of April 29 and earlier became the sole basis for the existing regulations.

After the expiration of the old treaty, Liang, on January 7, 1905, rejected the United States draft and submitted a second, more militant draft emphasizing reciprocity of treatment for the nationals of each country. Since the Department of Commerce and Labor would not consider making substantial concessions, the negotiations remained stalled until May, when Rockhill arrived in Peking to carry on negotiations there — to his dismay, in the middle of the boycott agitation.

In Peking, with the boycott still pending, Rockhill worked anxiously from June to August to reach a settlement. Although lacking "full powers" to negotiate a treaty, on June 22 he presented the American position on the Chinese draft of January 7, 1905. On July 1 Peking transmitted to Rockhill a new Chinese draft, which incorporated the principle of the reciprocal prohibiting of laborers. Rockhill returned an American draft to the *Wai-wu Pu* on July 8; the Chinese responded with a counterdraft on July 19. Rockhill replied with a new counterdraft on July 25, and Peking answered with another version on July 31. On August 2 Rockhill rejected the last Chinese proposal; but, on August 7, China again urged the acceptance of its earlier proposals which included admitting non-laborers, reciprocity on the question of admitting laborers, and allowing free Chinese immigration into Hawaii and the Philippines. In Rockhill's view a compromise was possible in a formula which defined the term *laborer* and allowed other Chinese to enter the United States, but the veto power of the Department of Commerce and Labor remained unchanged. Since the boycott had gone into effect on July 20, Rockhill suspended negotiations on August 14 on the grounds that attempts were being made to intimidate him. He charged the Chinese government with official approval of the boycott, and threatened to institute damage suits under the treaty of 1858. He also refused to resume treaty discussions until the boycott came to an end.

After Peking issued its edict on August 31, 1905, advising officials to terminate all boycott agitation, it pressed Rockhill to renew treaty discussions; but the American minister failed to obtain further authorization from the State Department, even though he invited it and solicited a clarification of his official status as negotiator. On September 2, 1905, A. A. Adee of the State Department sent to Metcalf the dispatch from Rockhill of July 28 "showing the situation of the question."[5] This was the dispatch which referred to article 4 of the Department of Commerce and Labor draft as the major stumbling block.[6] Metcalf, however, would not yield to this plan to return to a class-based policy.

On various levels, Chinese and Americans still got together to exchange views and to try to find an acceptable formula. One set of exchanges occurred in Shanghai between Rodgers and the boycott leader, Tseng Shao-ch'ing. Conferences also took place at both Shanghai and Hong Kong when Taft was visiting China. Indeed, from the Taft trip a news report was circulated in Washington on October 28 of a new treaty that would be ready to go to the Senate before Christmas. Based on Taft's conference with the Chinese merchants, the Roosevelt administration would introduce four modifications in the new treaty: a definition of *laborer* which would also admit clerks and salesmen; examinations in China to be accepted at the American ports of entry as final; no bar to section 6 (exempt class) Chinese from Hong Kong, Tonkin, and Singapore; and the end of detention sheds.[7] Once again nothing developed.

Official negotiations marked time as Roosevelt urged Congress in December 1905 to enact new legislation that would limit exclusion to skilled and unskilled laborers. Earlier, on October 1, Hang Shen-Hsiu and 1,241 merchants throughout China had notified Rockhill that they were declaring a truce in the boycott to give Congress time to enact legislation which would facilitate the conclusion of a new treaty. If Congress did not respond favorably during this truce period, Rockhill feared a renewal of the boycott. In fact, no truce was ever recognized in the Canton area, where a conciliatory Chinese element, in touch with American businessmen, in December made known without success its own terms for ending the boycott.[8]

By February 27, 1906, Hang had decided that Congress was not going to do anything. In an open letter in the *Peking and Tientsin Times*, he drew attention to the failure of Congress to go forward and revealed that Tseng, still head of the boycott association (*Wen-ming Chu Yueh She*, "Civilized Anti-exclusion Treaty Society"), had urged him to send to the Foreign Office petitions instructing Liang in Washington not to sign the new treaty.[9] Further information contained in his letter in the *Times* and one in *Chung Hua Pao* indicated that much probing of treaty issues had been going on in Washington.

Even if Congress had responded favorably to the president's recommendations, both the new nationalistic spirit in China and economic self-interest threatened to stand in the way of a fresh treaty settlement. Since October 1905, the Chinese Students Federation had demanded that Chinese be treated like all other immigrants. In addition, both Shanghai and Canton boycott leaders had made clear their desire to have at least some laborers admitted to the United States or into the Philippines and Hawaii. Within the United States, Chinese-Americans also hoped to loosen the restrictions on laborers. Representing the New York Chinese, for example, Attorney Max J. Kohler suggested that the new treaty admit skilled laborers. Such an inference could be drawn also from his statement in the *Tribune* "that a new treaty excluding only 'manual laborers' is demanded, not merely by public policy, but by law treaty faith and the immutable principles of justice and right."[10]

In contrast to Peking's eagerness in September 1905 to resume treaty negotiations, by February 1906 it was noticeably reluctant. Indications of this change in attitude were evident in an exchange of views between Rockhill and T'ang Shao-yi, the new American-educated under secretary in the Foreign Office. When they met on February 27, 1906, T'ang, a close associate of Yuan Shih-k'ai, informed Rockhill that he did not want to "patch up" the treaty of 1894 and that China wanted nothing which, in Rockhill's words, "did not give satisfaction to the people of China."[11] He further suggested that treaty discussions wait for expressions of American public opinion. Rockhill took T'ang's remarks to imply that China believed that all laborers should not be excluded. He parried with the statement that treaty questions should not be difficult to resolve, "as there was absolutely no discussion between them about the coming of laborers to the United States, which his Government [China] had not raised."[12]

When Rockhill's dispatch was received in Washington, Denby rightly foresaw more trouble ahead for the negotiations. T'ang, he wrote Root on April 2, was "notably resentful of America's attitude to the Chinese. He is a great friend of the Chinese Minister in Washington. His voice will be almost conclusive as to foreign affairs and it is to be noted that he is not in favor of a treaty."[13]

Since every treaty after the Burlingame treaty had produced further restrictions for Chinese-Americans and had been accompanied by arrests, deportations, or refusals to be readmitted, their attitude was bound to be negative. In February 1906 the "Chinese General Society for the Opposing of the New Treaty" of San Francisco had cash on hand amounting to $15,869.75.[14] With financial support going to an organization with such a name, the mood among Chinese-Americans, as with the government of China, appeared unfavorable for negotiating a new treaty. Nor did the adjournment of Congress, which had not made even a symbolic gesture in the direction of salving Chinese feelings, offer encouragement.

Liang and Root both realized that, without new legislation by Congress, the stalled treaty negotiations were doomed. All that remained was to find some formula for quietly dropping the matter. By

June 1906 the entire question had shifted its location from Peking to Washington, where Root now raised the subject. Since Congress had not taken further steps, Root remarked to Liang on June 11, treaty negotiations might appropriately be resumed. Liang replied without enthusiasm that he understood that Rockhill was working on the matter in Peking and that China would prefer legislation to a treaty. Undaunted, Root suggested a treaty along the lines of the Denby bill that would exclude laborers, retain the exempt classes but with more liberal interpretations, and station immigration officials from the United States at the main ports of China to examine and approve the credentials of departing Chinese. These provisions might be all right, responded Liang, if they could similarly be applied to Americans who traveled to China. No, replied Root, conditions were too different to permit that.[15]

Liang did not close the door entirely to further negotiations. His views expressed on June 11, he explained a few days later, were not the official policy of his government. What would be likely to appeal to his government was a reciprocity treaty which "might remove the odium of discrimination so objectionable in previous treaties."[16] Since Liang was planning a trip to Latin America and would be away during the summer months, he suggested that further treaty discussions be postponed until October. There the matter rested. In October 1906 Liang prepared a lengthy statement on the boycott as a reply to charges in February and May that the Chinese government had pretended to oppose the boycott while officially but quietly supporting it. In his answer he also disclosed the official position on the treaty. From the time that China had received the Bureau of Immigration draft of November 29, 1904, he had doubted the value of any further negotiations. His government's "experience with the previous immigration treaties" had "led it to fear that a new treaty would share the fate of the others at the hands of Congress, and it felt that its dignity would be better preserved by trusting to the sense of justice of your president and the voluntary action of your Congress."[17]

In place of encouraging further treaty discussions, Liang proposed taking measures like those outlined in the president's message: "If the Congress shall put his recommendations into the form of laws, and the Bureau of Immigration shall carry them out in the spirit of the Executive Order of June, 1905, the immigration question will be permanently settled, and an end be put to the troubles which have vexed the two Governments for a generation."[18] The Chinese government, it was clear, could not afford to accede to any treaty containing discriminatory features. American domestic legislation would have to assume the full responsibility. As it turned out, neither treaty nor legislative action resolved the impasse between the two countries. A third route — that of administrative reforms instigated by Roosevelt — served as a stopgap answer.

By the end of 1906, Roosevelt had effected changes relating to Chinese policy in personnel, administrative structure, and regulations. In some instances Chinese affairs were intermixed with Japanese relations and other questions, such as the general need for consular reform; however, the Chinese problem led to several reforms and contributed some of the motivation for others.

The most important personnel change made by Roosevelt was the shift of Metcalf from the Department of Commerce and Labor to the Navy Department. Roosevelt for some time had allowed Metcalf and Sargent to challenge his official position on exclusion and boycott matters. Indeed, Liang could and did taunt the president with these contradictions in his administration, duly noting that Sargent's testimony at the House Committee hearings in 1906 was "in marked contrast with the position of the president," and Metcalf's conduct was "even more serious." Why should Congress, he wondered, follow the president's recommendations, "while the head of the department having charge of the execution of the laws in question and his subordinates are telling the Congress that such measures are not required and would be hurtful to the interests of the United States"?[19]

Roosevelt did not have to be told of the disloyalty of Metcalf and Sargent; this was an old story. The question was what to do about the dilemma. He had carried on an ardent political courtship with California for too long to risk losing that state to the Democratic party now. Yet Metcalf was becoming more of a liability. Not only did he stand in the way of a reconciliation with the Chinese; the uproar in Japan over the school segregation of Orientals in San Francisco was another reason for obtaining a man less obviously prejudiced against Orientals. After a long hesitation, Roosevelt at last mustered up the courage to break the California-labor grip on the department. The switch came in October 1906. Because of a resignation, Charles Bonapart would leave the Navy Department to become the new attorney general, and Metcalf would become the new secretary of the navy. Metcalf had his choice of posts, explained the *New York Daily Tribune* tactfully, but he had decided that he would find the Navy Department "even more congenial than the Department of Commerce and Labor."[20] No transition could have been smoother, and Roosevelt retained his California following. At the same time the pro-Chinese had scored a major victory.

For the post of secretary of commerce and labor, Roosevelt selected a person who stood in striking contrast to his predecessor. Oscar Straus, immigrant from Germany, lawyer, businessman, diplomat, and the "first Hebrew" to hold a Cabinet post, was a man, suggested the *Tribune,* whose "sympathies may be relied upon to add to his efficient handling of the many difficult problems presented."[21] He assumed his office on December 12, 1906. The Chinese question was never given by Roosevelt as a reason for his selection. Straus said the matter of his appointment had been raised many months earlier. After a luncheon at the White House in January 1906, Roosevelt had asked Straus to wait in the Red Room; there he had told Straus that he wanted him in his Cabinet. Among other reasons, Roosevelt said, he wanted "to show Russia and some other countries what we think of the Jews in this country."[22] The Department of Commerce and Labor post was the one specifically mentioned, but Roosevelt spoke of not being sure until later which spot would be open. It was rumored that Jacob Schiff, the financier who had extensive interests in Japan as well as elsewhere, had suggested Straus to Roosevelt.[23]

From the outset Straus took a special interest in the explosive Japanese issue and did what he could to improve relations with that country. "I was especially gratified," he wrote the president on December 5, 1906, in a warm letter of praise for the president's annual message to Congress, "with the firm position you took on the Japanese matter."[24] The comment referred to Roosevelt's objections to interference by California in international affairs. The Japanese diplomat S. Uchida wrote Straus of his delight at Japan's having "such an influential friend in your national government."[25]

Similarly, Straus hoped to regain the goodwill of China. His ties were with the pro-Japanese and pro-Chinese easterners — with the humanitarian rabbi Simon Wolf, with the attorney for the New York Chinese, Max J. Kohler, and with the Asian-trade-minded Foord. No personal prejudice or political bonds were likely to turn Straus into an exclusionist.[26] "Happily, the gentleman to succeeed Secretary Metcalf," commented the *New York Journal of Commerce and Commercial Bulletin,* "will not bring . . . any of the limitations of a politician trained to regard the sentiments of the Pacific Coast as more important than the rest of the country."[27] He would also, it maintained, reduce the influence of the labor unions in the Bureau of Immigration. Straus, in his first annual report, enthusiastically endorsed the president's recommendation that all Chinese except laborers should be admitted.[28]

The findings of the Easley-Jenks-Reynolds commission, which had been activated by Roosevelt on February 24, 1906, were useful aids to Straus in effecting administrative reforms. Within certain limits the commission had done a thorough job. Its principal limitation had been its habit of conferring almost exclusively with educated Chinese and with well-to-do merchants, and thus it absorbed and presented the point of view of the upper-class Chinese. In his investigations James B. Reynolds had uncovered instances of fraud and bribery by immigration officials. One Chinese merchant, for example, could not get his son back into the country in 1906 without paying a bribe of $100. "Similar instances," related Reynolds later, "were told me by Chinese merchants and officials as well as by American missionaries."[29]

Straus began to remove dishonest persons from office; he also took an interest in upgrading the qualifications of interpreters. But the main outcome of the commission's report was a set of new regulations for the bureau, issued on February 26, 1907, under the signature of Sargent, and described as amendments to those released by Metcalf on February 5, 1906. Most notable in the new Straus-Sargent regulations was a liberalized definition of *student.* Young Chinese were no longer confined to university study but might enter the United States to attend elementary or preparatory schools. No longer was there a stipulation that a youth could only study what was not available in China. Furthermore, by inference, the student could remain in the United States after completing his education if he did not become a laborer.[30] Other new rules facilitated the travel of Chinese-Americans to and from China and provided travel privileges for the exempt classes of Chinese to and from the insular possessions and across the United States in transit. That Sargent remained the principal official in charge of administering the new rules should, however, not be overlooked entirely.[31]

In addition to these changes in the Department of Commerce and Labor, concurrent reforms in the consular system within the Department of State were also certain to help Chinese travelers to America. The consular reforms were long overdue; in China the evils connected with the spoils system had been especially evident. American consuls in China, wrote A. H. Smith, a bitter critic, were "the butt of every jest on the subject of the white man's so-called superiority over the Chinamen in the matter of 'squeeze.' " Knowing that they only had four to eight years in their posts, they took for granted "that any 'plunder' . . . to be made, should be promptly pocketed."[32] Their vulnerability had long supplied the Immigration Bureau with an excuse for conducting its own independent examinations at the ports of entry — a practice that was a major Chinese grievance. On July 27, 1906, Roosevelt initiated the reform program by placing the consular service under the Civil Service. The State Department then worked out rigorous examinations which candidates must pass.[33] On August 5 Congress raised salaries and allowed increases according to the new grading. Once the new program got underway immigration officials at American ports could not so easily challenge the papers of arriving Chinese.

Another significant change, the shift by China to a passport system, eventually came out of suggestions by Rockhill. When various local officials issued travel certificates, he informed Washington on August 15, 1905, the opportunities for fraud were great. He thought he could not possibly carry out the June 1905 mandate to check all Chinese applicants carefully before approving their requests to travel to the United States. If the Foreign Office alone issued travel permits, however, responsibility would at least be centralized and might allow the verifications by American authorities in China to be more systematic.[34] On February 28, 1906, during a discussion of treaty differences with the Chinese Foreign Office, Rockhill formally pressed China to switch to a regular passport system and urged the minister of Foreign Affairs to issue such credentials, "as a first step on the part of China."[35] Rockhill received encouragement from the State Department on April 27 when prospects for a future treaty had become dim.[36] Although conditions remained unchanged through 1906, China had little recourse but to move in that direction eventually.

By the end of 1906, even without the passport innovation, the administrative revisions effected on the American side were substantial. The reforms were manifested in China in the more efficient and professional reception accorded applicants for visas by a reformed consular service. In the United States the atmosphere had also become much improved. As a result of the Metcalf commission's recommendations of February 5, 1906, the despised Bertillon system had been abandoned, and delays in processing entering Chinese had been reduced. New federal facilities at San Francisco were replacing the detention shed of the Pacific Mail Steamship Company, and special privileges were being extended to upper-class Chinese in the new quarters. In 1907 further legal safeguards for entering Chinese were provided under Straus, and a more liberal classification of merchants, travelers in transit, and students was made. Tangible evidence of the new spirit was obvious in that the number of certificates rejected in 1906 was down to 6 percent, in contrast with 29 percent in 1905.[37]

Changes were also visible in the official treatment of Chinese-Americans. Efforts had been abandoned to force them out of the country. Domiciliary visitations by immigration officials were discontinued, and arrests and deportations of Chinese within the United States for illegal entry became rare. Regulations for leaving and returning to the United States were simplified; in addition, Chinese-Americans were assured of being readmitted into the United States. Although local prejudices might still lead to harassment, federal immigration authorities were learning that xenophobia and conscientious law enforcement were not synonymous.

In effect then, much of the Powderly policy, with the additions by Sargent, was terminated by presidential action in response to pressures emanating from the boycott. But administrative reforms were one thing; the exclusion principle was something else. The exclusion laws of 1902 and 1904 remained unchanged, and the failure of Congress to act in 1906 signified a continuation of those parts of Powderly's policy already sanctified by court decisions and precedents. Thus, the exclusion policy, as it had developed to 1905, continued after 1906 to be the cornerstone of American policy toward China. Although still eager to have the trade and goodwill of that country, Americans considered them less important. The lack of success in treaty negotiations was added confirmation of this point.

By the spring of 1906 fence mending had become the order of the day. It happened on both sides and on both official and unofficial levels. Gradually, a delicate balance was achieved. Since exclusion had been a constantly changing phenomenon, the balance had to be new and different. Although no specific end to the boycott was discernible, the Chinese government took vigorous measures after March 1, 1906, to suppress boycott agitation and to quell all anti-foreign disturbances. Rockhill, too, ceased to make complaints in Peking, and after June 1 Washington also seemed ready to drop claims for damages and demands for the punishment of officials. With the overt stage of the boycott at an end, both sides could pretend that it no longer existed in fact.[38]

Trade figures, however, told another story in 1906 and subsequently. In November 1906 the American Asiatic Association *Journal* printed the association's annual presidential address which disclosed that trade with China had been disappointing in the previous six months. The president, ignoring the boycott, intimated that perhaps the cause was overly high expectations of increased trade in Manchuria with the return of peace. Secretary Foord was franker to admit that the boycott might also be a factor but thought that the causes were "probably of a less sentimental origin."[39] For its own reasons the American Asiatic Association seemed resolved to depreciate the effects of the boycott and pretend that it no longer existed. From the vantage point of two years later, however, Straus wrote that, although the boycott might not have entirely accounted for a sharp drop in exports, the reduction "of fifty percent in two years is sufficiently startling to challenge attention."[40]

That businessmen had sustained some kind of setback in China was certain. James J. Hill, the railroad magnate, took an exaggerated view of the loss in terming the boycott "the greatest commercial disaster America has ever suffered." The European countries, he declared, had "practically monopolized the trade."[41] In the *United States Investor*, one writer soberly concluded that the China market depended on modifying the exclusion policy, but that priority would have to be given to American institutions. Businessmen, it therefore advised, would need to shift from the Chinese market to others.[42] While some businessmen appeared to be resigned to withdrawing altogether, the American Asiatic Association segment hoped to survive, and perhaps eventually recover from, the boycott by continuing its past practice of espousing the Chinese position on exclusion. "At the date of adjournment of Congress," reported Foord in the November 1906 issue of the *Journal*, "the sub-commitee was ready to report a bill, but the presentation of the report was delayed until the opening of the next session. At that time, the work of active agitation in favor of the passage of the Foster bill will be resumed."[43]

To recover lost ground, the hardheaded American merchants in Canton met with Chinese merchants and boycott representatives and agreed to work for the enactment of the terms set in December 1905 to ameliorate exclusion.[44] Businessmen were encouraged because knowledgeable Chinese were inclined to blame the policy on labor unions and to exonerate American merchants. While businessmen had to give up their dreams of a Chinese Eldorado, they found that they could continue to trade within modest limits circumscribed psychologically by the exclusion policy. Nevertheless, "there should be no illusions," adjudged the American Asiatic Association *Journal*, "about the consequences of . . . refusing to modify our Chinese Exclusion Acts."[45]

For the American churches the boycott period had also been a time of anxiety and crisis. The placards that proposed mob action on Sundays, when Christians were attending church services, "to tear down the chapels, and kill the Christians,"[46] were indeed unsettling. The Lienchow massacre of October 28, 1905, had been a time of severe testing. Indeed, it had started missionaries in South China moving toward the treaty ports. A few more such incidents might have precipitated the entire withdrawal of missionary personnel from the hinterland. In February 1906 alarmed church leaders met in New York but decided to keep their missionaries at their posts, while recognizing the "gravity of the present situation";[47] whether missionaries were making any converts under the circumstances was questionable. Within a year, reported one missionary who had traveled in China a great deal, Americans instead of being the best liked of foreigners had become the "best hated."[48] If the plans for a national church, projected in Shanghai in March 1906, should ever reach fruition, such a church, since it envisioned the elimination of foreign missionaries from China, would represent a threat to the missionary interest.[49]

Churchmen, even though sometimes asking for military protection, for the most part accepted and promoted the goals of the boycott leaders. Through petitions to congressional committees, forthright statements at the immigration conference of December 6-8, 1905, resolutions by missionary bodies, and testimony at congressional hearings, those Protestant churches with missions in China came to the front of the movement to secure better terms for Chinese immigrants. Moreover, the significance of their activities can be better judged when it is remembered that churchmen at that time normally avoided political involvement.[50] Churchmen were greatly relieved to discover by the end of 1906 that their worst fears had not been realized. Anti-American sentiment, while intense in some sections, was not universal. Robert R. Gailey, general secretary of the YMCA in Tientsin, for example, commented that Chinese had assured him personally that the boycott was a technique to accomplish an end and not an indication of hostility toward him or the United States.[51] With the decline of anti-missionary incidents, church leaders forgot about their earlier anxieties. Nevertheless, there was no reason to believe that the exclusion policy would soon cease to be a handicap for missionaries.

American educational institutions in China, whose fortunes

were intertwined with those of the missionaries but yet had separate interests, had also watched with foreboding the rise of the exclusion crisis. Claiming to comprise over 1,000 American schools and colleges, including the only women's colleges in China, and 12 of the 14 foreign colleges, American teachers and educators realized early the need for warding off the impending confrontation. Through the Educational Association of China, they voiced their concern to Roosevelt, and they helped students at Canton Christian College and Anglo-Chinese College in Foochow to draw up statements of protest to be sent to the president.

Since the original boycott plans had embraced the withdrawal of Chinese students and teachers from American schools, educators in China had special reason for alarm. Mass meetings and circulars appeared early in the colleges. Eight seniors left one college, and all of the seniors in one high school boycotted classes.[52] In some instances, Smith revealed, American mission schools had been badly disrupted.[53] American schoolmen were also worried that Japanese instructors and schools might displace Americans.

Yet the damage proved to be less than irreparable. Students placed a high value on their educational opportunity and, furthermore, they found the American educators sympathetic and cooperative. Less painful for students than leaving school was venting their wrath on American trade and forcing Chinese merchants to bear the brunt of the effort. And this students certainly did. The complaints of consuls and of Rockhill, and the warnings to students in the imperial edict of March 5, 1906, bore galling testimony to the effectiveness of their protests. Nevertheless, the fact that students chose to register their complaints in such a manner as not to disrupt their own schools was also significant. In 1905 more students than ever before were enrolled in Christian colleges, and at Canton Christian College construction went ahead, looking toward a time when the school would have 2,000 students and 60 acres;[54] at Anglo-Chinese College Bishop Bashford held a revival in which nearly all of the 300 students who were not already Christian said that they would become so. That a permanent loss of prestige for American education occurred, though difficult to assess in specific terms, is evident. The loss was dramatically symbolized by the forced resignation of Tenney as president of Tientsin University. American educational institutions, it seemed, could remain in China, but American leadership in education would thereafter be curtailed. As with trade and missionary activities, once again exclusion had set psychological limits, this time in the cultural realm, on American influence in China.

In the meantime, the AFL stood guard against any shifting of ground on Chinese exclusion by Congress. Exclusion early in 1907 became entangled with the question of the use of Chinese labor on the Panama Canal; but the plan to use the Chinese was abandoned, the AFL claimed, largely because of the "effort and energy" of Gompers.[55] The Japanese and Korean Exclusion League, required in 1905 and 1906 to engage in defensive action on the issue, defined its primary task thereafter as upholding Chinese exclusion "by its extension to Japanese and Korean immigrants."[56]

On the Chinese side, although the boycott leaders had failed to attain their principal goal of the elimination of discriminatory treatment, they had scored some gains on the American scene. The main features of the new settlement were threefold: 1) no more immigration would be allowed except on a temporary basis; but 2) visitors would receive courteous treatment; and 3) by implication, no further attempts would be made to force the departure of the existing Chinese-American minority.

If the exclusion-boycott issue were viewed briefly within the restrictionist context, an observer might suggest that the United States, without giving up its exclusion policy, had alternatives by which it might have settled the boycott earlier or have avoided it altogether. Not until the Powderly era had Chinese national sensibilities been severely aroused. A return to the 1898 posture then, when two to four thousand Chinese per year were admitted, offered one possible compromise. Another alternative was to have a literacy test, deliberately constructed in such a way as to bar Chinese. This idea emerged periodically from various sources. In August 1905, for example, Wu had seriously advocated it.[57] At that time the *New York Times* endorsed the same principle.[58] In effect, many Chinese were willing to accept almost any compromise that would avoid the overt racial-nationalistic discriminatory features of the prevailing policy. But the exclusionists adamantly defined the issue in black and white terms and insisted that the United States pay a needlessly high price to preserve the status quo.

Thus, the United States entered the 1900s with two policies, which were still continuing, though with some difficulty, in 1906. "We talk," wrote a former consul in 1906, "of maintaining the 'Open Door' . . . in China; it seems never to have occurred to our serene and self-satisfied souls that we have closed our own door to China and Chinamen."[59] But he was wrong. Many Americans fully realized the contradiction, and they deliberately made their choice. The trouble with China could be resolved, American businessmen told Taft in Hong

Kong, by repealing the exclusion act, but "we appreciate that this cannot be done."[60] To the *Chronicle*, "The weakening of the barriers erected against the admission of Chinese coolies for the defense of American labor and industries would be too great a price for all the trade we possess or may hope to acquire with China."[61]

Americans, not necessarily the same ones, chose to keep both policies, whether they were consistent or not. The open door policy in later years played a prominent part in the Taft administration, the Wilson administration, and in the 1920s and 1930s. As for the exclusion policy, after nearly two decades without change, in 1921 and 1924 Congress took further restrictive measures against the Chinese at the same time as it extended the policy to include other Orientals.[62] Exclusion, for all practical purposes, remained just as tight until, in 1943, as a wartime measure designed to boost the prestige of the Chinese government, China was allowed by the quota system 105 immigrants per year.[63] Not until 1965, in an era when the open door policy had lost all meaning, did a significant relaxation of the exclusion policy emerge in a new immigration law.[64]

14
Conclusion: The Continuing Problem of Policy Contradictions

"I have an impression," wrote Wu T'ing-fang, who believed in reincarnation, "that in one of my former existences I was born and brought up in the United States." But as for the exclusionist Occidentals, he hoped that they "in their next life . . . may be born in Asia or Africa, and that the injury that they are now inflicting on the yellow people they may themselves have to suffer in another life."[1] His remarks, contained in a book written in 1914, were a reminder that the exclusion policy remained for many years an omnipresent irritant in relations between the United States and China. The negative implications for the open door policy continued also.

Why was the "shotgun marriage" between these two contradictory policies allowed to take place at all? For one thing, the implicit inconsistency was not entirely obvious. The two policies appeared at different time periods and under different sponsorship; furthermore, on the surface they seemed to have no connection with each other. Congress gave birth to the exclusion policy; the executive branch formulated the open door policy. Second, in both cases China's reactions were not of prime importance to American policymakers. When the exclusion policy came to the fore, the main concern was such domestic factors as California's hysteria over the influx of Chinese to work for low wages. By contrast, when the open door policy was announced, the international balance of power — not domestic issues — was the major problem. At that moment the McKinley administration was trying to preserve the American position in China against the encroachment of world powers who were consolidating their spheres of interest. On both occasions China's feelings were of secondary importance; in both instances the American assumption was that China would be cooperative, especially if a paternalistic facade could be maintained. And with the open door policy the United States had hit upon a brilliant formula. It could pose as the savior of China while advancing its own economic and cultural interests. But here was the rub. China refused to cooperate or even to remain passive. Although the American stand was in favor of preserving China's territorial integrity, China still objected strenuously to the discriminatory nature of the exclusion policy and demanded at least some modification of that policy in return for trading privileges. Minister Wu and his successor, Liang Ch'eng, made clear that the United States would have to choose between trade and exclusion.

The open door policy, supported by influential names in industry and finance, and by churchmen, university heads, and statesmen, seemed capable of sweeping away major as well as minor obstacles. Dramatically presented and broadly gauged, the new slogan captured the imagination of statesman and common man alike. Scholars also focused much attention upon it.[2] The open door should have easily triumphed over the older exclusion policy, which was narrow and negative. But it failed to do so. On three separate legislative issues from 1900 to 1906, the forces behind the open door clashed with the defenders of exclusion and suffered defeat every time. The three cases in point were: the exclusion act of 1902, the exclusion act of 1904, and the abortive Foster bill of 1906. A brief review of these is enlightening.

The exclusion act of 1902, often regarded as a minor revision of earlier legislation, actually represented a new stage in the exclusion movement, not fully understood by Mary Coolidge and other scholars. This stage, moving beyond the barring of laborers, struck a blow against upper-class Chinese, particularly merchants and students. Under the leadership of Terence V. Powderly, the Bureau of Immigration made up rules, based on novel interpretations of treaty terms and past laws, which would choke off the remaining trickle of Chinese immigrants. They were also aimed at forcing Chinese residents to leave. Contrary to a widely held view that by 1900 the exclusion movement was losing strength, it actually entered upon its most dynamic and Sinophobic stage in the early 1900s. The Chinese minister frantically opposed the new trend by appeals to past treaty promises and to international law. He next resorted to lobbying techniques with congressmen. But despite his efforts, and those of his allies among the open door supporters, the new stage received legislative endorsement in the act of 1902, which not only allowed the bureau to bar all but a few upper-class Chinese but also applied as permanent policy the same rigorous standards to the newly acquired possessions of Hawaii and the Philippines.

In the exclusion act of 1904 China and the open door interests lost out again. The exclusionists, overriding the objections of the opposition, carried their cause even further, particularly by securing the elimination of all references to past treaties with China. Thus, immigration policy, freed of treaty restraints, came to rest entirely on domestic legislation. Frank B. Sargent, labor leader and successor to Powderly in 1902 as commissioner general, retained and enlarged upon Powderly's work by introducing additional regulations and new methods of harassment with the result that what had originally consisted of a class-based policy of restriction evolved into a restrictive policy of a national and racist type.

The third clash between exclusionists and open door advocates was a great deal more complex than the others and involved determined attempts by Chinese to secure a reversal of the ultra-restrictive policy. The Chinese government first sought a new treaty. Then a non-governmental boycott was initiated. Finally, while the boycott was in effect, pro-Chinese endeavored to get Congress to approve the Foster bill. The treaty negotiations were prolonged but unproductive. On the Chinese side the various drafts revealed a growing impatience with any form of racial and nationalistic discrimination. On the American side the negotiations highlighted the division between the State Department and the Department of Commerce and Labor. While the State Department was willing to return to the older policy of barring only Chinese laborers, the Department of Commerce and Labor attempted, in the earlier stages, to use the treaty route to tighten restrictions even further. As the general mood changed during the boycott period, it successfully resisted all efforts to negotiate milder restrictions.

The Chinese boycott, not well understood then, is still subject to widely varying interpretations. One must question the view that it began because of the exclusion policy in general or solely because Chinese national sentiment was aroused — or that it was initiated in China. Rather, bureau records indicate that the movement started in America with the Chinese-American community in desperation over a particular stage in the exclusion policy. The community became fearful that the Powderly-Sargent program might end up driving all Chinese-Americans out of America; Chinese-Americans of all class and cultural divisions, therefore, joined together to seek help from China. Appeals to the merchant guilds in China were successful.

Shanghai merchants, some of whom had experienced mistreatment in connection with the St. Louis Fair of 1904, had their own scores to settle. Students of Shanghai, Foochow, Canton, and elsewhere had similar reasons to join the cause. When the United States barred the laboring class alone, upper-class Chinese had less reason to be emotionally involved than when the policy affected all classes. But the new stage in the exclusion policy provided the irritant for touching off a general nationalistic reaction.

Bureau records indicate, throughout the period of the boycott, that Chinese-Americans played an active role. Money flowed across the Pacific Ocean to boycott headquarters in China. When boycott leaders in China showed an interest in accepting a compromise settlement, Chinese-Americans moved to block it. The boycott was their major bargaining tool, and they were determined to make the most of it. But their influence was dealt a devastating blow by the San Francisco earthquake of April 1906, which left the San Francisco Chinese destitute and preoccupied with the basic problems of survival. Bureau records among others reveal too that the Chinese Empire Reform Association made a significant contribution to the boycott in helping to organize, publicize, and coordinate the effort.

One common misconception is that the boycott was exclusively a commercial phenomenon. American diplomats, businessmen, and missionaries noted that Chinese students were dropping out of American schools in China, that some Chinese were making plans to establish a national Christian Church, and that others were distributing anti-American literature — all of which added up to a serious challenge to the cultural and intellectual leadership of Americans, as well as to their economic and political influence. Even on the commercial side, however, the results may have been more serious than is usually thought. The psychological blow dealt American businessmen must be taken into account also.

The boycott therefore emerges as a much greater threat to American policy than is generally assumed. Certainly at that time American policymakers saw it as a credible attack on American interests in China. It is not surprising that Roosevelt devoted as much time to it as he did. The impact of the boycott led him, in spite of loud protests from the anti-Chinese, to desert the exclusionist position and recommend to Congress the passage of new legislation that, by admitting all Chinese except members of the working class, would restore the former class-based immigration policy. Furthermore, while resorting to military gestures and warnings directed at the Chinese government, the president was also impelled, in a conciliatory gesture, to dismantle by executive action some of the Powderly-Sargent exclusionist regulations.

Congress, prompted by the boycott and the proposals of Roosevelt, also began to reconsider its position. Early in 1906 the Foster bill was a major attempt by the open door interests to modify the exclusion policy. A reinvigorated China lobby went to work once more. The American Asiatic Association, which took credit for originating the bill, energetically worked for its enactment. Church leaders and educators advocated it. Roosevelt and Secretary Root gave it their friendly assistance. But the opposition to the proposed law — which in essence opened the way for upper-class Chinese to enter the country — was too strong, and it failed to get out of committee.

But while the final results of the boycott, as it ground slowly to an official close, were meager on the Chinese side, some pro-Chinese gains were made, most notable those made by Chinese-Americans. The boycott broke the momentum of the intense pressure building up against them. It was a unique attempt to defend their civil rights, and without this intervention it is entirely conceivable that this minority group would have been forced out of the United States. In addition, Chinese-Americans had acquired the bargaining tool they would later need to offset the fact that first generation Chinese were not allowed to become naturalized citizens. Barred from participation in the normal democratic process — in contrast to most immigrants — they turned to lobbying techniques and court action. Appeals to their homeland and recourse to such novel devices as the boycott helped Chinese-Americans as well in protecting their interests.

Chinese merchants and students also achieved victories that, while limited, were important enough to encourage the resort to boycotts later. Nevertheless, in the 1905-1906 period the gains were peripheral. The broader goal of a drastic revision or even elimination of the discriminatory immigration policy sought by the Chinese and the open door interests was not attained.

How can the continuation of this abrasive type of exclusion be accounted for when such powerful forces were arrayed against it? The answer appears to be that an even more formidable combination was formed to promote and defend it. The labor movement, displaying an unusual degree of unity and intense feeling about the matter, was ably led by Gompers as head of the AFL. The Bureau of Immigration, as a planning agency for the coalition, made a major contribution also. The west coast, especially California, supplied a regional bloc of votes in Congress and a powerful voice in the Republican party. In addition, racist attitudes prevailed in the south, and race prejudice against Chinese, which was present to some extent in the north, further helped the exclusionist side. In the early 1900s a movement to restrict immigrants in general was also acquiring impressive strength. Thus, social, cultural, and political elements combined to give exclusion the edge over the open door.

The open door policy was, therefore, undermined by the exclusion policy, which served as a barrier to the extension of trade and cultural ties. Some historians have attributed the modest level of trade to the lack of capital investment in China and the failure of American businessmen to adjust to the peculiar features of the China market; but even if these problems had been overcome, the exclusion policy would have remained a handicap of some consequence.

In a broader sense, events during the years from 1900 to 1906 demonstrated that a policy of discrimination could produce an international crisis of serious proportions. At the same time, within the United States the policy induced political and social strains of considerable magnitude. Exclusion, both as an irritant to China and as a divisive factor internally — to say nothing of its incompatability with the open door policy — exacted a high price that later generations would continue to pay until Americans decided at last to slough off the racial myths of the early 1900s and the lingering subconscious predilections derived from them.

Notes

CHAPTER 1.

1. For convenient reference on the text of the open door notes, see Paul H. Clyde, ed., *United States Policy toward China: Diplomatic and Public Documents, 1839-1939* (New York, 1964), pp. 201-217. For earlier studies see Tyler Dennett, *John Hay: From Poetry to Politics* (New York, 1933), and A. Whitney Griswold, *The Far Eastern Policy of the United States* (New York, 1938). Renewed interest and reinterpretation occurred in the 1950s and 1960s.

2. Charles S. Campbell, Jr., *Special Business Interests and the Open Door Policy* (New Haven, 1951), p. 54. For a detailed study of the American Asiatic Association, see James John Lorence, "The American Asiatic Association, 1898-1925: Organized Business and the Myth of the Chinese Market" (Ph.D. diss., University of Wisconsin, 1970).

3. Further information is found in American Asiatic Association, 1900 (n.p., n.d), National Archives, Record Group 46, HR57A-F13.2. Hereafter National Archives will be cited as NA, and Record Group as RG.

4. U.S. Bureau of Foreign Commerce, Department of State, *Commercial Relations of the United States with Foreign Countries during the Year 1901* (Washington, D.C., 1902), p.11; Paul Varg, "The Myth of the China Market, 1890-1914," *American Historical Review* 73 (Feb. 1968): 757; Marilyn B. Young, *The Rhetoric of Empire: American China Policy 1895-1901* (Cambridge, 1968), p. 54.

5. "The Annual Meeting of the Association," *Journal of the American Asiatic Association* 1(Feb. 1900): 70. Hereafter cited as *JAAA*.

6. Ibid., p. 73.

7. *Missionary Review of the World* 13 o.s. (Aug. 1900): statistics on back of map foldout, next to p. 657. Including European societies, 54 societies were represented altogether with 527 ordained missionaries. These figures do not include Roman Catholic missionary activity. The American branch of the Roman Catholic Church was not involved in the China missions, but European Catholics were active. Hereafter cited as *MRW*.

8. Charles F. Remer, *Foreign Investments in China* (New York, 1968), p. 260.

9. Paul A. Varg, *Missionaries, Chinese, and Diplomats: The American Missionary Movement in China, 1890-1952* (Princeton, 1958), p. 136. See Paul A. Varg, *Open Door Diplomat: The Life of W. W. Rockhill* (Urbana, 1952), pp. 27-29.

10. *MRW* 13 o.s.: next to p. 657 (statistics on back of map foldout).

11. George F. Kennan, *American Diplomacy, 1900-1950* (New York, 1951), pp. 31-35.

12. William R. Braisted, *The United States Navy in the Pacific, 1897-1900* (Austin, Tex., 1958), p. 242. At one time McKinley toyed with the idea of getting territory in China. John W. Foster, *Diplomatic Memoirs* (Boston, 1909), 2: 257.

13. Thomas J. McCormick, *China Market: America's Quest for Informal Empire, 1893-1901* (Chicago, 1967), p. 128. See also William A. Williams, *The Tragedy of American Diplomacy* (Cleveland, 1959), and Walter LaFeber, *The New Empire: An Interpretation of American Expansion, 1860-1898* (Ithaca, 1963). For a helpful, brief, historiographical essay on the open door policy see John A. Garraty, "American Historians and the Open Door Notes," in Dorothy Borg, comp., *Historians and American Far Eastern Policy*, Occasional Papers of the East Asian Institute, Co lumbia University (New York, 1966), pp. 4-13.

14. "Editorials," *MRW* 14 o.s. (Sept. 1900): 717.

15. "General Missionary Intelligence," ibid., p. 728.

16. Jerry Israel, *Progressivism and the Open Door: America and China, 1905-1921* (Pittsburgh, 1971), pp. 3-30. See Jerry Israel, " 'For God, For China and For Yale'— The Open Door in Action," *American Historial Review* 75 (Feb. 1970): 806.

17. William W. Rockhill, "The United States and the Future of China," *Forum* 29 (May 1900): 328.

18. Young, *The Rhetoric of Empire*, p. 141.

19. Ho Yow, "The Attitude of the United States towards the Chinese," *Forum* 29 (June 1900): 385. Reactions to the open door policy were more negative and mixed in China than Chinese officials in the United States indicated. Three different responses were: ignore, welcome and use to China's advantage, stress its incompatibility with the exclusion policy. Chung-tung Chang, "China's Response to the Open Door, 1898-1906" (Ph.D. diss., Michigan State University, 1973), p. 153.

20. Quoted in "Should the Monroe Doctrine Take in Asia?" *Review of Reviews* 22 (July 1900): 79. Chang, "China's Response to the Open Door, 1898-1906," p. 20. See also Werner Levi, *Modern China's Foreign Policy* (Minneapolis, 1953), pp. 53-56.

21. Wu Ting-fang, "Mutual Helpfulness between China and the United States," *North American Review* 171 (July 1900): 8.

22. Ibid., p. 2.

23. Ho, "The Attitude of the United States towards the Chinese," p. 393.

24. Wu, "Mutual Helpfulness between China and the United States," p. 9.

25. *Literary Digest* 20 (Jan. 13, 1900): 35, cited in Marilyn B. Young, "American China Policy, 1895-1901" (Ph.D. diss., Radcliffe College, 1963), p. 161.

26. "The Annual Meeting of the Association," p. 74.

27. Ibid.

28. William W. Rockhill to Na-t'ung, June 22, 1905, NA, RG 59, Peking Legation Archives. Hereafter cited as PLA.

29. *New York Times*, Nov. 28, 1901, p. 1. Hereafter cited as *NY Times*.

30. Gunther Barth, *Bitter Strength: A History of the Chinese in the United States, 1850-1870* (Cambridge, 1964), p. 48.

31. Ibid., p. 62.

32. Ibid., pp. 30, 212-13.

33. Miller alludes to "cultural, racial, and medical fears of national dimensions." Stuart Creighton Miller, "An East Coast Perspective to Chinese Exclusion, 1852-1882," *Historian* 33 (Feb. 1971): 201. This article summarizes and criticizes earlier scholarship on the origins of anti-Chinese feeling. For a detailed study of the political uses of the anti-Chinese movement in California, see Alexander P. Saxton, *The Indispensable Enemy: Labor and the Anti-Chinese Movement in California* (Berkeley, 1971).

34. Clyde, *United States Policy toward China*, p. 85.

35. Ibid.

36. Marion T. Bennett, *American Immigration Policies: A History* (Washington, 1963), p. 301.

37. Shien-woo Kung, *Chinese in American Life: Some Aspects of Their History, Status, Problems, and Contributions* (Seattle, 1962), p. 66.

38. Tyler Dennett, *Americans in Eastern Asia: A Critical Study of United States' Policy in the Far East in the Nineteenth Century* (New York, 1922, 1941, 1963), p. 538.

39. Mary R. Coolidge, "Chinese Labor Competition on the Pacific Coast," *Annals of the American Academy of Political and Social Science* 34 (Sept. 1909): 341-42. Hereafter cited as *AAPSS*. See also Mary R. Coolidge, *Chinese Immigration* (New York, 1909), and Roderick D. McKenzie, *Oriental Exclusion: The Effect of American Immigration Laws, Regulations, and Judicial Decisions upon the Chinese and Japanese on the American Pacific Coast* (Chicago, 1928). McKenzie deals mainly with the 1924 laws and afterwards.

40. Elmer C. Sandmeyer, *The Anti-Chinese Movement in California* (Urbana, 1939), p. 109.

41. Ibid., pp. 63-64.

42. Rose Hum Lee, *The Chinese in the United States* (Hong Kong, 1960), p. 12.

43. Sandmeyer, *The Anti-Chinese Movement in California*, p. 68.

44. Chester L. Jones, "The Legislative History of Exclusion Legislation," *AAPSS* 34 (Sept. 1909): 352.

45. Dennett, *Americans in Eastern Asia*, p. 538.

46. Clyde, *United States Policy toward China*, p. 153.

47. Sandmeyer, *The Anti-Chinese Movement in California*, p. 93.

48. Dennett, *Americans in Eastern Asia*, p. 544.

49. Bennett, *American Immigration Policies*, p. 301.

50. Sandmeyer, *The Anti-Chinese Movement in California*, p. 97.

51. U.S. Congress, Senate, *A Compilation of the Laws, Treaty, and Regulations and Rulings of the Treasury Department Relating to the Exclusion of Chinese*, Sen. Doc. 291, 57th Cong., 1st sess., 1902, p. 19. The earlier laws are also contained in this compilation. Hereafter cited as Sen. Doc. 291, 1902.

52. Charles F. Holder, "America's Treatment of the Chinese," *North American Review* 171 (Aug. 1900): 218.

53. Ibid.

54. Dennett, *Americans in Eastern Asia*, pp. 546-48.

55. See footnote in Sen. Doc. 291, 1902, p. 19. See also Darrell H. Smith and Guy Herring, *The Bureau of Immigration: Its History, Activities, and Organization* (Baltimore, 1924), p. 20.

56. Sandmeyer, *The Anti-Chinese Movement in California*, p. 102.

57. Max J. Kohler, "Un-American Character of Race Legislation, Chinese and Japanese in America," *AAPSS* 34 (Sept. 1909): 285.

58. Clyde, *United States Policy toward China*, p. 156.

59. George M. Stephenson, *A History of American Immigration, 1820-1924* (New York, 1926), p. 262. For another standard work on immigration restrictions, see Roy L. Garis, *Immigration Restriction: A Study of the Opposition to and Regulation of Immigration into the United States* (New York, 1928).

60. Charles F. Holder, "The Dragon in America: Being an Account of the Workings of the Chinese Six Companies in America and Its Population of the United States with Chinese," *Arena* 32 (Aug. 1904): 120.

61. U.S. Congress, Senate, Committee on Immigration, *Hearings on Chinese Exclusion*, S2960, 57th Cong., 1st sess., 1902, p. 76. Hereafter cited as *Hearings*, S2960, 1902.

62. Robert Seager II, "Some Denominational Reactions to Chinese Immigration to California, 1856-1892," *Pacific Historical Review* 27 (Feb. 1959): 64.

63. Lee Chew, "The Biography of a Chinaman," *Independent* 55 (Feb. 19, 1903): 419. This article implies that this man arrived in America as a young man before the first exclusion act was passed.

64. U.S. Congress, Enclosure 6, *Exclusion of Chinese Laborers*, Sen. Doc. 162, 57th Cong., 1st sess., 1902, p. 41. Such an argument is hard to prove or disprove. It is likely, however, that Wu was exaggerating the impact upon trade of the exclusion policy.

65. See, for example, Enc. 3 in Rockhill to Elihu Root, Aug. 26, 1905, NA, RG 59, China Dispatches. Hereafter cited as CD.

66. Dennett, *Americans in Eastern Asia*, p. 544.

67. Ibid., p. 547.

68. See footnote in ibid, p. 548.

69. General background information on Chinese history for this and later chapters has been drawn from John K. Fairbank, Edwin O. Reischauer, and Albert M. Craig, *East Asia: The Modern Transformation* (Boston, 1965).

CHAPTER 2.

1. Mrs. S. L. Baldwin to Roosevelt, Nov. 25, 1901, NA, RG 85, Segregated Chinese Records, File Box 25. Hereafter, these records of the Immigration and Naturalization Service will be cited as SCR, and File Box as FB.

2. Terence V. Powderly to Baldwin, Dec. 3, 1901, SCR, Letter Book.

3. Baldwin to Powderly, Dec. 5, 1901, SCR, FB 26.

4. In writing about the American conception of China, Robert McClellan concludes: "The most consistent aspect of the image . . . was its inconsistency." Robert McClellan, *The Heathen Chinee: A Study of American Attitudes toward China, 1890-1905* (Columbus, 1970), p. 250.

5. Maldwyn A. Jones, for example, in *American Immigration* (Chicago, 1960), p. 263, observes that "the anti-Chinese movement had virtually run its course by the beginning of the twentieth century."

6. J. M. Scanland, "Will the Chinese Migrate?" *Arena* 24 (July 1900): 21.

7. Ibid.

8. For a history of the bureau, see Darrell H. Smith and Guy Herring, *The Bureau of Immigration: Its History, Activities, and Organization* (Baltimore, 1924).

9. Data on Chinese exclusion are omitted from Powderly's published autobiography. See Harry J. Carman, Henry David, and Paul N. Guthrie, eds., *The Path I Trod: The Autobiography of Terence V. Powderly* (New York, 1940). As commissioner

general of immigration from 1897 to 1902, his impact upon the exclusion policy was enormous. "In 1880, and again in 1892, I was at the head of the Knights of Labor," wrote Powderly, "when the Chinese exclusion laws were passed, and I made it my business to place every fact obtainable before the workingmen of the United States." Powderly to H. E. Garman, Dec. 16, 1901, Terence V. Powderly Papers, A1-108.

10. Coolidge, *Chinese Immigration*, p. 328.

11. Samuel Gompers, *Seventy Years of Life and Labor* (New York, 1925), 1: 522-23.

12. Arthur Mann, "Gompers and the Irony of Racism," *Antioch Review* 13 (June 1953): 208.

13. Fred Greenbaum, "The Social Ideas of Samuel Gompers," *Labor History* 7 (Winter 1966): 44.

14. Jones, *American Immigration*, p. 254.

15. U.S. Department of Justice, *Official Opinions of the Attorneys-General of the United States* (Washington, 1900), 22: 132.

16. Sen. Doc. 291, 1902, p. 35.

17. Ibid, p. 31.

18. Ibid., pp. 32-49. The new regulations were part of the *Compilation*, issued by Powderly on October 1, 1900.

19. An example of the wide range of conflicting precedents on matters pertaining to the Chinese is contained in an article by Stephen W. Nickerson, a pro-Chinese lawyer: "in the summer of 1882, Attorney-General Brewster decided (17 Op. Atty. Gen., 416) that Chinese laborers, in transit to or from China or some other country, could not lawfully be transported across the United States. . . . About six months later, this same official retracted his first opinion and came (17 Op. A.G., 483) to a contrary decision. In the spring of 1886, Attorney-General Garland decided (18 Op. A.G., 388) that the first opinion was correct. In the summer of 1889, Attorney-General Miller decided (19 Op. A.G., 369) that the second opinion was correct. Here we have four conflicting opinions in the short space of seven years." Stephen W. Nickerson, "The Dawning of a Wiser Chinese Policy", *North American Review* 188 (Dec. 1908): 919-20.

20. U.S. Department of the Treasury, Bureau of Immigration, *Annual Report of the Commissioner-General of Immigration for the Fiscal Year Ended June 30, 1901* (Washington, 1901), p. 49. Hereafter cited as *Annual Report . . . Immigration.* See also U.S. Congress, Senate, *Regulations Relating to Chinese Exclusion, etc.*, Sen. Doc. 300, 57th Cong., 1st sess., 1902, p. 4.

21. In a letter from Powderly to the secretary of the treasury, Lyman J. Gage, in which Powderly asked for a law to authorize inspectors to arrest Chinese. U.S. Congress, House of Representatives, *Amending Chinese Exclusion Laws*, House Doc. 471, 56th Cong., 2nd sess., 1901, p. 2.

22. Powderly to Collector of Customs, San Francisco, Feb. 13, 1901, SCR, Letter Book.

23. Ira M. Condit, *The Chinaman as We See Him and Fifty Years of Work for Him* (New York, 1900), p. 87.

24. Resolutions of Building Trades Council of the City and Council of San Francisco, Feb. 15, 1900, in SCR, FB 12. For all of the correspondence, see Packet no. 1094. Although the sworn statements are strong evidence in support of Dunn, the callous attitude known to prevail in San Francisco at that time, and the extent of uproar among the Chinese — who were ordinarily docile — suggest that Dunn was guilty.

25. Coolidge, *Chinese Immigration*, p. 288.

26. Ibid., p. 320.

27. *Annual Report . . . Immigration*, p. 49.

28. Ibid., p. 52.

29. U.S. Department of the Treasury, *Annual Report of the Secretary of the Treasury for the Fiscal Year Ended June 30, 1901* (Washington, 1901), p. 40.

30. Joshua K. Brown to Harold M. Sewall, Nov. 25, 1898, SCR, FB 11.

31. Alvey A. Adee to Wu T'ing-fang, Aug. 1, 1899, NA, RG 59, Notes to Chinese Legation. Hereafter cited as CL. For the diplomatic correspondence see also U.S. Congress, Senate, *Status of Chinese Persons in the Philippine Islands*, Sen. Doc. 397, 56th Cong., 1st sess., 1900.

32. Wu to John Hay, Sept. 12, 1899, Notes from CL.

33. Prince Ch'ing to Edwin H. Conger, Feb. 26, 1902, *Notes from China*, in U.S. Congress, House, *Protest of Chinese Government against Exclusion of Chinese from the Philippines*, House Doc. 562, 59th Cong., 1st sess., 1902.

34. For a study of the origins of anti-Chinese sentiment, see Stuart Creighton Miller, *The Unwelcome Immigrant: The American Image of the Chinese, 1785-1882* (Berkeley and Los Angeles, 1969). Miller, challenging the view that sinophobia originated in California, holds that it was present on a national basis even before 1882.

CHAPTER 3.

1. *New York Daily Tribune*, June 15, 1901, p. 1. Hereafter cited as *NY Tribune*.

2. Ibid.

3. Ibid.

4. John B. Gardner, "The Image of the Chinese in the United States, 1885-1915," *Dissertation Abstracts: Abstracts of Dissertations and Monographs* (Ann Arbor, 1961), 22: 1139.

5. Dennett, *Americans in Eastern Asia*, p. 602.

6. Linda P. Shin, "China in Transition: The Role of Wu T'ing-fang (1842-1922)" (Ph.D. diss., University of California at Los Angeles, 1970), pp. 239-40.

7. J. O. P. Bland, *Recent Events and Present Policies in China* (Philadelphia, 1912), p. 213.

8. Wu to Hay, Nov. 7, 1898, Notes from CL.

9. Wu to Hay, Dec. 12, 1898, ibid.

10. Wu to Hay, Nov. 15, 1899, ibid.

11. Hay to Wu, Dec. 5, 1899, Notes to CL.

12. Wu to Hay, Oct. 2, 1899, Notes from CL.

13. Wu to Hay, Jan. 11, 1900, ibid.

14. Wu to Hay, May 7, 1900, ibid.

15. Wu to Hay, July 9, 1900, ibid.

16. *NY Times*, July 10, 1900, p. 6.

17. Wu to Hay, Nov. 30, 1900, Notes from CL.

18. Stanley Jackson, Special Deputy Acting Collector, to Commissioner General of Immigration, Nov. 16, 1900, SCR, FB 16.

19. Lyman J. Gage to Hay, Dec. 10, 1900, SCR, Letter Book.

20. Hay to Wu, Dec. 5, 1900, Notes to CL.

21. George Campbell to Hay, March 14, 1900, SCR, FB 14.

22. Hay to Gage, Nov. 27, 1901, SCR, FB 26.

23. F. S. Stratton, Collector, to Frank V. Belt, Attorney, Jan. 12, 1901, SCR, FB 18.

24. Wu to Hay, Apr. 11, 1901, Notes from CL.

25. Wu to Hay, Dec. 26, 1900, ibid.

26. James R. Dunn, Inspector in Charge, to Collector of Customs, San Francisco, Jan. 25, 1901, SCR, FB 16.

27. Wu to Hay, July 20, 1899, Notes from CL.

28. Wu to Hay, March 9, 1900, ibid. See also Clyde, *United States Policy toward China*, p. 157.

29. Wu to Hay, March 9, 1900, Notes from CL. See also Clyde, *United States Policy toward China*, pp. 157-58.

30. See Hong Sling letter in Wu to Hay, Oct. 20, 1900, Notes from CL. Certificates were mandatory for Chinese laborers but were not required by law of merchants and others who were not laborers at the time of the registration date.

31. June 19, 1905, Diaries, John Hay Papers. William R. Thayer, ed., *The Life and Letters of John Hay* (Boston, 1915), 2: 406-7. Although Hay believed in Anglo-Saxon superiority, his views on race were "in most respects mild and moderate." Kenton J. Clymer, *John Hay: The Gentleman as Diplomat* (Ann Arbor, 1975), p. 67.

32. "The Annual Meeting of the Association," 1900, p. 74.

33. *NY Times*, Jan. 27, 1900, p. 3.

34. Ibid., Feb. 9, 1900, p. 3.

35. Ibid., Feb. 23, 1900, p. 9. In the same speech he suggested that the Monroe Doctrine — its non-colonization feature — be extended to China.

36. Ibid., Apr. 27, 1900, p.3.

37. Wu T'ing-fang, "China and the United States," *Independent* 52 (March 29, 1900): 754.

38. Ibid., p. 755.

39. Ho Yow, "The Attitude of the United States towards the Chinese," p. 387. Wu had to defend Ho Yow against charges of corruption later. Shin, "China in Transition," p. 236.

40. Wu T'ing-fang, "Mutual Helpfulness between China and the United States," p. 2.

41. Ibid., p. 9.

42. Ibid.

43. Ibid., p. 12.

44. *NY Times*, May 31, 1900, p. 1.

45. Quoted in International Typographical Union Resolutions, Poughkeepsie, New York, Nov. 1, 1901, to Congress, in NA, Legislative Records, Petitions, House Committee on Foreign Affairs, 57th Cong., 1st sess., 1901-1902, HR 57A-H7.3, FB 4818. Hereafter, Legislative Records are cited as LR, Petitions.

46. Senator B. Tillman, S.C., on his resolution to investigate the Chinese boycott. 59th Cong., 1st sess., Jan 29, 1906, *Congressional Record*, 40: 1673. Hereafter, *Congressional Record* is cited as *Cong. Rec.*

47. *NY Times*, July 3, 1900, p. 6.

48. Ibid.

49. Ibid., July 14, 1900, p. 2.

50. Ibid., Nov. 3, 1900, p. 6.

51. Ibid., Dec. 11, 1900, p. 8. For his speech of Dec. 20, see Wu T'ing-fang, "The Causes of the Unpopularity of the Foreigner in China," *AAPSS* 17 (Jan. 1901): 1-14.

52. *NY Times*, Feb. 9, 1901, p. 8.

53. Ibid., June 16, 1901, p. 3. *NY Tribune*, June 15, 1901, p. 1.

54. Enc. in Robert Watchorn to Powderly, March 25, 1902, Powderly Papers, A1-112.

55. Ho Yow, "Chinese Exclusion: A Benefit or a Harm?" *North American Review* 173 (Sept. 1901): 314-30. Ho Yow, "The Chinese Question," *Overland Monthly* 38 (Oct. 1901): 257.

56. "The Chinese Exclusion Bills," *JAAA* 2 (Feb. 1902): 22.

57. Walter Egbert to Roosevelt, Nov. 14, 1901, SCR, FB 25.

58. A. D. Cutler to Roosevelt, Nov. 25, 1901, SCR, FB 26.

59. Albert Whyte, Immigration Inspector, to Commissioner General of Immigration, Nov. 18, 1901, in Theodore Roosevelt Papers. This letter had been forwarded by Powderly to the president with a notation that Whyte was "one of the best men in the Immigration service." Whyte was reporting on his experience in Hawaii. He took the view that the delegation was part of a predatory class in Hawaii that was allowing the Islands to be "overrun by the scum of creation."

60. American Chamber of Commerce of Manila to House Committee on Foreign Affairs, Jan. 3, 1901, LR, Petitions, 59th Cong., 1st sess., 1901-1902, HR 57A-H7.3, FB 4822.

61. Chinese Residents in the Philippines to Senate Committee on Immigration, Dec. 7, 1901, ibid., S57A0J26, FB 110.

62. Nathan R. Johnson to McKinley, May 24, 1901, SCR, FB 20.

63. U. S. Congress, Senate, *Immigration of Chinese into the United States: A Pamphlet Containing a Collection of Excerpts and Arguments in Opposition to the Passage of a Law to Prohibit the Immigration of Chinese into the United States*, Sen. Doc. 106, 57th Cong., 1st sess., 1902, p. 6. Hereafter cited as Sen. Doc. 106.

64. *NY Tribune*, July 21, 1901, p. 1.

65. Ibid., Nov. 29, 1901, p. 9.

66. Rev. William M. Green to Powderly, Dec. 29, 1901, SCR, FB 26.

67. For petitions and letters, see LR, Petitions, House Committee on Foreign Affairs, 57th Cong., 1st sess., 1901-1902, HR 57A-H7.3. Another voice in the religious community deserving mention is Ira M. Condit, "John Chinaman in America," *MRW* 15 o.s. (Feb. 1902): 95-101.

68. *New York Journal*, Dec. 23, 1901.

69. LR, Petitions, House Committee on Foreign Affairs, 57th Cong., 1st sess., 1901-1902, HR 57A-H7.3.

70. "An Appeal," *JAAA* 2 (Feb. 1902): 38.

71. LR, Petitions, House Committee on Foreign Affairs, 57th Cong., 1st sess., 1901-1902, HR 57A-H7.3.

72. *San Francisco Chronicle,* Nov. 9, 1901, p. 6. Hereafter cited as *SF Chronicle.*

73. *Washington Globe-Democrat,* Nov. 7, 1901.

74 Hay to Roosevelt, Nov. 23, 1901, Roosevelt Papers.

75. *NY Tribune,* Nov. 28, 1901, p. 4. Isaac P. Noyes wrote a letter to the *Washington Post* in reply to Wu. Robert Watchorn, immigration official and confidant of Powderly, liked it and sent it to his chief. "Let China adopt Occidental and modern ways," wrote Noyes, "and she will not have cause to complain." *Washington Post,* Dec. 2, 1901, in Watchorn to Powderly, Powderly Papers, A1-112.

CHAPTER 4.

1. *NY Times,* Oct. 10, 1901, p. 8.

2. Ibid. The only southerners who showed any sympathy for Wu in Congress were connected with the cotton mills that exported goods to China. Aside from this small minority, the south saw the Chinese in racial terms. Little, if any, basis can be found in the records for the *NY Times'*s statement that the south was looking for cheap labor from China.

3. *SF Chronicle,* Nov. 9, 1901, p. 6.

4. Ibid.

5. Ibid.

6. Sandmeyer, *The Anti-Chinese Movement in California,* p. 106.

7. *American Federationist* 8 (Aug. 1901): 306.

8. "Executive Council Session," ibid. (Oct. 1901), p. 446.

9. Eva McDonald Valesh, "Three Notable Lines of Labor Work," ibid. (Nov. 1901), pp. 458-59.

10. Ibid., p. 458.

11. *SF Chronicle,* Nov. 14, 1901, p. 6.

12. American Federation of Labor, *Report of Proceedings of the 21st Annual Convention of the American Federation of Labor* (n.p., n.d.), p. 70. Hereafter cited as AFL, *Proc.* An effusive reaction to Roosevelt's statements on exclusion came to Powderly from the president of the Colorado Federation of Labor, a Republican, who was convinced that Colorado workingmen would vote for Roosevelt in the future. Garman to Powderly, Dec. 10, 1901, Powderly Papers, A1-108.

13. AFL, *Proc.,* p. 97.

14. Ibid., p. 155. The president of the Colorado Federation of Labor wrote Powderly of his disappointment that the Scranton convention "did not take a more decided stand against all Asiatic labor." Garman to Powderly, Jan. 20, 1902, Powderly Papers, A1-114.

15. "Executive Council Session," *American Federationist* 8 (March 1901): 94-95.

16. Powderly Papers, Scrapbook, 1900-1904.

17. *SF Chronicle*, Nov. 14, 1901, p. 6.

18. "A Memorial to the President of the United States of America on the Subject of Asiatic Labor," May 17, 1901, SCR, FB 20.

19. James R. Dunn to F. H. Larned, June 27, 1901, Powderly Papers, A1-107.

20. *San Francisco Call*, Nov. 21, 1901.

21. "California's Memorial to the President and the Congress of the United States for the Re-enactment of the Chinese Exclusion Law," Nov. 21-22, 1901, LR, Petitions, House Committee on Foreign Affairs, 57th Cong., 1st sess., 1901-1902, HR 57A-H7.3. Also in Sen. Doc. 191, 57th Cong., 1st sess., 1901-1902.

22. 56th Cong., 2d sess., *Cong. Rec.* 34: 2248.

23. 57th Cong., 1st sess., ibid., 35: 135 for Montana, p. 306 for Idaho. These two resolutions are identical. Both had been approved in March 1901.

24. Approximately 30 petitions are found in SCR, FB 25.

25. *NY Tribune*, Nov. 11, 1901, p. 12.

26. Ibid., Nov. 12, 1901, p. 9.

27. 59th Cong., 1st sess., *Cong. Rec.* 34: 4162-64. For the House petitions, see LR, Petitions, House Committee on Foreign Affairs, 57th Cong., 1st sess., 1901-1902, HR 57A-H7.3. For the Senate petitions, see LR, Petitions, Senate Committee on Immigration, 57th Cong., 1st sess., 1901-1902, S57A-K3. For petitions to the Treasury Department, see SCR, FB 25.

28. LR, Petitions, Senate Committee on Immigration, 57th Cong., 1st sess., 1901-1902, S57A-K3, FB 164.

29. Ibid., FB 4822 and others in S57A-K3. Maldwyn A. Jones and many others who have written on immigration have assumed that the issues of restricting European and Oriental immigration were kept separate even though the attitudes of race-consciousness in one case began "to be projected onto the other." *American Immigration*, p. 254. In 1902, however, the Daughters of Liberty were petitioning for restrictions in both cases. More ties may have existed than is generally realized. Higham limits his generalizations to the nineteenth century. John Higham, *Strangers in the Land: Patterns of American Nativism, 1860-1925* (New Brunswick, 1955), p. 167.

30. *SF Chronicle*, Jan. 7, 1902, p. 2.

31. See *Exclusion of Chinese Laborers*, Sen. Doc. 162, 57th Cong., 1st sess., 1901-1902.

32. Kirk Porter, *National Party Platforms* (New York, 1924), p. 216.

33. *NY Tribune*, Nov. 21, 1901, p. 3.

34. U.S. Congress, *A Compilation of the Messages and Papers of the Presidents* (New York, 1897-1901), 14: 6650.

35. Quoted in pamphlet, *Truth versus Fiction: Justice versus Prejudice: Meat for All, Not for a Few: A Plain and Unvarnished Statement Why Exclusion Laws against the Chinese Should Not be Re-enacted: Respect Treaties and Make General, Not Special, Laws* (n.p., n.d.), in LR, Petitions, House Committee on Immigration and Naturalization, 57th Cong., 1st sess., 1901-1902, HR 57A-F13.2. Also in Sen. Doc. 106, 57th Cong., 1st sess., 1901-1902. This pamphlet is a Chinese defense against an AFL pamphlet, and it voices the aspirations of the Chinese in America. Among other items, it includes a speech by Wu T'ing-fang. The Chinese Six Companies in San Francisco were raising a fund to fight exclusion by charging $1.00 per person. *NY Tribune*, Dec. 1, 1901, 2:4. Some of the financing of the pamphlet may have come from this fund. Another pro-Chinese pamphlet in the files of the House Committee on Immigration and Naturalization is a reprint of an article from *Public*, Dec. 14, 1901. Louis F. Post, *The Chinese Exclusion Act* (Chicago, n.d.).

36. Quoted in Howard K. Beale, *Theodore Roosevelt and the Rise of America to World Power* (Baltimore, 1956), p. 28.

37. "Memorandum," W. W. Rockhill to Secretary of State, Dec. 7, 1901, NA, RG 59, Reports of Bureau Officers, 1899-1911, vol. 10.

38. *NY Tribune*, Dec. 5, 1901, p. 2.

39. Powderly to George B. Cortelyou, Dec. 6, 1901, Roosevelt Papers. This bill was a drastic shift for Powderly, who called for reenactment of the existing law in "Exclude Anarchist and Chinaman!" *Colliers Weekly* (Dec. 14, 1901), Powderly Papers, Scrapbook, 1900-1904.

40. Gompers to Executive Council, Jan. 11, 1902, Gompers Papers, Letter Books.

41. Gompers to Boies Penrose, Jan. 20, 1902, ibid.

42. Roosevelt to Leslie M. Shaw, March 27, 1902, Elting E. Morison, ed., *The Letters of Theodore Roosevelt* (Cambridge, 1951), 3: 249. Hereafter cited as *Letters*.

43. "The Chinese Exclusion Bills," *JAAA* 2 (Feb. 1902): 22.

44. Campbell, *Special Business Interests and the Open Door Policy*, p. 24. Wu had helped to arrange the original railroad concession for this group. William R. Braisted, "The United States and the American China Development Company," *Far Eastern Quarterly* 11 (Feb. 1951): 158.

45. *SF Chronicle*, Jan. 25, 1902, p. 2.

46. 57th Cong., 1st sess., *Cong. Rec.*, 35: 3720.

47. *Hearings,* S2960, 1902, p. 19.

48. Ibid., p. 52.

49. Ibid., p. 12.

50. *NY Tribune,* Feb. 27, 1902. See also the petitions in the Senate Committee on Immigration files in Feb. 1902, LR.

51. 57th Cong., 1st sess., *Cong. Rec.* 35: 3808.

52. Wu to Hay, March 22, 1902, Notes from CL.

53. Prince Ch'ing to Edwin H. Conger, Feb. 26, 1902, in House Doc. 562, 57th Cong., 1st sess., 1901-1902. *NY Tribune,* March 12, 1902, p. 4.

54. *NY Tribune,* March 7, 1902, p. 9. The Board of Foreign Missions of the Presbyterian Church notified the Senate of its opposition to the Mitchell bill. See Board . . . to Hon. William P. Frye, Apr. 11, 1902, LR, Petitions, 57th Cong., 1st sess., 1901-1902, S57A-K3, FB 165.

55. *Washington Times,* Apr. 5, 1902, p. 2.

56. 57th Cong., 1st sess., *Cong. Rec.* 35: 3723.

57. Ibid., p. 3877.

58. Ibid., p. 3945.

59. *NY Tribune,* Apr. 17, 1902, p. 1. For the vote defeating S2960, see 57th Cong., 1st sess., *Cong. Rec.* 35: 5243. For the Platt substitute vote see ibid., p. 4251.

60. 57th Cong., 1st sess., *Cong. Rec.* 35: 4762.

61. 57th Cong., 1st. sess., Apr. 29, 1902, *Senate Journal,* p. 362.

62. Wu to Hay, Apr. 29, 1902, Roosevelt Papers.

63. Hay to Wu, Apr. 30, 1902, Notes to CL.

64. Wen Hwan Ma, who leaned toward the interpretation that moderation had won out, wrote in his *American Policy toward China as Revealed in the Debates of Congress* (Shanghai, 1934), p. 112: "The adoption of the Platt proposal marked a distinct defeat of the extreme exclusionists and an indication that public opinion in America was in favor of a faithful adherence to treaty obligations." For an older study of Congressional actions on exclusion, see Tien-lu Li, *Congressional Policy of Chinese Immigration or Legislation Relating to Chinese Immigration to the United States* (South Nashville, 1916).

65. George F. Hoar, *Autobiography of Seventy Years* (New York, 1903), 2: 124.

66. John W. Foster, *American Diplomacy in the Orient* (Boston, 1903), p. 305.

67. "Current Comment," *JAAA* 2 (May 1902): 73.

68. "Editorial," *American Federationist* 9 (June 1902): 298.

69. *San Francisco Examiner,* Apr. 30, 1902, p. 16. Republican exclusionists were more inclined to be satisfied with the outcome.

CHAPTER 5.

1. Wu to Hay, May 19, 1902, Notes from CL.

2. Quoted in David J. Hill to Wu, July 22, 1903, Notes to CL.

3. Hill to Wu, July 31, 1902, ibid.

4. Chew, "The Biography of a Chinaman," p. 422.

5. Ibid., p. 423.

6. John Barrett to Roosevelt, Apr. 30, 1902, Roosevelt Papers.

7. "Any person who knows anything about the administration of Chinese affairs in the Treasury Department knows that Mr. Gage had practically nothing to do with it. It is left to the Commissioner of Immigration." John W. Foster, *Hearings,* S2960, 1902, pp. 64-65.

8. *NY Times,* Jan. 29, 1905, 4: 1.

9. *NY Tribune,* March 23, 1903, p. 2. Powderly, a former friend, was not happy to see Sargent accept his job. Nor were Powderly's cronies. One called Sargent "essentially a 'Know-nothing' and sometimes I think he is an out and out exclusionist." Watchorn to Powderly, Nov. 26, 1905, Powderly Papers, A1-112.

10. Oliver P. Merryman, Feb. 15, 1902, *Hearings,* S2960, 1902, p. 431.

11. *Dictionary of American Biography,* s.v. "Sargent, Frank P."

12. Roosevelt to Philander C. Knox, Aug. 1, 1903, Morison, *Letters,* 3: 539.

13. *Annual Report . . . Commissioner General of Immigration,* 1903, p. 112.

14. Ibid., p. 102.

15. Ibid., p. 5.

16. *NY Tribune,* Nov. 26, 1902, p. 6.

17. *Annual Report . . . Commissioner General of Immigration,* 1903, p. 99.

18. House Doc. 847, 59th Cong., 1st sess., 1905-1906, p. 129.

19. John W. Foster, "The Chinese Boycott," *Atlantic Monthly* 97 (Jan. 1906): 118-27.

20. Stephen W. Nickerson, "Our Chinese Treaties; and Legislation, and Their Enforcement," *North American Review* 181 (Sept. 1905): 376.

21. House Doc. 847, 59th Cong., 1st sess., 1905-1906, p. 128.

22. F. H. Larned, Acting Commissioner General to the Secretary of the Treasury, May 14, 1902, SCR, FB 35.

23. *NY Tribune*, Sept. 21, 1901, p. 3.

24. Luella Miner, "Chinese Students and the Exclusion Laws," *Independent* 54 (Apr. 24, 1902): 976. According to Wu, an influential friend secured the postponement. Wu to Hay, Dec. 9, 1901, Notes from CL.

25. Miner, "Chinese Students and the Exclusion Laws," p. 977.

26. Luella Miner to James R. Dunn, Sept. 19, 1902, SCR, FB 35.

27. Miner, "American Barbarism and Chinese Hospitality," *Outlook* 72 (Dec. 27, 1902): 986.

28. Sargent to the Secretary of the Treasury, Sept. 5, 1902, SCR, FB 35.

29. Sargent to Edmund B. Fairfield, Sept. 15, 1902, ibid.

30. See correspondence in ibid.

31. Quoted by Miner, "The Strange Adventures of Mr. Fay and Mr. Kung," *Advance* (Dec. 11, 1902), p. 696, in SCR, FB 35. For the Immigration Bureau's defense of its position, see House Doc. 847, 59th Cong., 1st sess., 1905-1906, p. 128.

32. Miner, "The Strange Adventures of Mr. Fay and Mr. Kung," p. 696.

33. Miner, "Chinese Students and the Exclusion Laws," p. 978.

34. *NY Tribune*, July 20, 1903, p. 2.

35. International Missionary Union to the Secretary of the Treasury, June 20, 1902, SCR, FB 30.

36. *Pacific Commercial Advertiser* (Honolulu), Apr. 30, 1902, in Roosevelt Papers. See also the debates on Chinese exclusion in 1902 in the *Congressional Record*.

37. "World's Fair Commissioner Barrett," *JAAA* 2 (May 1902): 96.

38. "Asia at St. Louis," *JAAA* 3 (Aug. 1903): 201.

39. Wong Kai Kah, "A Menace to America's Oriental Trade," *North American Review* 178 (March 1904): 414-24; also reprinted as part of a pamphlet prepared by the Commercial Club of Indianapolis in the interest of obtaining a commission to look into the problems of the exempt classes of Chinese and provide for their protection. SCR, FB 85.

40. Department Circular no. 5, Jan. 7, 1903, SCR, FB 53.

41. Liang to David R. Francis, May 15, 1903, ibid.

42. Francis B. Loomis, Acting Secretary of State, to the Secretary of Commerce and Labor, July 6, 1903, SCR, FB 45.

43. Roosevelt to the Secretary of Commerce and Labor, July 6, 1903, ibid.

44. Cortelyou to Roosevelt, July 18, 1903, ibid.

45. *NY Times*, July 4, 1903, p. 6.

46. "Current Comment," *JAAA* 3 (Aug. 1903): 194.

47. Jin Fuey Moy to Sargent, Sept. 14, 1903, SCR, FB 45.

48. Cortelyou to Francis, Jan. 4, 1904, ibid.

49. Wong Kai Kah, "A Menace to America's Oriental Trade," pp. 414-24.

50. Commercial Club, Indianapolis, "A Menace to America's Trade in the Far East" (n. p., n. d.), in SCR, FB 85. Hugh H. Hanna, prominent political figure and business leader, much impressed by Wong, was behind this with some secret assistance from Hay. Hugh H. Hanna to Hay, Dec. 29, 1903, Hay Papers.

51. "Current Comment," *JAAA* 4 (May 1904): 98.

52. Ibid. (Apr. 1904), p. 66.

53. Ibid.

54. Francis A. Carl to Liang, March 21, 1904, Notes from CL.

55. Emil S. Fischer, "China at the Louisiana Purchase Exhibition," *JAAA* 4 (May 1904): 100.

56. Ibid.

57. Apr. 25, 1904, Hay Diary, Hay Papers.

58. "Chinese Exclusion," *Outlook* 76 (Apr. 23, 1904): 964.

59. Chester Holcombe, "The Restriction of Chinese Immigration," *Outlook* 76 (Apr. 23, 1904): 975.

60. Charles Stewart Smith, "Chinese Exclusion," *JAAA* 4 (May 1904): 122.

61. *Annual Report . . . Commissioner General of Immigration*, 1904, p. 884.

62. Ibid.

63. For a copy of the letter, see House Doc. 847, 59th Cong., 1st sess., 1905-1906, pp. 45-50.

64. Rev. E. R. Donehoo, D. D., West End Presbyterian Church, to Roosevelt, June 17, 1905, SCR, FB 85.

65. George Sladovich to Victor H. Metcalf, June 15, 1905, ibid.

66. Hop Wo Lung to Cortelyou, June 29, 1903, SCR, FB 45.

67. *NY Times*, Dec. 30, 1901, p. 7.

68. Ibid., Jan. 4, 1902, p. 2.

69. Ng Poon Chew, "The Chinaman in America," *Independent* 54 (Apr. 3, 1902): 803.

70. *NY Tribune*, Dec. 5, 1905, p. 9.

71. *NY Times*, June 11, 1901, p. 2.

72. Ibid., May 13, 1902, p. 9. See his biography in *Biographical Dictionary of Republican China*, "Liang Ch'i-ch'ao."

73. *NY Times*, May 13, 1902, p. 9.

74. Ibid., Sept. 26, 1903, p. 6.

75. Ibid., Dec. 20, 1903, p. 24. The original Chinese title in 1899 was *Pao-huang hui;* it is more literally translated as "Protect the Emperor Society."

76. Ibid.

77. Ibid., Aug. 12, 1904, p. 1.

78. John Barrett, "America in China: Our Position and Opportunity," *North American Review* 175 (Nov. 1902): 657.

79. The prospects and problems connected with cooperation between China and America over Manchuria are examined in depth in Michael H. Hunt, *Frontier Defense and the Open Door: Manchuria in Chinese-American Relations, 1895-1911* (New Haven, 1973). Empress Dowager Tz'u-hsi's policy in the early 1900s was to balance "Russian expansionism against the interests of the commercial powers." Ibid., p. 55.

80. Hay to Shen Tung [Chentung Liang Ch'eng], Nov. 22, 1902, Notes to CL.

81. Wu to Hay, July 1, 1902, Notes from CL.

82. *SF Chronicle*, Nov. 11, 1901, p. 1.

83. *NY Times*, Aug. 10, 1902, p. 3.

84. "Current Comment," *JAAA* 2 (Aug. 1902): 170.

85. Edwin H. Conger to Hay, Jan. 15, 1904, CD. For a summary of Wu's career from 1903 to 1906, see Shin, "China in Transition," pp. 21-24. Shin characterizes him as "a member of an early modernizing elite," p. 24.

86. *NY Times*, Aug. 10, 1902, p. 3. Stress was placed on his baseball prowess. A former opponent maintained that he had "invented the curve ball" and referred to him as an outstanding pitcher. Ibid., Nov. 29, 1903, p. 7. He also attended Amherst College.

87. *NY Times*, Aug. 10, 1902, p. 3.

88. Philip C. Jessup, *Elihu Root* (New York, 1938), 2: 45. Earl Swisher in his *Chinese Representation in the United States, 1861-1912* (University of Colorado Studies, Series in History 5 [Boulder, 1967], p. 29) has assessed Liang Ch'eng as "probably the ablest diplomat China sent to the United States during the Empire." He also called Wu and Liang "two brilliant and versatile diplomats," p. 34.

89. *NY Times*, Apr. 5, 1903, p. 13.

90. Ibid., Sept. 30, 1903, p. 8.

91. See correspondence and other records on this incident in SCR, FB 85, 12,164-C. Chow subsequently became minister of finance in the Chinese government.

92. Ibid.

93. Telegram quoted in Adee to Liang, Sept. 29, 1803, Notes to CL.

94. Metcalf to Roosevelt, June 7, 1905, SCR, FB 85. See also Metcalf to Roosevelt, June 7, 1905, Roosevelt Papers. Hay partly blamed Chow in his reply to Liang, Jan. 15, 1904, Notes to CL.

95. Liang to Hay, Nov. 30, 1902, Notes from CL. Loomis to Liang, Dec. 8, 1903, Notes to CL. Foster, "The Chinese Boycott," pp. 125-26. He was tied to a fence by his queue.

96. Liang to Hay, Nov. 10, 1903, Notes from CL.

97. Clyde, *United States Policy toward China*, pp. 222-30; U.S. Congress, House, *Papers Relating to the Foreign Relations of the United States*, 1903 (Washington, 1904), pp. 91-119. Hereafter cited as FR. For a discussion of the various commercial treaties negotiated, see Hosea B. Morse, *The International Relations of the Chinese Empire* (New York, 1918), 3: 369-74. For a treatment of the American treaty utilizing Chinese archival materials, see Hunt, *Frontier Defense and the Open Door*, pp. 68-76. Hunt found American negotiators poorly informed about various aspects of their subject, especially the location of cities in Manchuria, p. 71. Wu was one of the Chinese negotiators.

98. "The Annual Meeting," *JAAA* 3 (Nov. 1903): 296.

99. *NY Times*, Dec. 19, 1903, p. 1.

100. "The Annual Meeting," *JAAA* 2 (Nov. 1902): 269.

101. Miner, "The Strange Adventures of Mr. Fay and Mr. Kung," p. 698.

102. Conger to Hay, Jan. 25, 1904, CD.

CHAPTER 6.

1. Conger to Hay, Jan. 25, 1904, CD. For a survey of events leading to the termination of this treaty, see George E. Paulson, "The Abrogation of the Gresham-Yang Treaty," *Pacific Historical Review* 40 (Nov. 1971): 456-77. The article holds that if Roosevelt had intervened earlier he could have saved the treaty.

2. Conger to Hay, Feb. 6, 1904, Confidental, CD.

3. Hay to Conger, Feb. 11, 1904, NA, RG 59, Instructions from the Department of State to the Legation in Peking. Hereafter cited as CI.

4. Hay to Conger, Feb. 19, 1904, ibid.

5. Conger to Hay, March 1, 1904, CD.

6. Ibid. The third article concerned the exempt classes and the right of transit for laborers.

7. Ibid.

8. Conger to Hay, March 10, 1904, CD.

9. Conger to Hay, March 15, 1904, ibid.

10. Conger to Hay, Apr. 4, 1904, ibid.

11. Conger to Hay, Jan. 21, 1904, ibid.

12. Conger to Hay, Apr. 20, 1904, ibid.

13. Ch'ing to Conger, Apr. 1, 1904, Enc. 2, ibid.

14. Conger to Ch'ing, Apr. 11, 1904, Enc. 3, ibid.

15. Ch'ing to Conger, Apr. 19, 1904, Enc. 4, ibid.

16. Notation in Conger to Hay, Jan. 25, 1904, ibid.

17. *NY Times*, March 24, 1904, p. 5.

18. Hay to Conger, Apr. 2, 1904, CI.

19. A spokesman for the Legislative Committee of the Knights of Labor had appeared in the House chambers to demand that Livernash be made chairman of the Committee on Labor. Speaker Cannon ordered the man removed "to applause and later congratulations." *NY Times*, Dec. 6, 1903, p. 6. Historians have paid little attention to Livernash. After serving one term in the House, he was editor of the *Denver News* for a short time. He was also prominent in the founding of the Japanese-Korean Exclusion League in California in 1905. From 1909 to 1912 he lived in France. After that, he settled in Belmont, California, to study and write until his death in 1938. Upon his return from France, he changed his name to De Nivernais. "Edward J. Livernash, 1866-1938," *Biographical Directory of the American Congress, 1774-1961* (Washington, 1961), p. 1226. His connection with the Japanese-Korean Exclusion League is omitted from the *Biographical Directory*.

20. *SF Chronicle*, Apr. 1, 1904, p. 3.

21. 58th Cong., 2nd sess., *Cong. Rec.* 38: 4083-85. Ralston & Siddons, "Opinion That Denouncement of Treaty of 1894 with China Opens United States to Unrestricted Chinese Immigration." Apr. 1, 1904, Sen. Doc. 242, 58th Cong., 2nd sess., 1904-1905, 6, no. 4591.

22. Apr. 4, 1904, Hay Diaries, Hay Papers.

23. Roosevelt to Cortelyou, Jan. 25, 1904, Morison, *Letters*, 3: 709.

24. Apr. 5, 1904, Hay Diaries, Hay Papers. Beale sharply criticized the action as "abandoning statesmanship for West Coast politics." Beale, *Theodore Roosevelt and the Rise of America to World Power*, p. 215.

25. O. H. Platt to Roosevelt, Apr. 5, 1904, Roosevelt Papers.

26. Apr. 8, 1904, Hay Diaries, Hay Papers.

27. Apr. 8, 1904, 58th Cong., 2nd sess., *Cong. Rec.* 38: 4478.

28. *SF Chronicle*, Apr. 6, 1904, p. 3.

29. *NY Tribune*, Apr. 10, 1904, p. 2.

30. Ibid., Apr. 17, 1904, p. 3. See also 58th Cong., 2nd sess., *Cong. Rec.* 38: 5031.

31. AFL, *Proc.*, 1902, p. 132.

32. Ibid., pp. 89, 156. "Extracts from Minutes of Executive Council Meeting, Washington, D.C., January 19-24, 1903," *American Federationist* 10 (March 1903): 204; "Editorial," ibid. (Feb. 1903), p. 94; Edward Rosenberg, "Chinese Workers in China," ibid. (Aug. 1903), pp. 651-55; Rosenberg, "New Japan and Its Workers," ibid. (Dec. 1903), p. 1273; Rosenberg, "Labor Conditions in Hawaii," ibid. (Dec. 1903), pp. 1265-70.

33. AFL, *Proc.*, 1903, p. 87.

34. Ibid., 1904, p. 30.

35. 58th Cong., 2nd sess., *Cong. Rec.* 38: 5031.

36. Ibid., p. 5033.

37. Ibid., pp. 5033-34.

38. Ibid., p. 5036.

39. *SF Chronicle*, Apr. 19, 1904, p. 3.

40. Apr. 18, 1904, 58th Cong., 2nd sess., *Cong. Rec.* 38: 5031.

41. *SF Chronicle*, Apr. 21, 1904, p. 1.

42. Ibid.

43. Ibid.

44. "Current Comment," *JAAA* 4 (May 1904): 98.

45. *SF Chronicle*, Apr. 22, 1904, p. 4.

46. Apr. 23, 1904, 58th Cong., 2nd sess., *Cong. Rec.* 38: 5416.

47. Ibid., p. 5418.

48. Ibid., p. 5419.

49. Ibid.

50. Ibid., p. 5731. For the Cullom motion, see ibid., p. 5420. See also Li, *Congressional Policy of Chinese Immigration*, pp. 104-7. Ma, in *American Policy toward China*, p. 113, overlooks that the Senate struck out sections 6-13 of the Hitt bill. Harbaugh calls the signing of the bill by Roosevelt "one of the weakest actions of his presidential career." William H. Harbaugh, *Power and Responsibility: The Life and Times of Theodore Roosevelt* (New York, 1961), p. 296.

51. Samuel Gompers, "Chinese Exclusion," *Independent* 54 (Apr. 28, 1904): 947.

52. Ibid., p. 948.

53. "Labor Legislation," *American Federationist* 11(June 1904): 509.

54 "Current Comment" (1904), p. 98.

55. *FR*, 1904, pp. 118-46. Morse, *The International Relations of the Chinese Empire*, 3: 427-81.

56. *SF Chronicle*, Apr. 11, 1904, p. 6.

57. Ibid., Apr. 12, 1904, p. 4.

58. *Annual Report . . . Commissioner General of Immigration*, 1904, p. 885.

59. "Current Comment" (1904), p. 98. Foord urged that the regulations be a part of the treaty so as to spell out and limit the actions of the officials.

60. For one letter of inquiry about Metcalf, see Roosevelt to Marvin Hughitt, June 6, 1904, Morison, *Letters* 4: 821.

61. Roosevelt to Metcalf, June 16, 1904, ibid., p. 837.

62. Porter, *National Party Platforms*, p. 262.

63. *NY Times*, Aug. 27, 1904, p. 12.

64. *China Mail*, June 10, 1904.

65. U.S. Congress, House, Committee on Foreign Affairs, *Hearings on Chinese Exclusion*, 59th Cong., 1st sess., 1905-1906, p. 74. Hereafter cited as House *Hearings*, Exclusion, 1906.

66. For letters and telegrams between July 2 and July 18, see SCR, FB 87. For the bureau's defense of its activities, see House Doc. 847, 59th Cong., 1st sess., 1906, p. 146. Note that in this case the Portuguese citizenship of a Chinese was disregarded; Miss Soong was admitted in the end as a student according to the treaty with China and the administrative regulations of the Bureau of Immigration. Race had become the determining principle in light of this precedent. See also House *Hearings*, Exclusion, 1906, pp. 193-94.

67. *Oregon Journal,* July 17, 1904. For the inspector's report, see J. H. Barbour to Commissioner General of Immigration, July 20, 1904, SCR, FB 85.

68. Frederick W. Sutterle to Roosevelt, July 27, 1904, SCR, FB 85.

69. Mrs. Emma E. Fong to Roosevelt, Aug. 10, 1904, ibid.

70. John Goodnow, Feb. 7, 1905, "Memorandum for Mr. Loomis," in NA, RG 59, Reports of Bureau Officers, 1899-1911, 10, no. 22.

71. Liang to Hay, Aug 12, 1904, Notes from CL.

72. Liang to Hay, Aug. 8, 1904, ibid. Also U.S. Department of Commerce and Labor, NA, RG 85, 52320/27.

73. Rockhill to Hay, Aug. 12, 1904, SCR, FB 98.

74. Ibid.

75. Ibid.

76. For the original draft with Rockhill's proposed revisions indicated, see Department of Commerce and Labor, RG 85, 52320/27.

77. Hay to Rockhill, Oct. 6, 1904, SCR, FB 98.

78. Ibid.

79. Rockhill to Sargent, Oct. 7, 1904, William W. Rockhill Papers. Rockhill was director of the Bureau of American Affairs, but he was also adviser to the Department of State, which had no Far Eastern division as such. Varg, *Open Door Diplomat,* p. 51.

80. Department of Commerce and Labor, RG 85, 52320/27.

81. Ibid.

82. Richard K. Campbell to Sargent, Oct. 26, 1904, ibid.

83. Sargent to Campbell, Nov. 1, 1904, ibid.

84. Campbell, "Memorandum," Nov. 1904, ibid.

85. Ibid. See also Rockhill to Campbell, Nov. 1, 1904, SCR, FB 98, and Rockhill to Campbell, Nov. 1, 1904, Rockhill Papers.

86. Nov. 18, 1904, Hay Diaries, Hay Papers.

87. Nov. 22, 1904, ibid.

88. Nov. 25, 1904, ibid.

89. Nov. 28, 1904, ibid. An entry the day before (Sunday) indicated that Hay had been informed that the other department had completed its study and was ready to report. Nov. 27, 1904, ibid.

90. Nov. 29, 1904, ibid.

91. Ibid.

92. Hay to Liang, Nov. 29, 1904, Notes to CL.

93. Campbell to Commissioner General, "Memorandum," n.d., Department of Commerce and Labor, RG 85, 52320/27.

94. Dec. 2, 1904, Hay Diaries, Hay Papers.

95. Dec. 5, 1904, ibid.

96. Dec. 19, 1904, ibid.

97. Dec. 23, 1904, ibid.

98. Hay to Conger, Dec. 5, 1904, CI.

99. Liang to Hay, Jan. 7, 1904, Notes from CL.

100. Rockhill to Adee, Jan. 9, 1905, Rockhill Papers.

101. Rockhill to Secretary, Jan. 12, 1905, ibid.

102. Department of Commerce and Labor, RG 85, 52320/27.

103. Metcalf to Secretary of State, Jan. 12, 1905, ibid.

104. *Annual Report ... Commissioner General of Immigration*, 1905, p. 78.

105. Ibid., p. 81. Those who were admitted in the exempt class category are as follows: 1898: 5698; 1899: 3925; 1900: 3802; 1901: 1784; 1902: 1273; 1903: 1523; 1904: 1284; 1905: 1348. See chart 6 opposite p. 84 in ibid. Note especially the sharp drop between 1900 and 1901.

106. Loomis to Liang, Apr. 13, 1905, Notes to CL.

107. In this case, the Supreme Court ruled that the final authority in exclusion questions was the Secretary of Commerce and Labor.

CHAPTER 7.

1. "Current Comment," *JAAA* 5 (May 1905): 98.

2. "Seventh Annual Dinner of the Association," *JAAA* 4 (Jan. 1905): 364.

3. Hay to Secretary of Commerce and Labor, Jan. 20, 1905, SCR, FB 85. Packet no. 12,264 contains several letters pertaining to this matter.

4. J. Wilson Evans, Pacific Commercial Museum, to Secretary of State, Feb. 14, 1905, ibid.

5. John Goodnow to Francis B. Loomis, Nov. 17, 1904, ibid. See also U. S. Department of State, NA, RG 59, Consular Dispatches, Shanghai. Hereafter cited as Shanghai D. The petitions contained names from Shanghai, Peking, Foochow, Wuhu, and elsewhere.

6. Wilbur T. Gracey, Vice Consul in Charge, to H. H. D. Peirce, Third Assistant Secretary of State, Nov. 29, 1904, Nanking D. See also SCR, FB 85.

7. Edgar Quackenbush et al. to Secretary of State, n.d., in SCR, FB 85. The petition ended up in the files of the Bureau of Immigration. The movement began in Soochow, China, on Oct. 25, 1904. J. B. Feam became the chairman. The news was given to the *North China Daily News* to get wider circulation. Copies of the petition were obtainable at the Presbyterian Mission Press. "The Chinese Exclusion Act," *JAAA* 4 (Jan. 1905): 367.

8. Gracey to Peirce, Nov. 29, 1904, Nanking D.

9. Ibid.

10. Resolution of Convention of Superintendents, Missionaries, and Teachers of New England, Nov. 17-18, 1904, to Department of Commerce and Labor, SCR, FB 85.

11. John Fryer to Benjamin I. Wheeler, Apr. 19, 1905, SCR, FB 85.

12. Proclamation by Chung, Acting Consul General for California, on statement by Minister Liang, translated by J. Endicott Gardner, Inspector and Interpreter at San Francisco, Apr. 30, 1905, SCR, FB 85.

13. Ibid.

14. In *Chung Sai Yat Po*, May 16, 1905, San Francisco, SCR, FB 107. In all, 21 frantic telegrams were received by the Chinese Foreign Office between May 9 and 13 from Chinese-Americans. Chang, "China's Response to the Open Door, 1898-1906," p. 116.

15. Li, *Congressional Policy of Chinese Immigration*, p. 108. On June 30, 1905, the bureau was seeking a law which would require the registration of Chinese who were in the United States on January 1, 1900, and then authorize the bureau to deport all who had entered after that time and were not in the exempt classes. As another tack, the bureau was seeking a ruling from the courts to allow this. *Annual Report . . . Immigration*, 1905, p. 100. From June to June, 1,402 arrests of Chinese who were suspected of unlawful residence had been made, and 647 had been deported. *Annual Report*, p. 90. The Chinese had vigorously protested and threatened to boycott.

16. W. S. Harwood, "The Passing of the Chinese," *World's Work* 9 (Dec. 1904): 5626-31.

17. Charles F. Remer, *A Study of Chinese Boycotts with Special Reference to Their Economic Effectiveness* (Baltimore, 1933), p. 21. William Martin, Consul General at Hankow, to Loomis, May 29, 1905, Hankow D.

18. Quoted by Charles Stewart Smith from an earlier conversation with Li in *NY Tribune*, Apr. 25, 1904, p. 6.

19. Samuel L. Gracey to Peirce, June 8, 1905, Foochow D. Another copy of the minutes of the Shanghai meeting was sent by Schwerin to Roosevelt, July 13, 1905, SCR, FB 85; Chang Ts'un-wu, *Chung Mei Kung-yueh Feng-ch'Ao (Agitation Concerning the Sino-American Labor Treaty, 1905)* (Taipei, 1966), p. 43; Margaret Field, "The Chinese Boycott of 1905," *Papers on China*, East Asian Research Center (Harvard University, 1957), p. 65.

20. S. L. Gracey to Peirce, June 8, 1905, Foochow D. This information is based on a translation of the circulars.

21. *North China Daily News*, May 16, 1905, in Martin to Loomis, May 29, 1905, Hankow D.

22. Julius G. Lay to Hay, May 26, 1905, Canton D.

23. Ibid.

24. Lay to Loomis, May 31, 1905, ibid.

25. S. L. Gracey to Peirce, June 8, 1905, Foochow D. His son, Wilbur, was also a consul.

26. Schwerin to Roosevelt, July 13, 1905, SCR, FB 85.

27. Hay to Secretary of Commerce and Labor, June 23, 1905, ibid.

28. Henry B. Miller, Consul General at Yokohama, Japan, to Loomis, Aug. 8, 1905, Roosevelt Papers.

29. Rockhill to Secretary of State, July 6, 1905, CD.

30. Enc. 1 in CD.

31. Rockhill to Secretary of State, July 6, 1905, CD.

32. "A Statement of Objections to the Proposed American Chinese Exclusion Treaty," May 23, 1905, PLA.

33. James L. Rodgers, Consul General at Shanghai, to Loomis, Aug. 24, 1905, Shanghai D.

34. Lay to Rockhill, June 19, 1905, Rockhill Papers. A curious case in February, before the boycott was a public issue, was that of Wah Sang, who had come to the United States as a student. He had studied theology and had been ordained as a Methodist minister. In Texas he was arrested and then deported on the grounds that a minister was a laborer. Li, *Congressional Policy of Chinese Immigration*, p. 116.

35. Lay to Rockhill, June 19, 1905, Rockhill Papers.

36. "Exclusion Troubles," *Literary Digest* 30 (June 24, 1905): 925.

37. Quoted in ibid.

38. The Bureau of Immigration denied any unjust treatment or lack of courtesy. The inspector had been following regulations. The fault lay in the failure of the aliens to

have the proper certificates. House Doc. 847, 59th Cong., 1st sess., 1905, pp. 134-36. A member of the Legation in Peking, who later had a long and distinguished career in the diplomatic service, recalled the incident with chagrin in his memoirs. See William Phillips, *Ventures in Diplomacy* (Boston, 1952), pp. 27-28. Rodgers refers to the impact in Shanghai, in Rodgers to Secretary of State, July 27, 1905, Shanghai D.

39. Rodgers to Secretary of State, July 27, 1905, Shanghai D. Chang, *Chung Mei Kung-yueh Feng-ch'Ao*, p. 86.

40. One of Tseng's interests was to oppose footbinding. Beale, *Theodore Roosevelt and the Rise of America to World Power*, p. 216. Ma and Ku Chung were the two student leaders with whom Tseng worked. Rodgers to Loomis, Sept. 15, 1905, Shanghai D; Field, "The Chinese Boycott of 1905," pp. 68-69.

41. *NY Tribune*, Aug. 16, 1905, p. 1.

42. Ibid., Aug. 22, 1905, p. 12. A follower of K'ang records that the Reform Association began its campaign against the laws in 1903, and in 1904 it called on its branches in the United States to support a petition to the government in Peking to oppose continuing the existing treaty. Jung-pang Lo, *K'ang Yu-wei: A Biography and Symposium* (Tucson, 1967), pp. 270-71. Iriye gives the date 1903 for the first Honolulu editorial. Akira Iriye, "Public Opinion and Foreign Policy: The Case of Late Ch'ing China," in *Approaches to Modern Chinese History*, ed. Albert Feuerwerker, Rhoads Murphey, and Mary C. Wright (Berkeley and Los Angeles, 1967), p. 232. Schiffrin gives a 1902 date. Harold Z. Schiffrin, *Sun Yat-sen and the Origins of the Chinese Revolution* (Berkeley and Los Angeles, 1968), p. 291.

43. Rodgers to Loomis, Aug. 24, 1905, Shanghai D.

44. John Endicott Gardner to Commissioner of Immigration, San Francisco, Aug. 7, 1905, SCR, FB 85.

45. Reported in *NY Times*, Feb. 1, 1905, p. 8. Field terms it a "mouthpiece for Tseng Shao-ch'ing." Field, "The Chinese Boycott of 1905," p. 71. She does not connect it with the Reform Association, but she doubts any Japanese tie. The newspaper, she says, began in 1904 and was edited by Ch'en Ming. Ibid., pp. 71-72.

46. Lay to Loomis, July 10, 1905, Canton D.

47. Rockhill to Secretary of State, Aug. 24, 1905, CD. Field, "The Chinese Boycott of 1905," pp. 71-72. See also Iriye, "Public Opinion and Foreign Policy," pp. 228-29.

48. Chang, *Chung Mei Kung-yueh Feng-ch'Ao*, p. 63.

49. Ibid., p. 65.

50. Iriye, "Public Opinion and Foreign Policy," pp. 224-25.

51. Chang, *Chung Mei Kung-yueh Feng-ch'Ao*, pp. 47-48. See also Shin, "China in Transition," p. 361.

52. From a speech in Chicago on May 20, 1905, quoted in Beale, *Theodore Roosevelt and the Rise of America to World Power*, p. 218.

53. Lloyd Griscom to Rockhill, June 23, 1905, Rockhill Papers. On February 10, 1906, a Japanese official in the United States pointed out at a banquet that Japan would consider it foolish to risk the friendship of the United States for such a small gain. Why, he asked, should Japan single out the United States in place of a more hostile power? *NY Times*, Feb. 11, 1906, p. 5.

54. *SF Chronicle*, July 25, 1905, p. 6. This article also contained the view of J. E. Wilkie, secret service agent, that the boycott was started by "British and German traders in Hongkong and Shanghai to injure our trade in China."

55. Meribeth E. Cameron, *The Reform Movement in China, 1898-1912* (New York, 1931), p. 184.

56. H. B. LaRue to Metcalf, Dec. 20, 1904, SCR, FB 85.

CHAPTER 8.

1. Foord to Roosevelt, May 16, 1905, SCR, FB 85. See also "Correspondence," *JAAA* 5 (June 1905): 132.

2. See correspondence in SCR, FB 85, Packet no. 12,264. The *San Francisco News Letter* article did not believe that a boycott would occur but advocated admitting cheap Chinese labor.

3. Committee representing American Members of the Educational Association of China to Roosevelt, May 19, 1905, SCR, FB 85.

4. S. B. Gracey to Peirce, June 7, 1905, ibid. See also Gracey to Pe.

5. O. F. Wisner to Rockhill, July 15, 1905, in Rockhill to Hay, July 26, 1905, Enc. 3, CD. A letter to Roosevelt from Wisner and 32 other citizens of Canton reinforced the Chinese letter in calling for a treaty which would admit non-laborers, especially students. "We are ambitious," it emphasized, "to see our country acting as headmaster." U.S. Citizens of Canton to Roosevelt, July 17, 1905, Roosevelt Papers.

6. Edward S. Ling, Chairman of the Committee for Students and Teachers of the Anglo-Chinese College, Foochow, China, to Roosevelt, June 2, 1905, SCR, FB 85.

7. Rockhill to Hay, June 21, 1905, CD.

8. Davidson to James N. Jameson, President, American Association of China, in "American Association of China," *JAAA* 5 (July 1905): 165-66.

9. "A Statement of Objections to the Proposed American Chinese Exclusion Treaty," May 23, 1905, PLA.

10. Ibid.

11. Thomas Sammons, Consul General at Newchwang, to Loomis, June 19, 1905, Newchwang D.

12. Rockhill to Hay, June 17, 1905, CD.

13. Ibid.

14. "Memorandum," n.d., SCR, FB 90. Campbell probably prepared this unsigned statement.

15. Quoted in Rockhill to Secretary of State, July 26, 1905, CD.

16. Rockhill to Ch'ing, June 17, 1905, PLA.

17. Telegram from the gentry and people of Nanking to Rockhill, June 19, 1905, PLA. Apparently, "Supplementary Exclusion Treaty" referred to the policy of excluding members of the privileged classes.

18. "Memorandum, Conference at the Wai Wu Pu," June 22, 1905, PLA.

19. Ibid.

20. Ibid.

21. Ibid.

22. Ibid.

23. *NY Times*, June 28, 1905, p. 4.

24. Rockhill to Ch'ing, June 24, 1905, PLA.

25. Rockhill to Hay (Confidential), July 1, 1905, Roosevelt Papers.

26. Rockhill to Hay, July 1, 1905, CD.

27. Ch'ing to Rockhill, July 1, 1905, PLA.

28. For the American draft of July 8 and the Chinese draft of July 19, see "Chinese Counter-draft," July 19, 1905, PLA. On July 12 Rockhill urged Roosevelt to return the Boxer indemnity to China. Griswold, *The Far Eastern Policy of the United States*, p. 124.

29. Peirce to Rockhill, July 7, 1905, CI.

30. Rockhill to Secretary of State, July 14, 1905, CD. A notation by the State Department provided for the referral of this telegram to W.H. Libby of Standard Oil Company.

31. Rockhill to Secretary of State, July 15, 1905, CD.

32. See letter and enclosures in Rockhill to Secretary of State, July 25, 1905, ibid.

33. Ibid.

34. Ibid.

35. Ibid.

36. Rockhill to Hay, July 6, 1905, Enc. 4, CD.

37. Barrett to Roosevelt ("Personal and Confidential"), June 17, 1905, Roosevelt Papers.

38. *North China Daily News*, July 21, 1905, in Rockhill to Secretary of State, July 26, 1905, CD.

39. Rockhill to Na-t'ung, July 25, 1905, PLA.

40. Ibid.

41. Rockhill to Secretary of State, July 26, 1905, CD. This communication did not go to the Department of Commerce and Labor until September 14, according to a notation.

42. Peirce to Diplomatic and Consular Officers of the United States in China, June 26, 1905, CI.

43. Rockhill to Ch'ing, July 28, 1905, PLA. The press comment by Chinese in Canton was, "Why didn't the President do this before?" Lay to Loomis, Aug. 9, 1905, Canton D.

44. Na-t'ung to Rockhill, July 31, 1905, PLA.

45. Enc. in Na-t'ung to Rockhill, ibid. The parentheses contain explanations by the Legation translator, E. T. Williams.

46. Rockhill to Secretary of State, July 28, 1905, in Department of Commerce and Labor, RG 85, 52320/27.

47. Ibid.

48. Rockhill to Secretary of State, July 26, 1905, CD.

49. *SF Chronicle*, July 29, 1905, p. 2.

50. S. L. Gracey to Loomis, Aug. 5, 1905, Foochow D; Lay to Loomis, Aug. 1, 1905, Canton D.

51. Rockhill to Secretary of State, Aug. 2, 1905, CD.

52. Rockhill to Secretary of State, July 6, 1905, ibid. From Canton Cheshire commented, "What do you think of that pot-bellied Minister of the Wai Wu Pu—Na Tung? Fancy! the stand he took against Yuan Shih kai, when he recommended to the Throne the advisability of the Imperial Decree being issued stopping the agitation." Cheshire to Rockhill, Aug. 16, 1905, Rockhill Papers.

53. Rockhill to Secretary of State, Aug. 4, 1905, CD.

54. Adee to Rockhill, July 26, 1905, CI.

55. Rockhill to Ch'ing, Aug. 2, 1905, PLA.

56. The President and Ministers of the Board of Foreign Affairs to Rockhill, Aug. 7, 1905, PLA.

57. Ibid.

58. Phillips, *Ventures in Diplomacy*, p. 18.

59. Rockhill to Secretary of State, Aug. 4, 1905, CD.

60. Adee to Rockhill, Aug. 5, 1905, CI.

61. Rockhill to Ch'ing, Aug. 7, 1905, PLA.

62. Ibid. Article 15 of the treaty of 1858 stated in part: "At each of the ports open to Commerce, citizens of the United States shall be permitted to import from abroad and sell, purchase, and export all merchandise of which the importation or exportation is not prohibited by the laws of the Empire." Clyde, *United States Policy toward China*, p. 52.

63. Rockhill to Ch'ing, Aug. 14, 1905, PLA.

64. Ch'ing to Rockhill, Aug. 26, 1905, ibid.

CHAPTER 9.

1. Edwin Maxey, "Our Policy toward China," *Arena* 33 (May 1905): 510.

2. Holcombe, "The Question of Chinese Exclusion," *Outlook* 80 (July 8, 1905): 619.

3. Ibid., p. 614.

4. "Political Boycotts," *Independent* 59 (Aug. 17, 1905): 404.

5. "Current Comment," *JAAA* 5 (May 1905): 98.

6. *NY Times*, June 13, 1905, p. 8. For the memorial see "The Administration of the Chinese Exclusion Laws," *JAAA* 5 (July 1905): 167-68.

7. "The Administration of the Chinese Exclusion Laws," p. 168. See also "Current Comment," p. 162.

8. See clipping on "Banquet sponsored by the American Hardware Manufacturers Association, Hot Springs, Va.," in William H. Taft Papers, Series 9A, Addresses and Articles.

9. "Commencement Address at Miami University," June 15, 1905, ibid.

10. Henry C. Lodge to Roosevelt, June 18, 1905, Roosevelt Papers.

11. Roosevelt to Metcalf, June 16, 1905, Morison, *Letters* 4: 1236. North, a lawyer on the side, prided himself on strictly enforcing the laws and was one of the highest paid bureau officials. H. H. North to Powderly, May 23, 1901, Powderly Papers, A1-109.

12. June 19, 1905, Morison, *Letters* 4: 1240.

13. June 19, 1905, Diaries, Hay Papers.

14. *NY Times*, June 15, 1905, p. 1.

15. "Memorandum," n.d., Department of Commerce and Labor, RG 85, 52320/27.

16. *NY Times*, June 20, 1905, p. 8.

17. Portland Chamber of Commerce to Roosevelt, June 23, 1905, SCR, FB 85; *NY Tribune*, June 25, 1905, p. 2.

18. *NY Times*, June 24, 1905, p. 4.

19. Taft to Roosevelt, June 20, 1905, Taft Papers, Series 8, Secretary of War, Semi-official.

20. *NY Times*, June 24, 1905, p. 4.

21. Ibid.

22. Metcalf to Roosevelt, June 24, 1905, Roosevelt Papers. See also Department Circular no. 81 in ibid. or SCR, FB 85.

23. *SF Chronicle*, June 26, 1905, p. 4.

24. "Current Comment," p. 162.

25. Max J. Kohler to Roosevelt, June 26, 1905, SCR, FB 85.

26. Metcalf to Kohler, July 1, 1905, ibid.

27. John Endicott Gardner to James R. Garfield, ibid. Gardner's abilities as an interpreter were highly regarded by the bureau. His opportunities to advance were probably blocked because he had a Chinese wife.

28. *NY Tribune*, July 9, 1905, p. 3. The other two members of the commission were Edward W. Sime, solicitor, and Lawrence O. Murray, assistant secretary.

29. See report in North to Acting Commissioner General of Immigration, June 30, 1905, SCR, FB 85.

30. Ibid.

31. *NY Times*, June 29, 1905, p. 4.

32. From the *Havana Post*, July 7, 1905, in B. D. Washburn to Sargent, July 7, 1905, SCR, FB 85.

33. *NY Times*, June 25, 1905, p. 3.

34. Fleming D. Cheshire to Rockhill, June 27, 1905, Rockhill Papers.

35. *NY Tribune*, Aug. 17, 1905, p. 2.

36. Gardner to Garfield, July 1, 1905, SCR, FB 85.

37. *NY Tribune*, June 28, 1905, p. 3.

38. Ibid., June 29, 1905, p. 8.

39. Ibid. See also Lo, *K'ang Yu-wei*, pp. 198-99. For details on K'ang's speechmaking, see Robert L. Worden, "A Chinese Reformer in Exile: The North American Phase of the Travels of K'ang Yu-wei, 1899-1909" (Ph. D. diss., Georgetown University, 1972), p. 153 et passim.

40. Quan Yick Nam to Roosevelt, Aug. 3, 1905, Roosevelt Papers.

41. "Response to a toast by Mr. Sargent, at a dinner given by the Chinese Consul-General of Hawaii, at Honolulu," June 27, 1905, ibid.

42. Taft to Roosevelt, June 25, 1905, ibid.

43. "Extract from Chinese Newspaper in Hong Kong," June 30, 1905, ibid.

44. "General Notice of the Consolidated Chinese Six Companies at San Francisco," J. Endicott Gardner, July 14, 1905, SCR, FB 107.

45. *NY Tribune*, July 20, 1905, p. 1.

46. Ibid., July 2, 1905, p. 5.

47. See translations from the *Chinese World* (San Francisco), July 18, 1905, in SCR, FB 85.

48. *NY Times,* May 16, 1905, p. 8, and May 19, 1905, p. 5. See also Shih-shan Henry Tsai, "Reaction to Exclusion: Ch'ing Attitudes toward Overseas Chinese in the United States, 1848-1906" (Ph. D. diss., University of Oregon, 1970), pp. 311-12, a study of the structure and functioning of Chinese diplomacy.

49. See Enc. in Metcalf to Secretary of State, Jan. 22, 1906, SCR, FB 85; Field, "The Chinese Boycott of 1905," p. 82.

50. Enc. in Gardner to Commissioner General, Aug. 10, 1905, SCR, FB 85.

51. *Tai Tung Yat Bo (Ta-t'ung Pao)*, July 14, 1905, SCR, FB 85. This newspaper was under the control of a follower of Sun Yat-sen at this time. Lo, *K'ang Yu-wei*, p. 270.

52. See circular dated July 24, 1905, in SCR, FB 107. Although not mentioning Canton, it seemed to assume Canton's support. It was more noteworthy that backing was also coming from other parts of China.

53. Gardner to Commissioner of Immigration, July 28, 1905, SCR, FB 85.

54. Schwerin to Commissioner General, Aug. 1, 1905, ibid.

55. J. M. W. Farnham to Roosevelt, Aug. 7, 1905, ibid.

56. Gardner to Commissioner General, ibid.

57. Ibid.

58. Ibid.

59. *SF Chronicle*, July 1, 1905, p. 4.

60. Enc. in Gardner to Commissioner General, Aug. 10, 1905, SCR, FB 85.

61. *NY Tribune,* Aug. 6, 1905, p. 3.

62. Charles Mehan to Commissioner General, Aug. 23, 1905, SCR, FB 85.

63. Mehan to Commissioner General, March 10, 1906, ibid.

64. Rockhill to Elihu Root, Sept. 8, 1905, CD.

65. *NY Tribune,* Aug. 20, 1905, p. 3.

66. Adee to Rockhill, Aug. 15, 1905, CI.

67. Ibid.

68. *NY Tribune,* Aug. 14, 1905, p. 6.

69. Adee to Rockhill, Aug. 16, 1905, CI.

70. Loomis to Barnes, Aug. 26, 1905, Roosevelt Papers.

71. Rockhill to Loomis, Aug. 24, 1905, CD; Aug. 26, 1905, ibid.; Sept. 1, 1905, ibid.

72. *NY Tribune,* Aug. 10, 1905, p. 9.

73. Braisted, "The United States and the American China Development Company," p. 161.

74. Lay to Rockhill, Oct. 31, 1905, Rockhill Papers.

75. Jessup, *Elihu Root* 2: 44. The study of Root by Richard Leopold, *Elihu Root and the Conservative Tradition* (Boston, 1954), is too brief to cover the boycott issue. Useful information on Root's personality can be found in Lloyd C. Griscom, *Diplomatically Speaking* (New York, 1940), p. 268.

76. George C. Perkins to Roosevelt, Aug. 30, 1905, Roosevelt Papers.

77. Wheelwright to Roosevelt, Aug. 31, 1905, ibid.; S. H. Piles and Levi Ankenny to Roosevelt, Sept. 2, 1905, ibid.; J. Parker to Loomis, Sept. 2, 1905, ibid.

78. Loomis to Roosevelt, Sept. 1, 1905, Roosevelt Papers.

79. Taft to Roosevelt, Sept. 4, 1905, ibid. Roosevelt asked Perkins's help to get more liberal legislation from Congress. Roosevelt to Perkins, Aug. 31, 1905, Morison, *Letters* 4: 1327-28.

80. Gossipy sidelights of the Taft trip are contained in Alice Roosevelt Longworth, *Crowded Hours: Reminiscences of Alice Roosevelt Longworth* (New York, 1933), and Francis M. Huntington Wilson, *Memoirs of an Ex-Diplomat* (Boston, 1945).

81. Lay to Loomis, Aug. 16, 1905, Canton D.

82. Longworth, *Crowded Hours,* p. 92.

83. Roosevelt to Taft in Hong Kong, Sept. 3, 1905, Taft Papers, Series 4, Taft-TR.

84. "Remarks at the banquet given by the Viceroy in Canton," Sept. 4, 1904, ibid., Addresses and Articles, vol. 3. The viceroy gave health reasons for not being present.

85. House *Hearings*, Exclusion, 1906, p. 190.

86. Taft to Roosevelt, Sept. 4, 1905, Taft Papers, Series 4, Taft-TR; Roosevelt to Taft, Sept. 5, 1905, ibid.

87. Lay to Loomis, Sept. 12, 1905, Canton D.

88. Taft to Root, Oct. 4, 1905, NA, RG 59, Miscellaneous Letters to State Department. Hereafter cited as Misc. Letters.

89. *NY Tribune*, Oct. 4, 1905, p. 3. Rockhill called the 1884 act "practically impossible to carry out." Rockhill to Secretary of State, Aug. 15, 1905, CD. See also Rockhill to Secretary of State, Aug. 15, 1905, Misc. Letters.

90. *NY Tribune*, Oct. 5, 1905, p. 3.

91. Ibid., Aug. 30, 1905, p. 3.

92. Ibid., Oct. 11, 1905, p. 1.

93. Metcalf to Secretary of State, Oct. 30, 1905, Misc. Letters.

94. Fred W. Carpenter to Silas McBee, *The Churchman*, Oct. 19, 1905, Taft Papers, Series 8, Secretary of War, Semi-official.

95. "Atlanta Speech," Oct. 20, 1905, Roosevelt Papers.

96. T. C. Friedlander to Roosevelt, Sept. 5, 1905, ibid.

97. Roosevelt to Friedlander, Nov. 23, 1905, Morison, *Letters* 5: 90. He was misleading, however, in holding that the abuses which had produced the complaints then current went back to previous administrations. The use of the Bertillon system, for example, had begun with Sargent after 1902.

98. Ibid., p. 91. Root wrote some of the blunter parts of this letter. Jessup, *Elihu Root* 2: 46.

99. See draft in Root to Liang, Nov. 8, 1905, Elihu Root Papers, Letter Books.

100. Taft to Liang, Oct. 27, 1905, Taft Papers, Series 8, Secretary of War—Personal letters.

101. Root to Liang, Nov. 8, 1905, Personal, Root Papers, Letter Books.

102. Liang, "Commercial Relations between the United States and China," *Harper's Weekly* 49 (Dec. 23, 1905): 1860.

103. For example, see Nickerson, "Our Chinese Treaties, and Legislation, and Their Enforcement," pp. 369-78.

104. "Immigration—First Draft," Sept. 23, 1905, Roosevelt Papers, Speeches.

105. Chinese Students Federation to Roosevelt, Oct. 9, 1905, Misc. Letters.

106. Rockhill to Root, Nov. 3, 1905, CD.

107. Beale, *Theodore Roosevelt and the Rise of America to World Power*, p. 239.

108. U.S. Congress, *A Compilation of the Messages and Papers of the Presidents* (New York, 1902-1908), 15: 7009.

109. "Current Comment," p. 290. Foord's remarks were a reaction to the speech in Atlanta, which contained much that was also in the annual message. Foord approved the December speech, though suggesting that skilled laborers should also be admitted. See ibid., p. 322.

110. Japanese and Korean Exclusion League to George C. Perkins, Aug. 5, 1905, LR, Petitions, Senate Committee on Immigration, 59th Cong., 1st sess., 1905-1906, S59A-J46, FB 105.

111. Charles E. Neu, *An Uncertain Friendship: Theodore Roosevelt and Japan, 1906-1909* (Cambridge, 1967), p. 23. See also Roger Daniels, *The Struggle for Japanese Exclusion* (Berkeley and Los Angeles, 1961).

112. *SF Chronicle*, June 10, 1905, p. 6.

113. Ibid., June 14, 1905, p. 6.

114. Ibid., June 17, 1905, p. 6.

115. Ibid., June 27, 1905, p. 6.

116. Barrett to William Loeb, Jr., Sept. 8, 1905, Roosevelt Papers.

117. *NY Times*, June 25, 1905, p. 3.

118. July 28, 1905, Diaries, Garfield Papers.

119. Quoted in the *NY Times*, Aug. 2, 1905, p. 8.

120. Ibid.

121. AFL, *Proc.*, 1905, p. 171.

122. "Abstract of Minutes of the Executive Council Meeting, Held at Scranton, Pa., June 12-16 . . . 1905," *American Federationist* 12 (Aug. 1905): 539.

123. *NY Tribune*, July 13, 1905, p. 3. AFL, *Proc.*, 1905, p. 31.

124. *NY Times*, July 26, 1905, p. 6. Its editorial on Powderly's statements charged: "If the Americans do not know how tricky the Chinese are, they at least know how tricky POWDERLY is," ibid.

125. Samuel Gompers, "Talks on Labor," *American Federationist* 12 (Oct. 1905): 762. In contrast with the AFL's belief that Wu and the Chinese government were behind

the boycott, the *Chronicle* (July 7, 1905, p. 6) accused the American Asiatic Association of fomenting it. By August the *Chronicle* (Aug. 4, p. 6) had swung to the belief that Japan was behind it.

126. Gompers, Editorial, *American Federationist* 12 (Nov. 1905): 834.

127. AFL, *Proc.*, 1905, p. 30.

128. Ibid., p. 191.

129. "Theodore B. Wilcox on Oriental Trade," JAAA 5 (Sept. 1905): 240-42. "Hon. John Barrett on American Asiatic Trade," *JAAA* 5 (Oct. 1905): 268-72.

130. *SF Chronicle*, Aug. 20, 1905, p. 18.

131. *NY Tribune*, Dec. 12, 1905, p. 12. See also Gompers, Editorial, *American Federationist* 13 (Feb. 1905): 96.

132. *NY Tribune*, Dec. 16, 1905, p. 3.

133. Ibid., Dec. 17, 1905, p. 2.

134. *SF Chronicle*, Dec. 6, 1905, p. 4.

135. Ibid., Dec. 7, 1905, p. 1.

136. See Enc. in Thomas Sammons to Bacon, Jan. 19, 1906, Newchwang D., and the *SF Chronicle*, Dec. 7, 1905, p. 1. On July 15 Roosevelt had written Griscom in Japan that the League only represented a small segment and referred to Livernash as a "labor agitator." Roosevelt to Griscom, July 15, 1905, Morison, *Letters* 4: 1274-75.

137. *SF Chronicle*, Dec. 7, 1905, p. 1.

138. Ibid., Dec. 6, 1905, p. 4.

CHAPTER 10.

1. Roosevelt to Rockhill (Confidential), Aug. 22, 1905, Rockhill Papers.

2. Ibid.

3. Morse, *The International Relations of the Chinese Empire* 3: 435; Griswold, *The Far Eastern Policy of the United States*, p. 124.

4. The consul general at Canton admitted that boycott meetings were being held as late as January 8, 1907. *NY Times*, March 22, 1907, p. 4. See also Edward J. M. Rhoads, *China's Republican Revolution: The Case of Kwangtung, 1895-1913* (Cambridge, 1975), pp. 90-91.

5. Longworth, *Crowded Hours*, p. 100.

6. Phillips, *Ventures in Diplomacy*, p. 24.

7. Ibid., p. 25; Varg, *Open Door Diplomat*, p. 60.

8. Phillips to Joseph Choate, quoted in Beale, *Theodore Roosevelt and the Rise of America to World Power*, p. 245.

9. Rockhill to Root, Sept. 5, 1905, CD.

10. Ibid.

11. Rockhill to Root, Sept. 27, 1905, ibid.

12. No book has been published in English which deals with the 1905 boycott. In Chinese, see Chang, *Chung Mei Kung-yueh Feng-ch'Ao* (Taipei, 1966). In English, see Margaret Field, "The Chinese Boycott of 1905," *Papers on China* 11 (1957): 63-98; Akira Iriye, "Public Opinion and Foreign Policy: The Case of Late Ch'ing China," in *Approaches to Modern Chinese History*, ed. Albert Fuerwerker, Rhoads Murphey, and Mary C. Wright (Berkeley and Los Angeles, 1967), pp. 216-38; Jessie Ashworth Miller, "China in American Policy and Opinion, 1906-1909" (Ph.D. diss., Clark University, 1938); Anthony Milnar, "Chinese-American Relations with Especial Reference to the Imposition of the Boycott, 1905-1906" (Ph.D. diss., Georgetown University, 1948); Charles F. Remer, *A Study of Chinese Boycotts with Special Reference to Their Economic Effectiveness* (Baltimore, 1933).

13. Field, "The Chinese Boycott of 1905," p. 67.

14. Chang, *Chung Mei Kung-yueh Feng-ch'Ao.* p. 43.

15. Ibid., pp. 87-88.

16. Field, "The Chinese Boycott of 1905," p. 74.

17. Iriye, "Public Opinion and Foreign Policy," p. 221.

18. Field, "The Chinese Boycott of 1905," pp. 71-73.

19. Special Correspondent in Shanghai, "The Rising Spirit in China," *Outlook* 81 (Oct. 7, 1905): 316.

20. Field, "The Chinese Boycott of 1905," p. 76.

21. Chang, *Chung Mei Kung-yueh Feng-ch'Ao*, p. 147.

22. Ibid.

23. Ibid., p. 69.

24. Ibid., p. 203.

25. Ibid.

26. Iriye, "Public Opinion and Foreign Policy," p. 232.

27. Chang, *Chung Mei Kung-yueh Feng-ch'Ao*, pp. 153-54.

28. Ibid., pp. 211-14.

29. Rodgers to Bacon, Dec. 16 and Dec. 22, 1905, Shanghai D; Rockhill to Root, Dec. 23, 1905, CD. See also George Kennan, "China in Transition: The Anti-Foreign Rioting in Shanghai," *Outlook* 82 (Feb. 17, 1906): 351-57.

30. "Letter from Hang Shen-hsiu and more than a Thousand Others, Representing Chinese Merchants of every Province" to Rockhill, Oct. 1, 1905, PLA. Rockhill to Root, Oct. 4, 1905, CD. Department of Commerce and Labor, RG 85, 52320/27. In all, the signatures numbered 1,241. Signers included a few women and Manchu Bannermen.

31. Rockhill to Root, Oct. 4, 1905, CD.

32. Rodgers to Bacon, Jan. 10, 1906, Shanghai D.

33. Mason Mitchell to Bacon, Apr. 30, 1906, Chungking D. Hangchow, near Shanghai, felt the effects, but no significant incident occurred. Tension, after declining in December, again increased. Frederick D. Cloud to Bacon, Dec. 8, 1905, Hangchow D.

34. Murray Warner, House *Hearings*, Exclusion, 1906, p. 76.

35. Phillips, *Ventures in Diplomacy*, pp. 27-28. "General Missionary Intelligence," *MRW* 19 o.s. (July 1906): 544. William Hancock, Commissioner of Customs, believed the family head to be "the real instigator of the boycott," quoted in *NY Times*, March 3, 1906, p. 4. Hancock is not to be taken seriously here.

36. Rodgers to Rockhill, Sept. 1, 1905, Rockhill Papers. Field, "The Chinese Boycott of 1905," p. 69.

37. Field, "The Chinese Boycott of 1905," p. 69.

38. C. S. Walker, "The Army of Chinese Students Abroad," *World's Work* 13 (Jan. 1907): 8471.

39. Chang, *Chung Mei Kung-yueh Feng-ch'Ao*, pp. 220-21; Field, "The Chinese Boycott of 1905," p. 69; Tsai, "Reaction to Exclusion," p. 298.

40. U.S. Department of Commerce and Labor, *Annual Report of the Secretary of Commerce and Labor for 1907* (Washington, 1907), p. 143.

41. Rodgers to Bacon, March 31, 1906, Shanghai D.

42. Charles Denby, "Memorandum for the Secretary," May 8, 1906, ibid.

43. Chang, *Chung Mei Kung-yueh Feng-ch'Ao*, p. 239.

44. S. L. Gracey to Loomis, Aug. 18, 1905, Foochow D.

45. S. L. Gracey to Bacon, Nov. 29, 1905, ibid.

46. "General Missionary Intelligence," *MRW* 19 o.s. (July 1906): 554; *NY Times*, March 3, 1906, p. 4.

47. *NY Tribune*, Jan. 13, 1906, p. 8.

48. March 14, 1906, House *Hearings*, Exclusion, 1906, p. 41.

49. S. L. Gracey to Peirce, June 8, 1905, Foochow D. On Foochow colleges and missions, see Kenneth S. Latourette, *A History of Christian Missions in China* (New York, 1929, 1967), pp. 404 ff.

50. S. L. Gracey to Peirce, June 4, 1905, Foochow D.

51. "General Missionary Intelligence," *MRW* 18 o.s. (Oct. 1905): 793.

52. Arthur H. Smith, *China and America To-Day: A Study of Conditions and Relations* (New York, 1907), p. 172. In traveling from Canton to Peking, the engineer-in-chief for the Canton-Hankow railroad, P. H. Ashmead, "found that the Chinese regarded the boycott as a patriotic movement, strongly supporting it, particularly in the South." See letter in *NY Times*, June 10, 1906, p. 8.

53. Rockhill to James W. Ragsdale, Feb. 14, 1906, in Ragsdale to Bacon, Feb. 21, 1906, Tientsin D.

54. *NY Tribune*, Feb. 5, 1906, p. 1; Ragsdale to Bacon, March 22, 1906, Tientsin D.

55. Wilbur T. Gracey to Peirce, Nov. 29, 1904, Nanking D.

56. An article written for a Boston newspaper, but the State Department decided not to release it for publication. S. L. Gracey to Bacon, Nov. 29, 1905, Foochow D.

57. Chang, "China's Response to the Open Door, 1898-1906," p. 101.

58. Ibid., p. 128; Chang, *Chung Mei Kung-yueh Feng-ch'Ao*, p. 67.

59. Hunt, *Frontier Defense and the Open Door*, pp. 126-27; Rodgers to Loomis, Aug. 12, 15, 21, 1905, Shanghai D.

60. Sammons to Loomis, July 26, 1905, Newchwang D.

61. See Martin to Jee, Oct. 4, 1905, in Martin to Bacon, Feb. 8, 1906, Hankow D.

62. For a review of the attitudes and policies of these two men, see Hunt, *Frontier Defense and the Open Door*, pp. 124-27, and Field, "The Chinese Boycott of 1905," pp. 84-86.

63. Rockhill to Ch'ing, Aug. 14, 1905, PLA; Ch'ing to Rockhill, Aug. 26, 1905, PLA. The published record of American diplomacy is in *FR*, 1905, pp. 204-304.

64. Chang, *Chung Mei Kung-yueh Feng-ch'Ao*, p. 167.

65. Rockhill to Secretary of State, Aug. 26, 1905, CD. Lay, however, reported on attempts to undercut American businessmen by the German commissioner of customs at Wuchow and the German consul at Swatow. Lay to Rockhill, Jan. 30, 1906, Rockhill Papers.

66. Sammons to Loomis, Aug. 2, 1905, Newchwang D.

67. Whitelaw Reid to Secretary of State, Nov. 15, 1905, *FR*, p. 503. Milnar describes the boycott at Singapore as spreading from Shanghai, taking an intense turn, and ending in June 1906. Milnar, "Chinese-American Relations with Especial Refer-

ence to the Imposition of the Boycott, 1905-1906," pp. 194-205. Much financial support came from Singapore. S. L. Gracey to Bacon, March 31, 1906, Foochow D. See also *SF Chronicle,* Dec. 5, 1905, p. 1. The Singapore Chinese had close ties with Amoy and formerly with Manila. Cheshire to Bacon, Jan. 6, 1906, Canton D. Schwerin reported on unloaded cargoes of American goods at Singapore. *NY Tribune,* Feb. 14, 1906, p. 5.

68. Rockhill to Secretary of State, Aug. 26, 1905, CD. American diplomats' perceptions of Chinese nationalism and their reactions receive special attention in Linda M. Papageorge, "The United States Diplomats' Response to Rising Chinese Nationalism, 1900-1912" (Ph. D. diss., Michigan State University, 1973).

69. Ch'ing to Rockhill, Aug. 26, 1905, PLA.

70. Cheshire, who was with Lay part of the time in Canton, was sharply critical of him. Cheshire to Rockhill, Feb. 17, 1906, Rockhill Papers. Varg faults him for his handling of the Lienchow settlement. Varg, *Missionaries, Chinese, and Diplomats,* pp. 127-28.

71. Lay to Rockhill, June 19, 1905, Rockhill Papers.

72. Enc. in Lay to Loomis, Apr. 20, 1905, Canton D.

73. Lay to Hay, May 20, 1905, ibid.

74. Lay to Hay, May 26, 1905, ibid.; Chang, *Chung Mei Kung-yueh Feng-ch'Ao,* p. 108.

75. Lay to Loomis, May 31, 1905, Canton D.

76. Lay to Rockhill, May 29, 1905, Rockhill Papers.

77. Lay to Loomis, June 15, 1905, Canton D.

78. Lay to Hay, May 26, 1905, ibid.

79. Cheshire to Rockhill, June 23, 1905, Rockhill Papers.

80. *NY Tribune,* July 5, 1905, p. 3.

81. Lay to Loomis, July 10, 1905, Canton D.

82. Ibid.

83. See translation in ibid.

84. See Alvey A. Adee's notation in Lay to Secretary of State, July 10, 1905, Canton D.

85. Lay to Secretary of State, July 22, 1905, ibid.

86. Ibid.

87. Lay to Secretary of State, July 24, 1905, ibid.

88. See Enc. 1, ibid.

89. See Enc. 2, ibid.; Chang, *Chung Mei Kung-yueh Feng-ch'Ao,* p. 193.

90. Lay to Loomis, Aug. 9, 1905, Canton D.

91. Ibid.

92. Lay to Loomis, Aug. 6, 1905, ibid.

93. Ibid. Lay's naive observation was that such people were not really interested in the boycott but were "forced to take part in it."

94. See Enc. 1, Lay to Loomis, Aug. 9, 1905, Canton D. See also Lay to Ts'en, Aug. 9, 1905, in Lay to Loomis, Aug. 10, 1905, ibid.

95. Lay to Loomis, Aug. 24, 1905, Canton D; Chang, *Chung Mei Kung-yueh Feng-ch'Ao*, pp. 195-96.

96. Lay to Loomis, Aug. 16, 1905, Canton D.

97. Lay to Loomis, Aug. 24, 1905, ibid.

98. Lay to Root, Sept. 12, 1905, ibid. Ma Ta-ch'en, former student in a western medical school and a Christian, was arrested. He was accused of being in Sun Yat-sen's party, but his accuser was then linked with K'ang Yu-wei's party. Chang, *Chung Mei Kung-yueh Feng-ch'Ao*, pp. 218-21. See also Rhoads, *China's Republican Revolution*, p. 87.

99. Enc. 1, Rockhill to Root, Sept. 18, 1905, CD.

100. Rockhill to Root, ibid.

101. Lay to Rockhill, Oct. 17, 1905, Rockhill Papers.

102. Rockhill to Ch'ing, Sept. 13, 1905, PLA.

103. Lay to Loomis, Sept. 12, 1905, Canton D.

104. Lay to Rockhill, Sept. 14, 1905, ibid.

105. Lay to Loomis, Sept. 14, 1905, ibid. According to Papageorge, Rockhill was afraid that if the United States actually used military force, the boycott might explode "into a wholesale anti-foreign, anti-dynastic movement that might endanger foreign lives and property and probably topple the Manchu dynasty." Papageorge, "The Diplomats' Response to Rising Chinese Nationalism, 1900-1912," p. 135.

106. P. S. Heintzleman to Lay, Sept. 28, 1905, in Lay to Loomis, Sept. 28, 1905, Canton D.

107. Rodgers to Loomis, Nov. 15, 1905, Shanghai D.

108. Heintzleman to Root, Dec. 4, 1905, Canton D. The funeral service at Canton was held at Sir Chai-Hok-Tong College. Thousands also attended this service. At Fat-shan a public garden was planned in his honor, and a bronze statue was erected. S. L. Gracey to Bacon, Nov. 29, 1905, Foochow D. See also Lay to Loomis, Oct. 30, 1905, Canton D.

109. Lay to Rockhill, Oct. 19, 1905, Rockhill Papers.

110. Lay to Loomis, Oct. 30, 1905, Canton D.

111. Lay to Rockhill, Oct. 31, 1905, Rockhill Papers.

112. Rockhill to Ch'ing, Oct. 30, 1905, PLA; Enc., Rockhill to Root, Nov. 4, 1905, CD.

113. Rockhill to Root, Nov. 4, 1905, CD.

114. Enc. 3, Rockhill to Secretary of State, July 26, 1905, ibid.

115. William Ashmore, "The Probable Effects of Japan's Success on Missions in Asia," *MRW* 18 o.s. (Oct. 1905): 727.

116. For the first report, see Lay to Root, Nov. 3, 1905, Canton D. For the final official report, see Enc. in Lay to Bacon, Dec. 26, 1905, ibid.

117. Lay to Root, Nov. 8, 1905, Canton D.

118. Edward C. Machle to Henry V. Noyes, Oct. 28, 1905, Enc. 7, ibid.

119. Enc. in Lay to Bacon, Dec. 26, 1905, ibid. A recent study maintains that the boycott had nothing to do with the massacre. Edward J. M. Rhoads, "Nationalism and Xenophobia in Kwangtung (1905-1906): The Canton Anti-American Boycott and the Lienchow Anti-Missionary Uprising," *Papers on China* (1962), p. 177.

120. Lay to Rockhill, Dec. 18, 1905, Rockhill Papers.

121. Rockhill to Root, Nov. 4, 1905, CD.

122. Heintzleman to Root, Dec. 4, 1905, Canton D.

123. Ibid.

124. Lay to Bacon, Dec. 19, 1905, ibid. For the version of an American businessman in the locality, see *NY Times*, Feb. 12, 1905, p. 2. S. L. Gracey described Hong Kong as a "reflex of Canton spirit." Gracey to Bacon, Dec. 19, 1905, Foochow D. Shiffrin, *Sun Yat-sen*, pp. 211-13.

125. Lay to Bacon, Dec. 19, 1905, Canton D. *NY Tribune*, Dec. 11, 1905, p. 2. "China and America," *Outlook* 81 (Dec. 23, 1905): 952.

126. See translation of article in a Canton newspaper, in Lay to Bacon, Dec. 19, 1905. Canton D. William Burtt, representative of a Spokane milling firm, held later that William Jennings Bryan, who had made a speech at a banquet in his honor in China, had played into the hands of the group opposing compromise by declaring that American labor would never allow Chinese workers to enter America. *NY Times*, Feb. 12, 1906, p. 2. Internal revolutionary forces were at work and were doubtless more significant. See Iriye, "Public Opinion and Foreign Policy," p. 225.

127. Rockhill to Ch'ing, Dec. 4, 1905, PLA. Enc. 1, Rockhill to Root, Dec. 5, 1905, CD. Bacon's notation on January 16, 1906, was: "Rockhill's dispatch has a good ring to it and I do not see any evidence of his having become too proChinese as some people think."

128. Lay to Root, Dec. 30, 1905, Canton D.

129. Lay to Bacon, Jan. 3, 1906, ibid.

130. Cheshire to Bacon, Jan. 6, 1906, ibid.

131. *SF Chronicle*, March 15, 1906, p. 1.

132. Letter dated Jan. 19, in Lay to Bacon, Feb. 10, 1906, Canton D.

133. John Fowler to Department of State, Feb. 21, 1906, Chefoo D.

134. Cheshire to Bacon, Jan. 6, 1906, Canton D.

135. Lay to Bacon, Feb. 26, 1906, ibid.

136. See Lay to Root, March 15, 1906, ibid. Lay to Bacon, March 22, 1906, ibid.

137. Lay to Bacon, March 5, 1906, Canton D. Rhoads, *China's Republican Revolution*, pp. 92-93.

138. Lay to Bacon, June 17, 1906, Canton D.

139. Ibid.

140. Enc., Lay to Bacon, Dec. 26, 1905, ibid.

141. "Where the Shoe Pinches," *MRW* 18 o.s. (Nov. 1905): 860.

CHAPTER 11.

1. *NY Times*, Aug. 18, 1905, p. 1.

2. *NY Tribune*, July 1, 1905, p. 4.

3. Edward S. Bragg to Bacon, Jan. 17, 1906, Hong Kong D.

4. May 26, 1906, *Cong. Rec.*, 59th Cong., 1st sess., 40: 7508.

5. "Current Comment," *JAAA* 5 (Jan. 1906): 353.

6. Ibid.

7. "Current Comment," *JAAA* 6 (Feb. 1906): 2.

8. *SF Chronicle*, Jan. 15, 1906, p. 1.

9. See petitions in LR, Petitions, House Committee on Foreign Affairs, 59th Cong., 1st sess., 1905-1906, 56-H7.4. The Fruit Growers of California, seemingly not related to the other groups, sent in its periodic request for agricultural laborers also.

10. Resolution of Presbyterian ministers meeting at Troy, N.Y., Feb. 27, 1906, to Hon. William H. Draper, ibid.

11. Gustav H. Schwab, chairman, Committee on Foreign Commerce and the Revenue Laws, to Hon. Robert R. Hitt, chairman, Committee on Foreign Affairs, Feb. 2, 1906, in LR, Petitions, House Committee on Foreign Affairs, 59th Cong., 1st sess., 1905-1906, 56-H7.4. The petition of September 5, 1905, of the American members of the Educational Association of China from Shanghai was also among the petitions in the committee files.

12. "Breakfast to the Imperial Chinese Commission," *JAAA* 6 (Feb. 1906): 12. He endorsed the "spirit" of the bill rather than the specific provisions, however, and he said nothing to indicate that Chinese-Americans would be satisfied.

13. Ibid.

14. Ibid., p. 14.

15. Ibid., p. 13.

16. *NY Tribune*, Feb. 14, 1906, p. 5.

17. Ibid., Feb. 15, 1906, p. 2.

18. John W. Foster, who had been part of the China lobby in 1902, presented the Chinese position vigorously in "The Chinese Boycott," *Atlantic Monthly* 97 (Jan. 1906): 118-27.

19. House *Hearings*, Exclusion, 1906, p. 6. By making such concessions, Roosevelt appeared to hope that he could win over the anti-Chinese. *NY Tribune*, Feb. 13, 1906, p. 2.

20. On January 8, 1906, Taft wrote a letter of introduction to Root for McKinlay and called him "as familiar as any Member of Congress with all of the details of the Chinese question." McKinlay had been with Taft on his Philippines trip and had been "of the utmost assistance . . . in Hongkong and Shanghai in introducing Chinamen whom he had known in San Francisco. . . . Mr. McKinlay suggests that there is a possibility of the whole California delegation agreeing to certain amendments of the law which will straighten out the feeling in China, and at the same time not abate the strictness of the exclusion of the coolie class." Taft suggested calling in Denby for a conference with McKinlay. McKinlay, he thought, could be helpful "in reaching a solution that we should all like to have." Taft to Root, Jan. 8, 1906, Elihu Root Papers. See also ibid., Taft Papers, vol. 8, Secretary of War, semi-official.

21. House *Hearings*, Exclusion, 1906, p. 7.

22. Ibid., pp. 13-14.

23. *NY Tribune*, Feb. 19, 1906, p. 2.

24. Ibid.

25. Ibid., March 11, 1906, p. 4.

26. James J. Lorence, "Business and Reform: The American Asiatic Association and the Exclusion Laws, 1905-1907," *Pacific Historical Review* 39 (Nov. 1970): 433.

27. House *Hearings*, Exclusion, 1906, p. 20.

28. Ibid., pp. 54-56.

29. Ibid., pp. 92-93.

30. Ibid., p. 67.

31. Ibid., p. 43.

32. Ibid., p. 53.

33. Everis A. Hayes to Sargent, March 31, 1906, SCR, FB 87. Up to this point, K'ang and the Chinese Empire Reform Association had been more closely involved in the movement. In 1904 Sun had been backed by the Hawaiian Triads in seeking support and funds in the United States but had not won the American Chinese away from K'ang and Liang Ch'i-ch'ao. In 1905 he traveled in Europe to win the support of students and was chosen in that year to head the Revolutionary Alliance, which was centered in Tokyo and made up mainly of students. Harold Z. Schiffrin, "The Enigma of Sun Yat-sen," in Mary C. Wright, ed., *China in Revolution: The First Phase, 1900-1913* (New Haven, 1968), pp. 461-62. In a speech in Japan in August 1905, which was printed and widely distributed, he referred to the boycott approvingly as a movement to block a new exclusion treaty and noted that Europeans as well as Americans were frightened by its success. See pamphlet in Chinese entitled *Speech of Sun Yat-sen*, in North to Sargent, Apr. 5, 1906, SCR, FB 87. He did not take personal credit for the movement, however, and his biographers have not ascribed to him a significant role in it. See, for example, the excellent study by Harold Z. Schiffrin, *Sun Yat-sen and the Origins of the Chinese Revolution* (Berkeley and Los Angeles, 1968).

34. Sargent to Hayes, Apr. 11, 1906, SCR, FB 87. See also North to Sargent, Apr. 5, 1906, SCR, FB 87. Since Sun had lied about being born in Hawaii, he was subject to deportation when he gave his testimony if the truth had been known.

35. Apr. 9, 1906, House *Hearings*, Exclusion, 1906, p. 105.

36. Ibid., p. 129.

37. McKinlay to Warner, March 29, 1906, ibid., p. 90.

38. *SF Chronicle*, March 22, 1906, p. 4. William Griffith, ed., *The Roosevelt Policy: Speeches, Letters and State Papers Relating to Corporate Wealth and Closely Allied Topics by Theodore Roosevelt* (New York, 1919), 2: 356-62.

39. Apr. 9, 1906, House *Hearings*, Exclusion, 1906, p. 148.

40. *SF Chronicle*, Apr. 3, 1906, p. 1.

41. Ibid., Apr. 4, 1906, p. 6.

42. Ibid., Apr. 12, 1906, p. 4.

43. "Memorandum of an interview between the Chinese Minister, Sir Chentung Liang-Cheng, and the Secretary of State, at the State Department, Monday, June 11, 1906," in Notes from CL.

44. *SF Chronicle*, Apr. 12, 1906, p. 4.

45. Ibid., Apr. 14, 1906, p. 1.

46. *Cong. Rec.*, 59th Cong., 1st sess., 40: 7098.

47. Dec. 7, 1905, ibid., p. 214.

48. Jan. 29, 1906, p. 1672. Tillman's resolution was timed to offset Chinese official discouragement. The *New York Times*, Jan. 12, 1906, p. 8, was upset over rumors that Liang had notified Peking that there was no hope of getting Congress to act. Tillman then introduced his resolution for the first time on January 25 to coincide with a visit to the Senate gallery by Chinese dignitaries. Ibid., Jan. 26, 1906, p. 8.

49. *Cong. Rec.*, 59th Cong., 1st sess., 40: 1673.

50. March 13, 1906, ibid., p. 3749.

51. H. N. Spencer to Honorable Julius C. Burrows, Feb. 9, 1906, in LR, Petitions, Senate Committee on Immigration, 59th Cong., 1st sess., 1905-1906, S59A-J46, FB 105.

52. U.S. Senate, *Hearings before the Committee on Immigration of the United States Senate on the Boycott of American Manufactured Goods by the People of China,* 59th Cong., 1st sess., 1905-1906 (Washington, 1906), p. 22. Hereafter cited as *Hearings . . . Boycott.*

53. Ibid., p. 7. Two months after Denby reported the boycott was about dead, the *New York Times* revealed that the export of cotton goods in May was down to one third of what it had been the year before. Other exports were low too. *NY Times,* June 6, 1906, p. 8.

54. *Hearings . . . Boycott,* p. 37.

55. Ibid., pp. 39-46.

56. "Current Comment," *JAAA* 6 (May, 1906): 97.

57. Chancellor and Six Deans to E. J. Burkett, May 19, 1906, LR, Petitions, Senate Committee on Foreign Relations, 59th Cong., 1st sess., 1905-1906, S59A-J33.

58. Sen. Doc. 449, 59th Cong., 1st sess., 1905-1906, p. 2.

59. Root to Liang, May 28, 1906, Notes to CL.

60. *SF Chronicle,* Dec. 6, 1905, p. 4.

61. Quoted from one of identical letters sent to California congressmen and members of the House Committee on Foreign Affairs, n.d. (received Jan. 27), in LR, Petitions, House Committee on Foreign Affairs, 59th Cong., 1st sess., 1905-1906, HR 59A-H7.4.

62. Japanese and Korean Exclusion League resolution, Feb. 4 and Feb. 14, 1906, ibid.

63. Resolution to Rep. Needham, n.d. (received March 15, 1906), in LR, Petitions, House Committee on Foreign Affairs, 59th Cong., 1st sess., 1905-1906, HR 59A-H7.4.

64. Apr. 9, 1906, House *Hearings,* Exclusion, 1906, p. 168.

65. AFL, *Proc.*, 1905, pp. 191, 30. Through death the AFL lost its powerful ally in the Senate, John H. Mitchell of Oregon.

66. Gompers, Apr. 9, 1906, House *Hearings*, Exclusion, 1906, p. 153. The timing of the publication of a short book in California on the boycott in March 1906 by W. K. Roberts, a former clergyman, who had been in China as an employee of the Customs Service during the earlier stages of the boycott (to December 1905), was ideal from the standpoint of the anti-Chinese side. Ministers who took the hard line were rare people. Roberts expressed his belief in white superiority and the need to bar inferior races from the United States. He endorsed the use of gunboat diplomacy for China to curb the boycott and protect American citizens. Statements of an anti-Japanese type in the book were also tailored to the prejudices of the exclusionists. William K. Roberts, *The Mongolian Problem in America: A Discussion of the Possibilities of the Yellow Peril, with Notes upon American Diplomacy in Its Relation to the Boycott* (San Francisco, 1906).

67. *SF Chronicle*, Feb. 6, 1906, p. 5. Ten rules were cut out; three more liberal ones were added. House Doc. 847, 59th Cong., 1st sess., 1905-1906, p. 24.

68. Coolidge, *Chinese Immigration*, p. 308.

69. House Doc. 847, 59th Cong., 1st sess., 1905-1906, pp. 154-55.

70. U.S. Department of Commerce and Labor, *Reports of the Department of Commerce and Labor, 1905: Report of the Secretary of Commerce and Labor and Reports of Bureaus* (Washington, 1906), p. 50.

71. "Current Comment," *JAAA* 6 (June 1906): 130.

72. Apr. 9, 1906, House *Hearings*, Exclusion, 1906, p. 157.

CHAPTER 12.

1. Roosevelt to Root, Apr. 3, 1906, Root Papers.

2. Gompers, *Seventy Years of Life and Labor*, 2: 162.

3. Neu, *An Uncertain Friendship*, p. 36. See also Thomas A. Bailey, *Theodore Roosevelt and the Japanese-American Crises: An Account of the International Complications Arising from the Race Problem on the Pacific Coast* (Stanford, 1934).

4. Beale, *Theodore Roosevelt and the Rise of America to World Power*, p. 241. An earlier strengthening of naval power on the China coast happened on November 15, after the Lienchow trouble. Harbaugh, *The Life and Times of Theodore Roosevelt*, p. 285.

5. Roosevelt to Taft, Jan. 11, 1906, in Morison, *Letters*, 5: 133.

6. Beale, *Theodore Roosevelt and the Rise of America to World Power*, p. 240. But some of the press was not in favor of sending troops. Jessie Miller, "China in American Policy and Opinion, 1906-1909," pp. 73-74.

7. *NY Tribune*, Feb. 5, 1906, p. 1.

8. Rockhill to Root, Feb. 14, 1906, CD.

9. *NY Tribune*, Feb. 5, 1906, p. 1. Drew was not dismissed, but a Foochow petition had asked for his transfer. Rockhill to Root, Feb. 13, 1906, CD.

10. *NY Tribune*, Feb. 16, 1906, p. 9.

11. *SF Chronicle*, Feb. 13, 1906, p. 1.

12. Martin to Bacon, Feb. 8, 1906, Hankow D.

13. *NY Tribune*, Feb. 7, 1906, p. 1.

14. Ibid., Feb. 16, 1906, p. 9.

15. *SF Chronicle*, Feb. 12, 1906, p. 1.

16. *NY Tribune*, Feb. 13, 1906, p. 2. The reference to Germany implied that the center of trouble would be the Shantung peninsula, where German influence was greatest. Fowler's dispatches revealed a great deal of restlessness in that area.

17. Ibid., Feb. 17, 1906, p. 3.

18. Ibid., Feb. 24, 1906, p. 3.

19. *SF Chronicle*, Feb. 24, 1906, p. 4.

20. *NY Tribune*, Feb. 24, 1906, p. 3. Liang in Washington also tried to quiet fears of an anti-foreign uprising. Ibid., March 2, 1906, p. 8. Even the secretary of the viceroy in Canton made a calming statement. *SF Chronicle*, March 12, 1906, p. 1.

21. Roosevelt to Leonard Wood, Apr. 2, 1906, in Morison, *Letters* 5: 205. Wood's chief of staff had returned from China to Manila in March and on March 16 was reported in the press to believe that China was peaceful. *NY Times*, March 17, 1906, p. 1.

22. Roosevelt to Wood, Apr. 2, 1906, in Morison, *Letters* 5: 205.

23. Root to Liang, Feb. 14, 1906, Notes to CL.

24. Bacon to Rockhill, Feb. 21, 1906, CI.

25. Root to Rockhill, Feb. 26, 1906, ibid.

26. Rockhill to Ch'ing, March 1, 1906, PLA.

27. Rockhill to Root, March 5, 1906, CD. For the preliminary report by cable, see Rockhill to Root, March 2, 1906, ibid.

28. Enc. in Ch'ing to Rockhill, March 7, 1906, PLA. Rockhill to Root, March 7, 1906, CD.

29. Ch'ing to Rockhill, March 7, 1906, PLA.

30. Rockhill to Root, March 26, 1906, CD.

31. Rockhill to Root, April 5, 1906, ibid.

32. Rockhill to Root, Apr. 7, 1906, ibid.

33. Rockhill to Root, Apr. 23, 1906, ibid.

34. Rockhill to Root, Apr. 26, 1906, ibid.

35. Rockhill to Root, May 3, 1906, ibid.

36. Rockhill to Root, June 13, 1906, ibid.

37. Rockhill to Root, June 28, 1906, ibid.

38. Rockhill to Root, May 24, 1906, ibid.

39. Rockhill to Root, March 8, 1906, ibid.

40. Ibid.

41. Roosevelt to Rockhill, Aug. 22, 1905, in Morison, *Letters* 4: 1310.

42. *SF Chronicle*, Jan. 8, 1906, p. 4.

43. Ibid., Jan 14, 1906, p. 37.

44. Ibid.

45. *NY Tribune*, Jan. 25, 1906, p. 1. Rockhill was deeply disturbed over a confidential letter informing him that an attempt had been made to give a physical examination to the commissioners. Fearing repercussions, Rockhill asked permission to deny that this had ever happened. Root discovered that it had been the purser; no U. S. officer had made such an effort. Root did not follow through, and no crisis resulted. Rockhill to Root, Feb. 15, 1906, CD.

46. *SF Chronicle*, Jan. 15, 1906, p. 1.

47. *NY Tribune*, Feb. 13, 1906, p. 2. Olney's pro-Chinese views revealed a division within the Democratic party on this point. Clark was anti-Chinese, and Bryan had offended Chinese merchants and boycott leaders in China with his remarks at a banquet given in his honor there. Ibid., Feb. 12, 1906, p. 1; *NY Times*, Feb. 12, 1906, p. 2.

48. Roosevelt to Ralph M. Easley, Jeremiah W. Jenks, and James B. Reynolds, Feb. 24, 1906, in Morison, *Letters* 5: 165.

49. *NY Tribune*, Feb. 13, 1906, p. 2.

50. Quoted in "General Missionary Intelligence," *MRW* 19 o.s. (June 1906): 475. See also "Secretary Root on Chinese Relations," *JAAA* 6 (March 1906): 54.

51. Roosevelt to Taft, Apr. 23, 1906, Taft Papers, Series 4, Taft-TR, Jan. 1905-Apr. 1906.

52. *SF Chronicle*, Apr. 25, 1906, p. 2.

53. Ibid., Apr. 24, 1906, p. 2.

54. Ibid., May 23, 1906, p. 8. John C. Kennedy, however, holds that most of the aid to Chinese came from Chinese communities. Kennedy, *The Great Earthquake and Fire; San Francisco, 1906* (New York, 1963), p. 236.

55. Taft to Liang, July 9, 1906, Taft Papers, Secretary of War, Semi-official, vol. 51.

56. *SF Chronicle*, May 11, 1906, p. 1.

57. Extract from Chinese newspaper in Hong Kong, June 30, 1905, in June 30, 1905, Roosevelt Papers.

58. Rockhill to Roosevelt, July 7, 1905, ibid.

59. Jenks to Roosevelt, Aug. 10, 1905, ibid. Yu Chu Wang, *Chinese Intellectuals and the West, 1872-1949* (Chapel Hill, 1966), p. 510, gives the number of students in the United States in 1905 as 130.

60. Wilson to Secretary of State, Jan. 3, 1906, *FR*, 1906, p. 1072.

61. Smith, *China and America To-Day*, pp. 231-32.

62. Letter from thirty-three citizens to Roosevelt, July 17, 1905, Roosevelt Papers.

63. Ibid.

64. Ibid.

65. Jameson to Rodgers, Nov. 7, 1905, in "Correspondence," *JAAA* 5 (Jan. 1906): 357.

66. Chinese Students Federation to Roosevelt, Oct. 9, 1905, Misc. Letters.

67. Enc. in Rodgers to Bacon, Jan. 10, 1906, Shanghai D.

68. See translation in Ch'ing to Rockhill, March 5, 1906, PLA. Rockhill to Root, March 7, 1906, CD.

69. *NY Tribune*, Feb. 7, 1906, p. 1.

70. The idea did not appeal to the *Chronicle*, which thought that such students would return to China and work against foreign control in that country. *SF Chronicle*, March 19, 1906, p. 6.

71. Smith, *China and America To-Day*, p. 214.

72. Charles Vevier, *The United States and China, 1906-1913: A Study of Finance and Diplomacy* (New Brunswick, 1955), p. 62.

73. House Doc. 1275, 60th Cong., 2d sess., 1908-1909, pp. 3-5.

74. Varg, *Open Door Diplomat*, p. 81. Guy M. Walker to Metcalf, June 29, 1905, SCR, FB 85.

75. *NY Tribune*, Feb. 22, 1906, p. 3.

76. Jenks to Roosevelt, Aug. 10, 1905, Roosevelt Papers.

272   CHINESE EXCLUSION VERSUS THE OPEN DOOR POLICY

77. Jenks to Root, Oct. 2, 1905, Root Papers.

78. Jenks to Root, Oct. 13, 1905, ibid.

79. Ibid.

80. Jenks to Root, Oct. 14, 1905, ibid.

81. Roosevelt to Rockhill, Aug. 29, 1905, Rockhill Papers.

82. *SF Chronicle*, Jan. 15, 1906, p. 3. See also *SF Chronicle*, Jan. 16, 1906, p. 6.

83. Roosevelt to Arthur H. Smith, Apr. 3, 1906, in Morison, *Letters* 5: 206.

84. "What Can Be Done," *Outlook* 82 (March 31, 1906): 730-33. The editor was under the influence of Smith. Miller, "China in American Policy and Opinion, 1906-1909," p. 134.

85. "Is Conciliation 'Weakness'?" *Outlook* 83 (June 2, 1906): 256.

86. "General Missionary Intelligence," *MRW* 19 o.s. (Sept. 1906): 715.

87. Rockhill to Root, May 3, 1906, CD.

88. Vevier, *The United States and China, 1906-1913*, p. 62.

89. In 1907 Fu Chi Hao (Fei Chi Ho), one of Luella Miner's wards of 1901-1903, after a bitter review of his experiences in entering the United States, called the boycott "simply the beginning of the anti-American feeling." China would "never forget the bitterness of the cup of humiliation, of shame and degradation, forced upon her by Christian America." Fu Chi Hao, "My Reception in America," *Outlook* 84 (Aug. 10, 1907): 773.

90. Beale, *Theodore Roosevelt and the Rise of America to World Power*, p. 252. Michael H. Hunt, "The American Remission of the Boxer Indemnity: A Reappraisal," *Journal of Asian Studies* 31 (May 1972): 539-59.

CHAPTER 13.

1. Department of State, Circulars, Apr. 15, 1905.

2. *NY Tribune*, Jan. 10, 1906, p. 4.

3. These claims were collected from Chinese who had suffered financial loss by delays in landings, arrests, deportations, and accusations of not having registered. How seriously the Chinese officials took this course of action is not clear. It may only have been a ploy to convince Chinese-Americans of the concern of their government and keep them from turning to the anti-government reform parties. It might also have been thought of as a useful bargaining point with the United States government. For the proclamation by the acting consul general at San Francisco explaining the policy, see the translation by Gardner, Apr. 30, 1905, SCR, FB 85.

4. *NY Tribune*, Jan. 13, 1906, p. 3.

5. See note in Rockhill to Secretary of State, July 28, 1905, in Department of Commerce and Labor, RG 85, 52320/27.

6. Ibid.

7. *NY Times*, Oct. 29, 1905, p. 7; Taft to Root, Oct. 4, 1905, Misc. Letters.

8. *NY Tribune*, Dec. 11, 1905, p. 2.

9. See Enc. in Rockhill to Root, Feb. 28, 1906, CD.

10. *NY Tribune*, Jan. 15, 1906, p. 5.

11. Rockhill to Root, Feb. 28, 1906, CD.

12. Ibid.

13. See memorandum with ibid. T'ang was named premier by Yuan in March 1911 following the revolution in China. Jerome Ch'en, *Yuan Shih-k'ai, 1859-1916. Brutus Assumes the Purple* (Stanford, 1961), p. 140.

14. Acting Commissioner, San Francisco, to Commissioner General of Immigration, March 10, 1906, SCR, FB 85.

15. Memorandum of June 11 interview in Liang to Root, June 16, 1906, Notes from CL.

16. Liang to Root, June 16, 1906, ibid. Root viewed Liang's proposals at that time as "impractical." An insight into the attitudes in the State Department in late June is found in Denby's unofficial letter to Rockhill on matters which included the trademark and opium questions. "China," he wrote, "always undermines her own positions — she loves her coolies so that she is prepared to offend her best friend to secure an agitation on behalf of their entry into America, and yet she shows this affection by selling them into South African slavery at a few shillings a head." Denby to Rockhill, June 30, 1906, Rockhill Papers.

17. Liang to Root, Oct. 12, 1906, Numerical File, 108/80.

18. Ibid.

19. Ibid.

20. *NY Tribune*, Oct. 24, 1906, p. 1. See also ibid., Oct. 18, 1906, p. 1.

21. *NY Tribune*, Oct. 24, 1906, p. 1.

22. Oscar S. Straus, *Under Four Administrations: From Cleveland to Taft* (Boston, 1922), p. 210.

23. John M. Blum, *The Republican Roosevelt* (New York, 1967), p. 37. Schiff was head of Kuhn, Loeb and Company, which backed Harriman and Schwerin and their large transportation complex including the Pacific Mail Steamship Company. Vevier, *The United States and China, 1906-1913*, pp. 19-21 passim.

24. Oscar Straus to Roosevelt, Dec. 5, 1906, Oscar S. Straus Papers. See also Straus, *Under Four Administrations*, p. 219.

25. S. Uchida to Strauss, Dec. 15, 1906, Straus Papers.

26. Straus ruled on last resort Chinese appeal cases personally. Others were handled by a holdover from the Metcalf era, Lawrence O. Murray, who had won the confidence of Straus. Although Straus was not easily disillusioned, even he had his bitter moments. "You would be surprised," he wrote Kohler, after a year in office, "at the amount of prevarication, unreliability, fraud and subterfuge which creeps into these cases, so that it would prejudice the mind of a saint." But Straus then added, "I suppose this is largely due in part to the drastic provisions of the law, but it is the fact, none the less." Straus to Max J. Kohler, Feb. 26, 1908, Straus Papers.

27. Quoted in "Progressive Japan," *JAAA* 6 (Nov. 1906): 304.

28. The laws, he said in his report of June 30, 1907, were framed in such a manner as to be "regarded as involving a discrimination on account of race." *Annual Report of the Secretary of Commerce and Labor for 1907*, p. 142. Chinese, he said, were bound to find them offensive. Trade, he noted, had fallen off from 57 million in exports to China in 1905, to 44 million in 1906, to 26 million in 1907. Both commercial self-interest and friendly relations, he argued, were in danger. Only 857 new Chinese had entered the United States in the previous year. No harm and great good would come from adopting Roosevelt's formula. Ibid., p. 144.

29. James Bronson Reynolds, "Enforcement of the Chinese Exclusion Law," *AAPSS* 34 (Sept. 1909): 364.

30. Department of State, Circulars, "Amendments to the Regulations Governing the Admission of Chinese," Feb. 26, 1907, no. 143.

31. Sargent died in 1908. Instructions went out on March 25, 1907, to consular officials in China to check carefully on any persons seeking to come to the United States as students or members of the merchant class.

32. Smith, *China and America To-Day*, p. 182.

33. Wilson, *Memoirs of an Ex-Diplomat*, pp. 155-56.

34. Rockhill to Secretary of State, Aug. 15, 1905, CD.

35. Rockhill to Root, Feb. 28, 1906, CD.

36. Bacon to Rockhill, Apr. 27, 1906, CI.

37. Coolidge, *Chinese Immigration*, p. 308.

38. Attempts were made in 1907 to revive the boycott in Shanghai and in Canton, but officials impounded funds received from abroad and arrested boycott leaders. Reynolds, "Enforcement of the Chinese Exclusion Law," p. 363. Nickerson, "Dawning of a Wiser Chinese Policy," pp. 924-25. Wu was supporting the official action at that time.

39. "The Annual Meeting," *JAAA* 6 (Nov. 1906): 292.

40. Straus, "The Spirit and Letter of Exclusion," *North American Review* 187 (Apr. 1908): 485.

41. Quoted in Charles Chaile-Long, "Why China Boycotts Us," *World Today* 10 (March 1906): 314.

42. "Chinese vs. South American Markets," *United States Investor*, 17 (Jan. 27, 1906): 140-41, quoted in Morton V. Malin, "American Economic Interests in China, 1900-1908" (Ph.D. diss., University of Maryland, 1954), p. 153.

43. "The Annual Meeting," p. 295.

44. *NY Tribune*, Dec. 11, 1905, p. 2.

45. "Progressive Japan," *JAAA* 6: 303. The American share of foreign trade in China was 15 percent in 1905 and had dropped to 11.4 percent in 1914. Remer, *Foreign Investments in China*, p. 261. A position held by Varg and others is that American trade was not greater because Americans had failed to invest in China. Paul A. Varg, *The Making of a Myth: The United States and China, 1897-1912* (East Lansing, 1968), p. 47.

46. Gracey to Bacon, Nov. 29, 1905, Foochow D.

47. *NY Tribune*, Feb. 17, 1906, p. 3.

48. Enc., Testimony of Herman O. T. Burkwell, in Lay to Bacon, Dec. 26, 1905, Canton D.

49. "General Missionary Intelligence," *MRW* 19 o.s. (July 1906): 554.

50. "This was the only time during the decade, when they [missionaries] expressed themselves on a political question." Varg, *Missionaries, Chinese and Diplomats*, pp. 135-36.

51. May 1, 1906, *Hearings . . . Boycott*, p. 39.

52. "Anti-American Feeling in China," *Outlook* 80 (Aug. 12, 1905): 893.

53. Smith, *China and America To-Day* p. 171.

54. "General Missionary Intelligence," p. 232.

55. Thomas F. Tracy and Arthur E. Holder, "How Labor Fared in the 59th Congress," *American Federationist* 14 (Apr. 1907): 247.

56. Walter MacArthur, in *NY Times*, Dec. 9, 1905, p. 5.

57. *NY Tribune*, Aug. 10, 1905, p. 9.

58. *NY Times*, Aug. 9, 1905, p. 6.

59. Chaile-Long, "Why China Boycotts Us," p. 314.

60. Taft to Root, Oct. 4, 1905, Misc. Letters.

61. *SF Chronicle*, June 10, 1905, p. 6.

62. Lee, *The Chinese in the United States of America*, p. 14.

63. For a discussion of the background of the 1943 law, see Robert A. Divine, *American Immigration Policy, 1924-1952* (New Haven, 1957), pp. 147-52.

64. Complaints by immigration officials of abuses by the Chinese, and by the Chinese of over-zealous enforcement, continued periodically over the years. The boycott technique used by the Chinese also has its own fascinating history. In 1910 it was used against the United States over the lengthy detention of Chinese at the San Francisco immigration quarters. In 1911 one writer credited it with being decisive in forestalling loans by foreigners to the imperial government when the Sun Yat-sen side, with Wu as a prominent leader, threatened to employ it. John S. Thompson, *China Revolutionized* (Indianapolis, 1913), pp. 562-73. In 1935 George Bronson Rea, longtime resident in China, complained that Chinese illegally in the United States were ignored by federal authorities, because if they tried to deport the illegal residents they "would start an anti-American agitation and boycott of our trade in China that would bring to a swift termination all hopes of future profits." Rea, *The Case for Manchoukuo* (New York, 1935), p. 127. In 1914, after his participation in the successful 1911 Chinese revolution, Wu said nothing about boycott matters in his book about the United States, but referred at length to the "discriminatory laws" which were "a blot . . . on her otherwise good name, and her relations with China, though cordial, cannot be perfect." Wu Ting-fang, *America through the Spectacles of an Oriental Diplomat* (New York, 1914), p. 44.

CHAPTER 14.

1. Wu, *America through the Spectacles of an Oriental Diplomat*, p. 186. Incidents involving affronts included the following future leaders in the Chinese government: Sun Yat-sen, future president of the Chinese Republic; Soong Ai-ling, future sister-in-law of another president of China; her husband, H. H. Kung, a future minister of finance; and Chou Tzu-ch'i, another future minister of finance. Wu T'ing-fang, the bitterest enemy of exclusion, was to become premier in 1917.

2. Only six pages are devoted to Chinese exclusion in Griswold, *The Far Eastern Policy of the United States*, pp. 333-39. Nevertheless, the present study fully supports Griswold's assertion that "the Chinese boycott epitomizes the conflict of policy growing out of the immigration issue." P. 338.

Bibliography

To a great extent this study is based on various types of records in the National Archives. Diplomatic records for the period 1900-1906, made available on microfilm, are assembled chronologically and separately as notes, instructions, and dispatches. The notes from and to the Chinese Legation in Washington have abundant material on the exclusion question. In addition, they contain exchanges involving treaty negotiations as they began in Washington in 1904 and were then transferred to Peking in 1905. When the negotiations shifted to China, the dispatches and instructions reported the course of events on both the treaty and boycott problems.

An invaluable supplement to these diplomatic records is the Peking Legation Archives, which contain the texts of various treaty drafts and considerable background on the boycott problem. No less important are the consular dispatches from China. Those from Canton are especially useful in revealing a great deal both about the workings of the exclusion policy and about developments of the boycott. Shanghai was another important center. But also important are the dispatches from Amoy, Chefoo, Chungking (least important), Foochow, Hangchow, Hankow, Hong Kong, Nanking, Newchwang, and Tientsin.

Another helpful collection is the Miscellaneous Letter Files, which contain letters on exclusion, the treaty issue, and the boycott. Some information on exclusion is also found in the Reports of Bureau Officers, 1899-1911, vol. 10. Of lesser importance are the Department of State circulars and the consular reports. All of the above are part of the records of the Department of State in Record Groups 59 and 84.

In the National Archives, another set of records nearly as important as the diplomatic is the Bureau of Immigration records in Record Group 85. Among the bureau records, the Chinese Segregated Records collection contains a wealth of material of many types. Correspondence between immigration officials, for example, discloses the policy and methods of implementation in dealing with Chinese immigrants. Correspondence between the State Department and the departments containing the bureau adds further information. Exchanges with Chinese officials, with congressmen, and congressional committees are also there as well as the origin of provisions in treaty drafts on exclusion, and articles and newspaper clippings on exclusion. Many letters to the president were referred to the bureau to be answered and placed in its files, as were translations of items that originated in the San Francisco Chinese community. Indeed, the information in the files reveals that bureau officials gleaned a great deal of knowledge about Chinese policy from the San Francisco Chinese during the boycott and passed on this material to other branches of government. Pamphlets, and even a printed speech in Chinese by Sun Yat-sen, are in this collection. Petitions and resolutions sent to congressional committees in support of or opposed to exclusion are another key collection used in this study in the National Archives. More attention, however, will be given to these records, contained in Record Group 46, later.

Since the exclusion policy, treaty revision, and the boycott were dependent on legislative as well as executive decisions, I have given attention to records connected with that branch. The *Congressional Record* was useful. The hearings of the House Committee on Foreign Affairs and the Senate Committee on Immigration also contain valuable information. Most significant also in understanding the dynamics behind congressional actions are the many petitions and resolutions in the files of the House and Senate committees on foreign relations and immigration. Both the quantity and content of these communications were of major importance. House and Senate documents were also helpful but had to be handled with great care. One document deserving special emphasis because it gives the Bureau of Immigration's defense of the administration of exclusion regulations and expresses its convictions about the boycott is in U.S. Congress. House. *Compilation from the Records of the Bureau of Immigration of Facts Concerning the Enforcement of the Chinese Exclusion Laws.* House Document 847, 59th Cong., 1st sess., 1906.

The American Asiatic Association was behind the effort to promote the open door policy and to modify the exclusion policy. Its *Journal* was its voice and provided a running commentary on pro-Chinese political activities. A useful organ in following the thinking of the Protestant missionary movement — another major force on the pro-Chinese side — was the *Missionary Review of the World.*

One way of learning about the anti-Chinese side of the controversy is to read the AFL's main journal, the *American Federationist.* In addition, the AFL's convention debates and resolutions are available in the *Report of Proceedings* of its annual conventions. On the exclusionist side, the commissioner general of immigration also had his *Annual Report,* as did the secretary of the treasury and the secretary of the Department of Commerce and Labor. The California point of view and exclusionist activities centered in California can be discovered in the congressional debates and in the columns of the *San Francisco Chronicle.*

Points of view and policy statements by both sides also appeared frequently in the journals and the press of the day. Articles cited in the *Readers Guide to Periodical Literature* contributed much to this study. By using their helpful indexes, much information was also gleaned from the *New York Times* and the *New York Daily Tribune.*

In addition to archival materials, manuscript collections are indispensable. Many concern government officials who were making policy, such as the president, secretaries of state, secretary of commerce and labor, and the commissioner general of immigration. Since the American Federation of Labor was an important pressure group, the papers of President Samuel Gompers received attention also.

MANUSCRIPT COLLECTIONS:

Cambridge, Mass. Houghton Library, Harvard University. William W. Rockhill Papers.
Washington, D.C. Catholic University of America Archives. Terence V. Powderly Papers.

Washington, D.C. Library of Congress. James R. Garfield Papers; Samuel Gompers Letter Books; John Hay Papers; Theodore Roosevelt Papers; Elihu Root Papers; Oscar S. Straus Papers; William Howard Taft Papers.

GOVERNMENT DOCUMENTS:

U.S. Congress. *Biographical Directory of the American Congress, 1774-1961.* Washington, 1961.
U.S. Congress. *A Compilation of the Messages and Papers of the Presidents.* 20 vols. New York, 1897-1901, 1902-1908.
U.S. Department of Justice. *Official Opinions of the Attorneys-General of the United States Advising the President and Heads of Departments in Relation to Their Official Duties.* Vol. 22. Washington, 1902.
U.S. Department of State. *Commercial Relations of the United States with Foreign Countries.* 2 vols. Washington, 1902.
_____. *Papers Relating to the Foreign Relations of the United States, 1900-1907.* Washington, 1901-1908.

SELECTED BIBLIOGRAPHY:

Bailey, Thomas A. *Theodore Roosevelt and the Japanese-American Crises: An Account of the International Complications Arising from the Race Problem on the Pacific Coast.* Stanford, 1934.
Barth, Gunther. *Bitter Strength: A History of the Chinese in the United States, 1850-1870.* Cambridge, 1964.
Beale, Howard K. *Theodore Roosevelt and the Rise of America to World Power.* Baltimore, 1956.
Bennett, Marion T. *American Immigration Policies: A History.* Washington, 1963.
Bland, J. O. P. *Recent Events and Present Policies in China.* Philadelphia, 1912.
Blum, John M. *The Republican Roosevelt.* New York, 1954, 1967.
Boorman, Howard L., and Howard, Richard C., eds. *Biographical Dictionary of Republican China.* 4 vols. New York, 1968.
Borg, Dorothy, comp. *Historians and American Far Eastern Policy.* New York, 1966.
Braisted, William R. "The United States and the American China Development Company." *Far Eastern Quarterly* 11 (Feb. 1952): 147-65.
_____. *The United States Navy in the Pacific, 1897-1909.* Austin, 1958.
Cameron, Meribeth E. *The Reform Movement in China, 1898-1912.* New York, 1931, 1963.
Campbell, Charles S., Jr. *Special Business Interests and the Open Door Policy.* New Haven, 1951.
Carman, Harry J.; David, Henry; and Guthrie, Paul N., eds. *The Path I Trod: The Autobiography of Terence V. Powderly.* New York, 1940.
Chang, Chung-tung. "China's Response to the Open Door, 1898-1906," Ph.D. dissertation, Michigan State University, 1973.
Chang, Ts'un-wu. *Chung Mei Kung-yueh Feng-ch'Ao (Agitation concerning the Sino-American labor treaty, 1905).* Taiwan, 1966.
Ch'en, Jerome. *Yuan Shih-k'ai, 1859-1916: Brutus Assumes the Purple.* Stanford, 1961.
Clyde, Paul H., ed. *United States Policy toward China: Diplomatic and Public Documents, 1839-1939.* New York, 1964.

Clymer, Kenton J. *John Hay: The Gentleman as Diplomat.* Ann Arbor, 1975.
Condit, Ira M. *The Chinaman as We See Him and Fifty Years of Work for Him.* New York, 1900.
Coolidge, Mary R. *Chinese Immigration.* New York, 1909.
Daniels, Roger. *The Politics of Prejudice: The Anti-Japanese Movement in California and the Struggle for Japanese Exclusion.* Berkeley and Los Angeles, 1962.
Dennett, Tyler. *Americans in Eastern Asia: A Critical Study of United States' Policy in the Far East in the Nineteenth Century.* New York, 1922, 1941, 1963.
_____. *John Hay: From Poetry to Politics.* New York, 1934.
Divine, Robert A. *American Immigration Policy, 1924-1952.* New Haven, 1957.
Fairbank, John K.; Reischauer, Edwin O.; and Craig, Albert. *East Asia: The Modern Transformation.* Boston, 1965.
Field, Margaret. "The Chinese Boycott of 1905." *Papers on China* 11 (1957): 63-98. East Asian Research Center, Harvard University, 1957.
Foster, John W. *American Diplomacy in the Orient.* Boston, 1903, 1926.
_____. *Diplomatic Memoirs.* 2 vols. Boston, 1909.
Gardner, John B. "The Image of the Chinese in the United States, 1885-1915." Ph.D. dissertation, University of Pennsylvania, 1961.
Garis, Roy L. *Immigration Restriction: A Study of the Opposition to and Regulation of Immigration into the United States.* New York, 1928.
Gompers, Samuel. *Seventy Years of Life and Labor.* 2 vols. New York, 1925.
Greenbaum, Fred. "The Social Ideas of Samuel Gompers," *Labor History* 7 (Winter 1966): 35-61.
Griffith, William, ed. *The Roosevelt Policy: Speeches, Letters and State Papers Relating to Corporate Wealth and Closely Allied Topics by Theodore Roosevelt.* 3 vols. New York, 1919.
Griscom, Lloyd C. *Diplomatically Speaking.* New York, 1940.
Griswold, A. Whitney. *The Far Eastern Policy of the United States.* New York, 1938.
Harbaugh, William H. *Power and Responsibility: The Life and Times of Theodore Roosevelt.* New York, 1961.
Higham, John. *Strangers in the Land: Patterns of American Nativism, 1860-1925.* New Brunswick, 1955.
Hoar, George F. *Autobiography of Seventy Years.* New York, 1903.
Hunt, Michael H. "The American Remission of the Boxer Indemnity: A Reappraisal." *Journal of Asian Studies* 31 (May 1972): 539-59.
_____. *Frontier Defense and the Open Door: Manchuria in Chinese-American Relations, 1895-1911.* New Haven, 1973.
Iriye, Akira. "Public Opinion and Foreign Policy: The Case of Late Ch'ing China." *Approaches to Modern Chinese History.* Edited by Albert Feuerwerker, Rhoads Murphey, and Mary L. Wright. Berkeley and Los Angeles, 1967.
Israel, Jerry, " 'For God, For China and For Yale' — The Open Door in Action." *American Historical Review* 75 (Feb. 1970): 796-807.
_____. *Progressivism and the Open Door: America and China, 1905-1921.* Pittsburgh, 1971.
Jessup, Philip C. *Elihu Root.* 2 vols. New York, 1938.
Johnson, Allen, and Malone, Dumas, eds. *Dictionary of American Biography.* 21 vols. New York, 1928-1937.
Jones, Maldwyn A. *American Immigration.* Chicago, 1960.
Kennan, George F. *American Diplomacy, 1900-1950.* New York, 1951.
Kennedy, John Castillo. *The Great Earthquake and Fire: San Francisco, 1906.* New York, 1963.

Kung, Shien-woo. *Chinese in American Life: Some Aspects of Their History, Status, Problems, and Contributions.* Seattle, 1962.

LaFeber, Walter. *The New Empire: An Interpretation of American Expansion, 1860-1898.* Ithaca, 1963.

Latourette, Kenneth S. *A History of Christian Missions in China.* New York, 1929, 1967.

Lee, Rose Hum. *The Chinese in the United States.* Hong Kong, 1960.

Leopold, Richard W. *Elihu Root and the Conservative Tradition.* Boston, 1954.

Levi, Werner. *Modern China's Foreign Policy.* Minneapolis, 1953.

Li, Tien-lu. *Congressional Policy of Chinese Immigration or Legislation Relating to Chinese Immigration to the United States.* South Nashville, 1916.

Lo, Jung-pang, ed. and trans. *K'ang Yu-wei: A Biography and a Symposium.* Tucson, 1967.

Longworth, Alice Roosevelt. *Crowded Hours: Reminiscences of Alice Roosevelt Longworth.* New York, 1933.

Lorence, James John. "The American Asiatic Association, 1898-1925: Organized Business and the Myth of the Chinese Market." Ph.D. dissertation, University of Wisconsin, 1970.

_____. "Business and Reform: The American Asiatic Association and the Exclusion Laws, 1905-1907." *Pacific Historical Review* 39 (Nov. 1970): 421-38.

Ma, Wen Hwan. *American Policy toward China as Revealed in the Debates of Congress.* Shanghai, 1934.

McClellan, Robert. *The Heathen Chinee: A Study of American Attitudes toward China, 1890-1905.* Columbus, 1971.

McCormick, Thomas J. *China Market: America's Quest for Informal Empire, 1893-1901.* Chicago, 1967.

McKenzie, Roderick D. *Oriental Exclusion: The Effect of American Immigration Laws, Regulations, and Judicial Decisions upon the Chinese and Japanese on the American Pacific Coast.* Chicago, 1928.

Malin, Morton V. "American Economic Interests in China, 1900-1908." Ph.D. dissertation, University of Maryland, 1954.

Mann, Arthur. "Gompers and the Irony of Racism." *Antioch Review* 13 (June 1953): 203-14.

Miller, Jessie Ashworth. "China in American Policy and Opinion, 1906-1909." Ph.D. dissertation, Clark University, 1938.

Miller, Stuart Creighton. "An East Coast Perspective to Chinese Exclusion, 1852-1882." *Historian* 33 (Feb. 1971): 183-201.

_____. *The Unwelcome Immigrant: The American Image of the Chinese, 1785-1882.* Berkeley and Los Angeles, 1969.

Milnar, Anthony Lee. "Chinese-American Relations with Especial Reference to the Imposition of the Boycott, 1905-1906." Ph.D. dissertation, Georgetown University, 1948.

Morison, Elting E., ed. *The Letters of Theodore Roosevelt.* 8 vols. Cambridge, 1951.

Morse, Hosea B. *The International Relations of the Chinese Empire.* 3 vols. New York, 1910-1918.

Neu, Charles E. *An Uncertain Friendship: Theodore Roosevelt and Japan, 1906-1909.* Cambridge, 1967.

Papageorge, Linda M. "The United States Diplomats' Response to Rising Chinese Nationalism, 1900-1912." Ph.D. dissertation, Michigan State University, 1973.

Paulsen, George E. "The Abrogation of the Gresham-Yang Treaty." *Pacific Historical Review* 40 (Nov. 1971): 457-77.

Phillips, William. *Ventures in Diplomacy.* Boston, 1952.

Porter, Kirk H. *National Party Platforms*. New York, 1924.

Rea, George B. *The Case for Manchoukuo*. New York, 1935.

Remer, Charles F. *Foreign Investments in China*. New York, 1933, 1968.

_____. *A Study of Chinese Boycotts with Special Reference to Their Economic Effectiveness*. Baltimore, 1933.

Rhoads, Edward J. M. *China's Republican Revolution: The Case of Kwangtung, 1895-1913*. Cambridge, 1975.

_____. "Nationalism and Xenophobia in Kwangtung (1905-1906): The Canton Anti-American Boycott and the Lienchow Anti-Missionary Uprising." *Papers on China* 16 (1962): 154-97. East Asian Research Center, Harvard University, 1962.

Roberts, William K. *The Mongolian Problem in America: A Discussion of the Possibilities of the Yellow Peril, with Notes upon American Diplomacy in Its Relation to the Boycott*. San Francisco, 1906.

Sandmeyer, Elmer C. *The Anti-Chinese Movement in California*. Urbana, 1939.

Saxton, Alexander P. *The Indispensable Enemy: Labor and the Anti-Chinese Movement in California*. Berkeley and Los Angeles, 1971.

Schiffrin, Harold Z. *Sun Yat-sen and the Origins of the Chinese Revolution*. Berkeley and Los Angeles, 1968.

Seager, Robert II. "Some Denominational Reactions to Chinese Immigration to California, 1856-1892." *Pacific Historical Review* 28 (Feb. 1959): 49-66.

Shin, Linda P. "China in Transition: The Role of Wu T'ing-fang (1842-1922)." Ph.D. dissertation, University of California at Los Angeles, 1970.

Smith, Arthur H. *China and America To-Day: A Study of Conditions and Relations*. New York, 1907.

Smith, Darrell H., and Herring, H. Guy. *The Bureau of Immigration: Its History, Activities, and Organization*. Baltimore, 1924.

Stephenson, George M. *A History of American Immigration, 1820-1924*. New York, 1926.

Straus, Oscar S. *Under Four Administrations: From Cleveland to Taft*. Boston, 1922.

Swisher, Earl. *Chinese Representation in the United States, 1861-1912*. University of Colorado Studies: Series in History no. 5. Boulder, 1967.

Thayer, William R. *The Life and Letters of John Hay*. 2 vols. Boston, 1915.

Thompson, John S. *China Revolutionized*. Indianapolis, 1913.

Tsai, Shih-shan Henry. "Reactions to Exclusion: Ch'ing Attitudes toward Overseas Chinese in the United States, 1848-1906." Ph.D. dissertation, University of Oregon, 1970.

Varg, Paul A. *The Making of a Myth: The United States and China, 1897-1912*. East Lansing, 1968.

_____. *Missionaries, Chinese and Diplomats: The American Protestant Missionary Movement in China, 1890-1951*. Princeton, 1958.

_____. "The Myth of the China Market, 1890-1914." *American Historical Review* 73 (Feb. 1968): 742-58.

_____. *Open Door Diplomat: The Life of W. W. Rockhill*. Urbana, 1952.

Vevier, Charles. *The United States and China, 1906-1913: A Study of Finance and Diplomacy*. New Brunswick, 1955.

Wang, Yu Chu. *Chinese Intellectuals and the West*. Chapel Hill, 1966.

Williams, William A. *The Tragedy of American Diplomacy*. Cleveland, 1959.

Wilson, Francis M. Huntington. *Memoirs of an Ex-Diplomat*. Boston, 1945.

Worden, Robert L. "A Chinese Reformer in Exile: The North American Phase of the Travels of K'ang Yu-wei, 1899-1909." Ph.D. dissertation, Georgetown University, 1972.

Wright, Mary C., ed. *China in Revolution: The First Phase, 1900-1913.* New Haven, 1968.

Wu T'ing-fang. *America through the Spectacles of an Oriental Diplomat.* New York, 1914.

Young, Marilyn B. "American China Policy, 1895-1901." Ph.D. dissertation, Radcliffe College, 1963.

——————. *The Rhetoric of Empire: America's China Policy, 1895-1901.* Cambridge, 1968.

Index

Adee, Alvey A., 122, 136, 201
American Asiatic Association: influence on Open Door policy, 16; and exclusion, 20, 45, 48, 50, 103, 210, 219; criticizes Bureau of Immigration, 73; praises Prince, 74; on Wu, 78; and commercial treaty of 1903, 82; opposes Hitt bill, 90; on act of 1904, 92; appraises treaty prospects, 92; on boycott, 112, 113, 127, 129; and Foster bill, 172, 175, 219; and Imperial Chinese Commission, 173; and trade decline, 210
American Asiatic Association of Japan, 16
American Association of China, 16, 113, 115, 195
American Baptist Missionary Union, 165
American Board of Foreign Missions, 175, 176
American Chamber of Commerce, Manila, 48
American China Development Company, 19, 78, 85, 98, 137
American Chinese Company, 95
American Federation of Labor (AFL), 233n35, 256-57n125, 268n65; size of, 30; adopts exclusion resolution, 54; and Powderly, 54, 67; and Roosevelt, 54, 60, 178; California wing of, 55; use of petitions, 56, 182; power of, 58, 219; for Kahn bill, 60; ties with Patterson, 86; exclusion actions, 1902-4, 88; on Hitt bill, 90; and Congress, 91-92; defends exclusion, 143, 213; and Japanese and Korean Exclusion

League, 183. *See also* Gompers, Samuel
Anglo-Chinese College, 114, 154, 212
Arthur, Chester, 24, 58
Ashmore, William, 165

Baldwin, Mrs. S. L., 28, 49
Bard, Thomas R., 55, 92
Barrett, John, 67, 72, 77, 120, 142
Bash, A.W., 196-97
Bashford, James W., 181, 212
Beattie, Andrew, 168, 186, 189, 190
Bertillon system, 68, 74, 80, 183, 192, 208, 255n97
Bird, O. F., 71
Blair, Henry W., 26
Boston Chamber of Commerce, 50, 61, 90
Boston: Police Raid of 1903, 29, 152; mass arrests, 68-69, 81
Boxer indemnity, 99, 114, 195-96, 197, 249n28
Boxer Rebellion, 18, 37, 39, 44, 47, 69, 77, 103, 139, 187-88
Boycott, 142, 219-20, 245n15, 256-57n125, 257n4, 260n52, 260n67, 263n119, 267n53, 275n41, 276n64; warning of, 28, 73, 75; Liang Ch'eng and, 78, 133; concern about, 90; previously used, 105; procedures, 106; Shanghai and, 106, 108-9, 120, 149; Canton and, 107, 137-38, 157-70, 181; spread of, 107-8; and K'ing family incident, 109; leaders and groups in, 109-12; Chinese government and, 111, 149, 204; Japan and, 111-12, 140; Americans and, 112; Rockhill and,

285

Delber L. McKee, professor of history at Westminster College, Pennsylvania, has the following degrees: A.B. (1946) from Hastings College; M.A. (1947) from the University of Wisconsin; and Ph.D. (1953) from Stanford University. He has also had a Fulbright-Hays Grant (1962) to the Summer Institute in Chinese Civilization, Taiwan.

The manuscript was edited by Marguerite C. Wallace. The book was designed by Gil Hanna, who also did the hand lettering. The typeface for the text is Janson, which originally dates from about 1690 and was cut by Nicholas Kis. The display face is Palatino, designed by Hermann Zapf about 1950.

The text is printed on Glatfelter Natural paper and the book is bound in Holliston's Crown Linen cloth over binders' boards. Manufactured in the United States of America.